Front-line Nurse

Front-line Nurse

British Nurses in World War II

ERIC TAYLOR

ROBERT HALE · LONDON

Photoset in North Wales by
Derek Doyle & Associates, Mold, Flintshire.
Printed in Great Britain by
St Edmundsbury Press Ltd, Bury St Edmunds, Suffolk.
Bound by WBC Book Manufacturers Limited,
Bridgend, Mid-Glamorgan.

Contents

To the memory of my mother, Edith, a nurse in the First World War and my father, Wilfred, who served in the Royal Army Medical Corps and later stimulated my interest in writing.

List of Illustrations

Illustration Credits

George Scott collection: 25–27, 32. QARANC Museum: 33–37, 42. RAF Museum: 38. Imperial War Museum: 41, 51–53. *Reading Evening News*: 47. Charles Whiting: 48. Pat Gould, CBE, RRC: 49–50.

All other illustrations are from the collections of nurses and others mentioned in this book.

Acknowledgements

I must first acknowledge the inspiration I received from those fine books, *A Nurse's War* and *Quiet Heroines* by Brenda McBryde. However, when I began researching for my own book the variety, number, and enthusiasm of those nurses who responded to my appeals in newspapers, magazines, and nursing journals, strengthened my belief that there certainly was room for another detailed record of wartime nursing history, concentrating on the experiences of nurses in the many theatres of operation in the Second World War.

These nurses generously told me their stories, shared their experiences with me and gave me permission to include their accounts in this book. *Front-line Nurse* would not have been possible without all these personal accounts.

My sincere thanks are due also to all officers in the Forces and civilian nursing services who have helped me in gathering material and in contacting the nurses concerned.

I am particularly grateful to Pat Gould, CBE, RRC, for her help with the accounts of nurses serving with Queen Alexandra's Royal Navy Nursing Service in Hong Kong and to Bette Anderson who so generously lent me accounts and guided me to other sources of information.

I most gratefully acknowledge the help I received from Major M.H. McCombe, Curator of the Queen Alexandra's Royal Army Nursing Corps Museum, and Major Jill Machray, Regimental Secretary, Q.A.R.A.N.C. and Mr Brian Fitzpatrick of the Museum staff. I should like also to thank Susan McGann, Archivist of the Royal College of Nursing.

I have received considerable assistance from the staff of the RAF Museum, Hendon and in particular, Anna McIlwaine in the RAF Archives.

Without reservation, my many requests for help have been met with courtesy and candour by staff of the Imperial War Museum, the Public Record Office at Kew, and the British Newspaper Library at Colindale. Without their efficient service this book would not have been so comprehensive.

I gratefully acknowledge the help I have received from Sir Harry

Secombe, CBE, especially for his amusing account of his own hospitalization in North Africa. I should like to thank also Malcolm Beaumont of the Department of Social Security, Professor Robert Barr Smith, College of Law, University of Oklahoma, and Michael Conway of the 1940 Association.

My thanks go also to all those publishers and agents, mentioned in the notes to chapters, who generously gave me permission to quote from their books. I am particularly grateful to Henry Holt and Company, Inc. for allowing me to include a long passage from Ernie Pyle's book *Here is Your War*.

For details of the personal experience of Nurse Joanna Stavridi in Greece and Crete I am indebted to her brother Valieri Stavridi and her sister, Mrs Hadjilazaro who gave me access to Joanna's letters and those from Colonel Hamilton-Fairley.

To all those front-line nurses, their husbands, service personnel and others who have communicated with me I express again the sincere thanks I have already given privately, especially to: Marie Floyd-Norris; Margaret Boyce; Iris Bower MBE, ARRC; Marjorie Bennett; Myra Roberts Jones; Mary and Maurice Pinkney; Pat Stephens; George Pfister, husband of the late Anne Pfister; Diana Sugden O'Brien; Violet Leather; Flora Urquhart; Eileen Haynes; the late Winifred Beaumont; Monica Carhart-Harris; Beryl Allinson; Hilary Lewis; Rosemary Hearn; Louise Robinson; Stella Spence; Wyndham Davidson; Alice Simonite; Norma Whitehead; Joyce O'Ryan; Monica Jackson; Joy Hobley; Jean Gaukroger; Noelle Starr; Alexandra Croll; J.C. Kilmister; Elizabeth Mungall; Pamela Thompson; Joan Morgan; Betty Wragg; Anne Templeman; Sylvia Suthren; Margaret Priestly; Teresa Gladwin; Nan Hewson; Peggy Edwards; Henrietta Lee; Margaret Pritchett; Irene Black; Margaret Brown; Kitty Hutchinson; Bill Dilworth; Helen Clark; Roger Keys; Harold Carr; Mollie Jennings; Winifred Reid; Edna Birkbeck; Sheila Bambridge; and Evelyn Cook.

As with my other books on the women who went to war, it is to my wife, Sheila that I owe a special debt for her invaluable help with the research, interviewing, and the meticulous checking and correction of drafts. My colleague the military historian Charles Whiting has led me to much useful material and I should like it to be known how much I valued the encouragement and accounts of hospital life in North Africa of a good friend, John Cooper, formerly of the Lancashire Fusiliers of 78th Division, who sadly died before the book was finished.

To all I express my sincere gratitude. The responsibility for any shortcomings or errors, is, of course, my own.

Glossary

AA	Anti-Aircraft (Ack-Ack)
ADMS	Assistant Director of Medical Services
ADS	Advance Dressing Station
ARRC	Associate of Royal Red Cross
BEF	British Expeditionary Force
BGH	British General Hospital
CAEC	Casualty Air Evacuation Centre
CCP	Casualty Clearing Point
CCS	Casualty Clearing Station
CO	Commanding Officer
DADMS	Deputy Assistant Director of Medical Services
DFC	Distinguished Flying Cross
DMS	Director of Medical Services
DSO	Distinguished Service Order
EMS	Emergency Medical Service
FANY	First Aid Nursing Yeomanry
FDS	Field Dressing Station
HQ	Headquarters
IGH	Indian General Hospital
LCI	Landing Craft Infantry
LCT	Landing Craft Tank
MC	Military Cross
MEF	Middle East Forces
MFH	Mobile Field Hospital
MO	Medical Officer
MTB	Motor Torpedo Boat
NAAFI	Navy, Army and Air Force Institute
NCO	Non-Commissioned Officer
NYD	Not Yet Diagnosed
OC	Officer Commanding
OR(s)	Other Rank(s)
OTT	Operating Theatre Technician
POW	Prisoner of War
PRO	Public Record Office
QM	Quartermaster

QAIMNSR	Queen Alexandra's Imperial Military Nursing Service (Reserve)
QARANC	Queen Alexandra's Royal Army Nursing Corps
QARNNS	Queen Alexandra's Royal Naval Nursing Service
RAMC	Royal Army Medical Corps
RAP	Regimental Aid Post
RASC	Royal Army Service Corps
RMO	Regimental Medical Officer
RNH	Royal Naval Hospital
RRC	Royal Red Cross
RTO	Railway Transport Officer
SEAC	South East Asia Command
SIW	Self-inflicted Wound
SMO	Senior Medical Officer
TANS	Territorial Army Nursing Service
TCV(s)	Troop-Carrying Vehicle(s)
VAD	Voluntary Aid Detachment
VC	Victoria Cross
WAAF	Women's Auxiliary Air Force
WRNS	Women's Royal Naval Service

1 Into France and Norway

With less than an hour's warning and no
word to our families, off we went. I found
it all rather exhilarating.
                    Eileen Haynes QAIMNSR

In September 1939, when Britain went to war with Nazi Germany, the
nation's nursing services – Forces and civilian – were in a position to
cope with the conflict which lay ahead. Which is far more than can be
said of the British Army.

The young men of the British Expeditionary Force who went across to
France in a holiday mood that hot summer of 1939 were, to quote the
army's most celebrated commander, Field Marshal Montgomery of
Alamein, '... totally unfit to fight a first-class war on the continent of
Europe.'[1]

Nurses, on the other hand, were in a far better state of readiness. On
1 September 1939 the mobilization orders for the nursing services of the
Navy, Army and Air Force were complete, and fourteen days later
three general hospitals were disembarking at Le Mans – Numbers 9, 2
and 3 – followed shortly by Number 11. During that week, too, numbers
1 to 4 ambulance trains arrived. Three medical officers, three nursing
sisters and between thirty and forty RAMC medical orderlies were
ready on each train to look after the flood of patients expected from the
front.[2]

The first of those nurses arriving in France travelled towards the front
by train. Amongst them was Eileen Hawkin (now Haynes). 'After
disembarking in Boulogne we set off. Our train had no corridor. We did
not stop for twenty four hours. I'll not go into details of how we coped
with these conditions, but one of us had a tin of fruit and a can opener,
so I'll leave it at that.'

Admittedly there were a few small hitches. The call-up of the
Territorial Auxiliary Nursing Service and the QA Reserves was so swift
that some nurses were arriving in France without uniform, and
Matron-in-Chief at the War Office had to issue a special order to stop

enterprising nurses ordering 'makeshift' uniforms from local French tailors.[3]

Crossing over to France with the BEF was a memorable time for nurses. Marjorie Bennett (then Doyle) remembers vividly:

> In a highly secret move our contingent of nurses crossed the Channel by night with a battalion of the 51st Highland Division. All port holes and windows were blacked out but below decks everywhere was brightly lit. We sat around singing all the popular songs of the time – the Gracie Fields hit of 'Wish me Luck as you Wave me Good-bye', and also the old ones 'Pack up your Troubles in your Old Kit Bag' and 'Tipperary' evoking the atmosphere of the First World War. Well, some of those nurses were old enough to remember that war. We danced Scottish reels to Scottish pipers until we gasped for breath. What a wonderful introduction to wartime life. The future looked really exciting. It was. But not in the way we expected. We breakfasted at dawn in Le Havre and set up the hospital in what had been a gambling casino there.
>
> A bizarre scene! The walls were covered in long mirrors and from the ceiling, ornate chandeliers dangled. The floor was highly polished marble mosaic which reflected the sparkling lights from above. Once the beds were installed with their bright red hospital blankets it really did look bright and gay.
>
> At first there were few patients. The shooting war had not begun. It was the time of the 'phoney war' as the newspapers sometimes called it. French divisions were sitting behind their so-called 'impregnable' Maginot line. And nothing happened.

The British Tommy in those days was physically healthy, and there was little sickness, but as a cold autumn passed into a bitterly cold winter, patients trickled in suffering from pneumonia or bronchitis.

Then, as troops got to know local girls, there was a dramatic increase in venereal disease. Eileen Hawkin Haynes, then at La Baulle Hospital recalled: 'We put our VD patients in an annexe. Their pay was cut and leave cancelled. RAMC orderlies coped wonderfully, but sometimes they asked for a QA volunteer to sort out a complication.'

General Montgomery, then commanding the Third Infantry Division, was so alarmed at the numbers reporting sick with VD he drafted a Divisional Order which very nearly ruined his military career. His solution to the VD problem was simple: firstly, the NAAFI should sell condoms; secondly, troops should be advised to visit clean brothels when they felt the need for sex; and thirdly, all soldiers should be taught how to buy French letters from local shops.[4] In his innocence, the puritanical Montgomery offended everyone from the Mothers' Union to the Army Council and beyond. His Divisional Order, however, had achieved what he wanted, since the VD problem diminished.

In those quiet months of the 'phoney war' nurses enjoyed a pleasant time. Naturally, hospitals received many invitations from neighbouring British and French units to attend officers' mess parties. 'Our Matron,' said Marjorie Bennett, 'was keen for us to accept in the interests of fostering good international relations.'

I played my part willingly. Often a French count would send a chauffeur-driven car to pick me up from the Sisters' Quarters. His limousine was well known. When we passed French traffic police they would give him a salute. I was always in my best grey and scarlet cape and felt like one of the Royal family.

One day I'd just come off night duty and decided to go shopping in the town instead of going to bed. I broke the golden rule for QAs in France and put on my civilian clothes.

I was drifting along looking in shop windows when suddenly a big French police car drew up alongside. A gendarme jumped out and barked, 'Get inside.' He blocked the pavement, arms spread and almost pushed me inside the car. I had no option. My schoolgirl French cut no ice with that big man. He had been alerted, I heard later, to be on the look out for a woman with a poor French accent wearing civilian clothes. A woman who sometimes dressed as a nurse and rode in a chauffeur-driven car with the count. A spy!

I was pushed into a cell amongst a few haggard-looking prostitutes. Every time I tried to ask why I was behind bars, all they would say was, 'A bientôt' or 'Attendez'. At dusk they took me into a room and began to fire questions at me. I tried to tell them I was English and they said they knew I was a spy.

After another two hours there was a commotion in the outer office and a red-tabbed British Army officer from the Judge Advocate General's Office came in. Again I was put in the interrogation room. This time the Army officer fired the questions. Where did I do my training? Gosport. What is the name of the Cathedral in Portsmouth? What is the full name of the hospital's commanding officer? ... and so on. A few minutes later there was another commotion and this time into the Gendarmerie strode the hospital CO and the Matron too.

It wasn't long before my irate escorts had me outside that stinking gaol. Apparently the French were sensitive about spies and Fifth Columnists[5] and felt sure that someone who wore a uniform one day and not the next, was up to no good. The Matron was annoyed. It was a disgrace! I had been stupid, disobeying routine orders by going out in civilian clothes. The colonel quietly asked if he could take me out to dinner!'

In this strange way the winter months passed. The twelve divisions of the British Expeditionary Force, commanded by Lord Gort VC, which had never exercised as an army together, settled into a routine of digging trenches and boasting in their marching song they would soon be hanging out the washing on Hitler's defensive Siegfried Line. Fortunately, perhaps because of their previous meticulous and rigorous training, RAMC personnel and nurses in each of the hospitals, ambulance trains and casualty clearing stations worked out contingency plans for various emergencies during those 'quiet' months when Hitler was planning another campaign.

In the early hours of 7 April 1940, German troops invaded Norway. One week later, 13,000 ill-equipped British and French troops landed at several points north and south of Trondheim. These virtually raw recruits were to help the Norwegian Army resist the well-trained German battalions in a country still in the grip of an Arctic winter. Nurses of Number 7 Casualty Clearing Station, hastily kitted out, went with them and landed at Harstad in the Narvik Fiord.

Sister Winifred Barnfather (now Reid) remembers how it was and shudders. 'We staggered ashore under lambskin Arctic overcoats, men's size only available, weighing fifteen pounds, men's special thermal socks and padded Balaclava helmets to wear under steel helmets. We looked just like a moving overcoat attached to a tin hat! It was bitterly cold and we slept in everything we had.' There was four feet of snow, and the temperature was zero which immediately presented the CCS with the problems of frostbite and amputations. At first the CCS was billeted at a school in Trondheim, but then in the middle of the night they were told to board small fishing-boats and move north to Harstad. 'We wondered what we were in for. At sea in small boats in freezing weather. Well inside the Arctic Circle. Awful. We set up our hospital in five separate buildings,' recalled Winifred Reid.

German aircraft dominated the skies. They bombed and machine-gunned everything which moved; Red Cross markings provided no protection. Hardly had the CCS opened operationally when they were ordered to move yet again. The Norwegian Army and the Allies, hopelessly outclassed and outnumbered, were in retreat. In great haste Number 7 CCS moved back to Trondheim, where, after hours of waiting on the dockside harassed by Stukas diving out of the skies with their sirens howling, they embarked in the hospital ship *Aba*, packed with wounded, and set sail for Britain.

Teresa Gladwin, who had gone to France with Number 6 Casualty Clearing Station in October 1939, remembers well those days of waiting for when the Germans would strike on their front: 'We were one of the most forward of the CCSs and billeted in a château in the village of Vaudricourt. We had specific orders to keep our panniers packed so that we would be ready to move quickly if the Germans attacked and broke through our lines.' The older medical staff got ready for the Spring. 'Then Hitler will start,' they said.

They were right. On 10 May, the storm burst: the long-expected German assault on the Low Countries began. A German artillery barrage of unprecedented violence rained down upon British and French lines as a prelude to the advance of 136 German divisions. The poorly equipped BEF fell back in disarray against superior German fire-power. Panzer columns cut through Allied Defences, leaving nurses in the forward casualty clearing stations and ambulance trains having to make their way back through enemy-held territory.

'As the most advanced CCS of the BEF we moved to Haalert, opened up in a school and were told to be ready to take 500 casualties that evening. Long before then, though, casualties began to pour into our reception area. But we had to move again and again with scarcely any time at all to tend to the wounded,' recalled Teresa Gladwin.

> One incident sticks out in my memory. We were in the Lille area when the whole unit was told to assemble for an urgent meeting. Our Commanding Officer told us we were being driven back so quickly that we would not be able to take all the wounded with us. 'I have 150 wounded men on my hands and I'm going to ask for volunteers. Any of you men who would be prepared to stay behind to look after them please take one step forward.' Without hesitation every one of those RAMC orderlies took that step forward. It was a moving moment. Sister K.D. Roberts said to me: 'We can't leave them. I'm going to stay.' I said, 'So will I.' However, out of the blue, a hospital train arrived and we were able to take all our wounded back to Blighty via Dunkirk. We had to leave all our beautiful equipment. A nice little find for the Germans.

Now, all over the front, convoy after convoy of wounded clogged the casualty clearing stations where doctors and nurses, working in steel helmets and often within shell-fire range, strove desperately to resuscitate, carry out urgently needed surgery and then evacuate casualties to base hospitals. No one escaped the onslaught. Sophia

Templeman, Matron of Number 1 BGH, recorded in her unit war diary
how clearly marked casualty clearing stations and ambulance trains in
her unit were bombed and strafed. In the confusion of the retreat 'to
previously prepared positions,' nurses often had to make their way back
to their own lines as the German armour pressed rapidly ahead, leaving
them cut off behind. Sisters of Number 6 Ambulance Train escaped on
foot, on French farm-carts and stolen bicycles back to Doullens, when
they were cut off at Albert. A frightening baptism of fire for them.[6]

It came as a shock to everyone that those easily identifiable
ambulance trains marked with prominent red crosses were attacked by
Luftwaffe pilots eagerly going for any target that came into their sights.
Seventeen nurses narrowly escaped death aboard Number 1 Ambulance
Train bringing wounded to the docks at Dieppe when it was bombed
and machine-gunned by German Air Force Stukas. In another
ambulance train, six Sisters who had survived the shelling of their
forward CCS with West Force and were later machine-gunned in their
ambulance train, volunteered to go back for more, despite the risks
involved. 'Their morale was excellent. They were prepared to go
anywhere to bring back wounded,' recorded Sophia Templeman in her
war diary.[7]

'At the hospital at La Baulle, casualties came by trainloads,' wrote
Eileen Haynes (then Hawkin). 'Some terrible cases, some had had
emergency amputations on their legs on the train, many had gas
gangrene, and we were so short of staff.'

> I remember one man particularly, who had half his abdomen
> missing and had been temporarily 'dressed'. After settling
> into his bed, he shot a terrific haemorrhage and asepsis took
> a back seat. I literally had to clench my fists and press them
> down into his wounds and call for morphia. While this went
> on, he asked me to write to his wife and tell her he loved her
> and insisted I keep a gold medal of Our Lady, which is still in
> my family. He died within hours.
>
> We worked all round the clock shipping the troops back to
> England – that is, those who were able enough to go – in
> order to make way for more who were lying on makeshift
> beds on the floor. We took our breaks when we could. We
> used the Winnett Orr treatment for wounds – we let flies
> settle on open wounds, and then put plaster on in the case of
> injured limbs. When the plaster cast was removed the
> wounds were as clean as a whistle. The maggot-flies were
> good for something!
>
> This went on and on. We had a strict curfew, but we also
> let our hair down now and again. I even remember my first
> taste of Cointreau in a toothmug! I have never touched it

since. I was given a tumblerful of it and I liked the sweet taste
but I paid for it later!

Further along the coast, at Le Havre, Sister Marjorie Doyle was on
the ward in the casino hospital when the Luftwaffe bombers struck.

It was suddenly a nightmare as glass chandeliers in our old
casino hospital swung crazily in the lofty ceiling, ornate wall
mirrors cracked and shattered. Hurriedly we wrapped
patients in blankets and slid them under the beds. Even in
the midst of all this one patient had the nerve to invite me to
get under the bed with him! I declined and ran to the Sister's
office. There I knelt and prayed to God for deliverance of all
patients and staff. But the response came from elsewhere.
New orders came: 'Evacuate the hospital at once!'

We wrapped up patients, put them into ambulances and
set off for a château at Fécamp on the coast fifty miles north
of Le Havre. By nine o'clock that evening we had dined on
bully beef and biscuits washed down with some French wine.
Heads were nodding before we even left the table. My
batman, a lovely Welsh lad called Evans, whispered in my
ear: 'I've put your camp bed in a small box room. You'll get a
good night's rest there, Ma'am. I'll call you in the morning.'
It seemed as though I had only dropped off to sleep when
Evans came bursting into the room shouting 'Quick Ma'am.
Get up. The Germans are coming!'

We drove away from the château at dawn and back to the
casino hospital we had so recently left at Le Havre. When we
arrived, the town was a smoking ruin, fires still burning all
over from city centre to the suburbs. Our former hospital was
gutted, a glowing heap of ashes and girders. The docks were
devastated. There was no possibility of sailing out of that
port.

We drove to the railway station. I was amongst several
nurses who had to travel in a commandeered coal cart. You
can imagine what a state my grey uniform was in by the time
we arrived. After hours of waiting on the platform, a hospital
train drew into the station. We hurriedly loaded all our
patients into whatever narrow space a stretcher would fit,
and climbed aboard ourselves. What a relief! The patients
were no longer our responsibility and we just slumped on the
floor, dead beat. But tired as we were we could not sleep for
the ear-rattling crack of anti-aircraft guns and the deeper
thunderclaps of bombs dropping all around.

Slowly we chugged our way through one small station after
another with platforms packed with refugees. We drew

slowly through great rolling clouds of black smoke into the dockyards of Cherbourg. The first thing I saw there shocked me. It was the top half of a sunken hospital ship, its huge red cross still standing out from the white hull. Unmistakably. I couldn't help thinking then that whoever had bombed that ship had done so deliberately.

However, there was another hospital ship berthed nearby and we started to load the patients. It was then a strange thing happened. I heard my name being called. I stopped and listened. Again it came: 'Hey! Marjorie!'. I looked round the loading area and over the debris and saw him, my younger brother Steven! We hugged and I asked him to come with us on the hospital ship. He could not leave his unit. I wondered if I should ever see him again. I had to go. Once on board, the ship sailed. We were given a cup of tea laced with rum. Most of us were asleep within minutes.

Back in northern France the German advance was then sweeping like a flood towards the Channel ports. Bombarding every obstacle, their Panzers thundered on, reducing towns, villages and farmhouses to flaming ruins and trapping the British Expeditionary Force and a part of the French Army around Dunkirk. By the last week in May, the situation was chaotic. Casualty clearing stations hardly knew which way to turn, as forward German army units tightened the encircling net around the BEF. Number 5 Casualty Clearing Station was heavily bombed whilst operations were in progress. The surgeon and theatre staff carried patients down to a cellar and continued the operations by candlelight.

In the church of St Blaise at Crombeke, twenty miles south-west of Dunkirk, Number 10 Casualty Clearing Station, which 48-year-old Matron Jean Mitchell had brought to France, was working under terrible conditions. Packed into the gloom of that dark church, lit only by a few candles and two hurricane lamps, and lying in the churchyard and field beyond, were over a thousand wounded men. Pews had been removed to make room for stretchers. Doctors and nurses stumbled between them, doing what they could for those in pain. There was no food and very little water. Colonel Tristram Samuel, commanding Number 10 CCS, now faced a new and formidable problem. The situation was hopeless. His orders from Dunkirk were clear: 'Can take no more wounded. Stand fast until you fall into the hands of the Germans.' They were not going to get out. They would be prisoners of war.

His mind was made up. He would send the nurses back. First, though, there was one last task for them to do. They went round every casualty, giving out army field service cards to be completed with number, rank and name and posted back to England. Tears were running down the nurses' cheeks. The men then knew. They were to be left to the Germans. Hurriedly, the nurses then left.

Time passed with agonizing slowness. Then, just as the first light of dawn glowed through the stained-glass windows, Colonel Samuel rolled down his sleeves, straightened his tie, donned his jacket and put on his cap. He carefully adjusted the Red Cross band on his sleeve and marched from the church. He was ready for the formality. Surrender.

At Rosendael, three miles east of Bastion, Major Philip Newman, commanding the CCS there, was in a similar predicament, sorting out the rows of badly wounded soldiers. He had already received his orders. Many would just have to be left for the Germans to treat. Others might just make it to the docks at Dunkirk. But the ominous order from Major-General Harold Alexander had left him with another terrible decision: which of the nursing orderlies and medical officers should he leave with those wounded, to become, perhaps for many years, prisoners of war? He looked at the message again: 'One doctor and ten other ranks must stay behind with them.' Major Newman made up his mind. Chance would decide the destiny of doctors and nursing orderlies. In the light of flaring acetylene lamps, the padre drew names from a hat. One of the first drawn out to stay was that of Major Philip Newman.

Just as they were all reconciled to their fate, a new order came from General Alexander: 'All those wounded who were semi-ambulant should have a chance to get away on the last trucks.' Miraculously, men heaved themselves off their backs and crawled, hopped or used makeshift crutches from farmyard rakes and brushes to get to the trucks. Newman and the orderlies who had drawn the unlucky bits of paper from the hat settled down to await their fates.

Norman Woodhouse, of the East Yorks, recalled that reprieve:

> I wasn't in any great pain then, my leg was splinted and I'd been given an injection. Those nurses didn't seem real, nor the noise. I must have dozed part of the time because it was broad daylight when I was lifted onto the Ambulance Train. I then began to see and hear things more clearly. We were on our way, rattling over rails and points. We'd not gone very far when bits of wood, splinters and bullets came hurtling through the roof. Men cried out. None of us could move. A nurse came through carrying padding and bandages. She stooped over patients, staunching blood and applying thick field dressings. They were marvellous. Wonderful.[8]

Doctors and nurses on those trains worked wonders. Surgeons carried out emergency operations, Sisters replaced blood-caked dressings and fed the critically wounded casualties. By the end of the short campaign, nine out of the fourteen hospital trains operating in France would be lost through bombing or capture.

Whole units were cut off, but still casualties had to be treated. Improvisation was the order of the day. Captain William MacDonald, a medical officer separated from his unit on the beaches, sterilized wounds with petrol, and, lacking Thomas splints for compound fractures, secured shattered femurs with rifles. RAMC nursing orderlies ransacked abandoned houses for sheets.

In a last supreme effort to bring back as many of the wounded as possible, two British hospital ships, clearly identified as such, were sent across the Channel by daylight after an uncoded message, deliberately meant to be intercepted by the Germans, was transmitted, announcing their mission. One of these hospital ships was sunk; the other was so badly damaged it had to turn back.

Other rescue ships made it to the breakwater in the harbour. A seemingly endless flow of troops shuffled down it, and, amongst them, stretcher-bearers dodged back and forth as fast as they could, carrying their wounded on to the ships. On one trawler, Surgeon-Lieutenant David Brown, formerly of the destroyer *Whitehall*, having no surgical instruments available, amputated legs and arms with the engine-room's hack-saw. sterilized with blazing chloroform.[9] Amy Goodrick, with a Mae West life-jacket strapped firmly across her chest, braved shell splinters stabbing into the deck of the hospital ship *Dinard* to fetch water and food for wounded men who had neither eaten nor drunk anything for days.[10] For thirteen days, hospital ships ran the gauntlet across the Channel between Dover and French ports.

Eileen Hawkin and her party realized they had no hope of getting off from those Normandy ports, so they drove to St Nazaire where two ships still had room for them. 'They were horribly overcrowded with not enough life belts to go round but we were only too pleased to sail away. We were just gathering speed when the Luftwaffe bombers came in low. They sank the sister ship and we stopped to pick up survivors. It was the one time I realized just how much my life was in danger. At other times we'd been too busy to notice.'

In a letter to her Matron-in-Chief, one sister told how surgeons from Number 16 General Hospital carried out emergency operations during the crossing, and how one soldier had his leg amputated immediately he was brought on board. On their next crossing, when they could not get to the quay because other ships were loading casualties from a hospital train there, they started to sail out of the harbour but were attacked by German dive-bombers. 'Salvos of bombs fell on either side of the ship, pieces of bomb cases splintered the deck. Our hospital ship markings were plainly visible but we were as much a target as any other ship,' she wrote.[11]

Indeed, the Luftwaffe's orders were clearly worded, as Cajus Bekker recorded: 'The Luftwaffe nominated Dunkirk as its main target, and for the first time ordered both Luftflotten to operate at maximum strength against the town and harbour.'[12] The stream of bombers never let up.

Neither town nor harbour was given any breathing space. Beneath all the smoke and dust from the fires and collapsing buildings the town itself was hardly recognizable as more bombs fell on the inferno. The long eastern mole was a prime target. There, nurses and medical teams worked furiously to load as many of the wounded on to the hospital ships berthed there before the mole itself was destroyed.

A senior Sister of the QAIMNS, describing the scene dispassionately in a letter to Matron-in-Chief, Katharine Jones, told how the quay was broken up and on fire in places, yet ships' officers, crew and RAMC personnel all helped to carry patients the length of the quay under machine-gun fire from the air. Soon all beds on the ship were filled, and patients were put on makeshift beds on the floor. Nurses renewed dressings, which had not been done for days, and fed those who could eat, whilst all the time, bombs fell around their ship. 'The Sisters with me were most helpful. They looked after their patients splendidly under difficult circumstances. The constant machine-gun fire and bombs did not in any way detract from their efficiency,' she concluded.[13]

Time and time again the cool efficiency of those nurses was noted. A captain of a hospital ship wrote after the evacuation of Dunkirk: 'We had numerous narrow escapes and nerve-racking experiences. During all this our Sisters were really splendid. Never a sign of excitement or panic. They just carried on under the able leadership of our Matron, calmly and efficiently.'[14]

'Calmly and efficiently'. That just about sums up the way those nurses worked in all theatres of war and under the most testing conditions.

When the 'miracle' of Dunkirk was over, it was noted that shortly after the first six nursing sisters had landed at Cherbourg with the BEF in September 1939, more than a thousand others had joined them. In various ways they all got back to Britain in 1940 and, despite the many ordeals, most of them volunteered for further service overseas.[15] This was a great tribute not only to their courage but also to the training which had prepared them for the harsh reality of front line service.

Back in England, no one knew what those men and women of the BEF had been through. Perhaps it was just as well. As Montgomery wrote in his memoirs, 'It was not understood that the British Army had suffered a crushing defeat and that our island home was now in grave danger.'

Facing that danger very soon would be the nurses, servicemen and women and civilians alike.

2 Front-line Britain

We had quite a few cases with nervous disorder – 'shell shock'. These were treated with doses of paraldehyde which put them to sleep and we would wake them every four hours, toilet them, make them drink a pint of fruit juice, give them another dose of paraldehyde. This treatment lasted about thirty-six hours. They seemed to recover sufficiently to return to duty.

Alexandra Croll QARNNS
Royal Naval Depot, Lowestoft

With France defeated, Britain was the only enemy standing in Hitler's way towards his aim of permanent domination of Europe. On 17 July 1940 he issued a directive to commanders of the German Army, Navy and Air Force. It read: 'Since England, in spite of her hopeless military situation shows no signs of coming to an understanding, I have decided to prepare for, and if necessary to carry out an invasion of Britain.'[1] Nurses in Britain were now to be in the front line and dealing with new kinds of casualties.

'Our hospital at Belmont, Surrey, was next to the railway line to London. We had just received survivors from the SS *Lancastrian* sunk by the Luftwaffe off Dunkirk beaches, when we had our own first raid,' recalled Joy Hobley, then a VAD (Mobile). 'A direct hit on the hospital killed one nurse and took the arm off another nurse.'

The situation for Britain was grim. Somehow, the 'miracle' of Dunkirk had aroused the whole British nation. Few, however, knew how perilous their position was. The troops brought home from France were far from being a well-equipped fighting force. And Britain now stood alone. The future would depend upon the Royal Air Force, for Hitler had said there would be no invasion until German air superiority was achieved.

And so the Battle of Britain began. Reichsmarschall Hermann Goering, who had arrogantly boasted his Air Force would bomb Britain to its knees without any help from the German Army or Navy, unleashed 2,000 war planes. He aimed to smash Fighter Command and its capability of defending Britain, and also break the nation's morale and its will to continue fighting.

In all this, nurses were going to play a vital part.

Whilst Luftwaffe bombers concentrated on Fighter Command and coastal radar stations, bombs also fell on unexpected places. At that time, Sister Iris Jones (later Ogilvie and now Bower) was stationed at St Athan RAF Hospital, in the Vale of Glamorgan, Wales. She had trained at St Mary's Hospital, Paddington, London, with her friend Mollie Giles, and together they had applied to join Princess Mary's RAF Nursing Service, but it was a strange quirk of fate that decided their success at the interview for the Service. To this day, Iris is still astonished that such a small fact could determine the whole of her future life, as she musingly recalled:

> The interview was awe inspiring. At the head of a long table sat an impressive Air Marshal. Alongside were senior officers and the Matron-in-Chief, Dame Gladys Taylor. The other applicants were all from Barts or Guys and we did not give ourselves much chance. When I was being interviewed I felt I was not doing very well. Then when the Air Marshal asked me if I spoke any foreign languages I didn't think my school certificate French would be good enough so I said, 'Yes, I speak Welsh.' Nobody said a word. But the Air Marshal had a twinkle in his eye when he looked at me. I was asked to wait outside.
>
> When everybody had been through an officer came out and told me that my application was approved. 'Do you know why?' he asked. I shook my head. 'Because the Air Marshal's mother speaks Welsh!' he said.

Iris was enjoying life at St Athan, and it was not too far from her home in Tremain, near Cardigan. One night she was doing her rounds, when the quiet of the hospital headquarters was disturbed by the frantic ringing of the telephones: an air raid alert. Sirens screamed their warning, but there was not time to do anything much with the patients before the first of the bombs fell on the RAF camp and hospital. Iris felt stunned by a noise beyond all comprehension, the continuous explosions of bombs smashing at her ears and nerves, numbing her brain. Then came a terrifying roar. A high-explosive bomb hit the hospital wing at the far end of the corridor in which she was walking.

A shiver of fear shot through her body. Screams came from that direction. She would have to do something. But what? She started to run towards the bombed building, but suddenly her feet gave out from

under her. She felt herself falling a long way down. She was in a deep
bomb crater. She clawed her way upwards and into the building which
once had been a ward. Bombs were still falling. Patients were crying,
moaning and shrieking in pain and horror. There was a heart-stopping
sound of panic.

She worked with speed, helping some patients to take cover under
their own beds and reassuring others the worst was over. Soon, indeed,
it was. Nurses, doctors and orderlies rallied each other, and before long
the hospital was back to its normal routine. Mercifully, casualties were
few. But the higher authorities felt gallantry should be recognized. Iris
Jones received the award of Associate of the Royal Red Cross. 'I didn't
do anything more than anyone else would have done. I just happened to
be in the right place at the right time,' she said.

Not many months later she just happened to again be in the right
place at the right time. She had been posted to Torquay, Devon, where
a hospital for RAF officers had been established in the Palace Hotel. It
was a 'safe area' where aircrew with faces 'fried' and bodies badly
mutilated when their aircraft was shot down in flames could recover
between plastic surgery operations carried out in East Grinstead's
Queen Victoria Hospital. There, Dr Archibald McIndoe was giving new
hope to those terribly scarred young men who came to him. He rebuilt
entire faces, eyes, ears, limbs and more. In between each operation, a
period of rest and careful nursing was essential.

Convalescing slowly at Torquay at that time was Richard Hillary, a
young fighter pilot whose plane had been shot down in flames over the
Kent coast. In the quiet ambience of Torquay, where patients could
gaze upon the tranquil sunlit waters of Tor Bay, no better place could
have been found for him to write his famous book *The Last Enemy*. Or
so it seemed.

It was on one of those tranquil sunny mornings that Sister Iris Jones
was walking to her ward with a very pretty Australian girl, known as
Tinkle Bell, of the Voluntary Aid Detachment. Everyone liked Tinkle
Bell. Together they were chattering away when a medical officer came
towards them from the wards. He asked, 'Can you spare a moment,
Sister? There's just one or two things I need to check with you before
you go to your ward.' Iris smiled and sent Tinkle Bell on her way alone,
whilst she went with the medical officer. They had just turned the corner
of the corridor when they heard the roar of aeroplane engines. Through
the big bay windows they saw a flight of German bombers thundering
across the bay from Brixham, their black German crosses clearly visible.
Iris and the medical officer both dived for cover under the nearest bed.

Under anaesthetic on the operating table then was Flight Lieutenant
Peter Swan, whose aircraft had crashed after a mock attack by a Bristol
Beaufighter. Though Swan had managed to bale out, he had hit the tail
of his own aircraft and smashed both legs. Already he had spent a year
in the RAF hospital at Halton, Buckinghamshire, and he was eager to

get back to Bomber Command. This final operation would put him well on the road to recovery.

The first bomb hit the hospital and others followed. When the noise subsided, Iris and the medical officer crawled from under the bed into the dust and debris of the corridor. Now they could hear cries and moans. Rubble was still tumbling down. They dashed along the corridor towards where a small ward had been. There was just now a gaping hole in the ground. Iris was struck by the horror of what she then saw. A thin arm with a frilly cuff at the end protruded from a pile of heavy masonry. There was no doubt in her mind. Lying crushed beneath all the concrete and metal was Tinkle Bell.

When Peter Swan emerged from his anaesthetic he found himself covered in blood from the anaesthetist's wounds. Swan himself was not touched. He went on to become one of the war's outstanding Pathfinder pilots, winning the DFC and DSO in 1944 and a bar to his DFC in 1945. (He died, aged seventy-five, in November 1995 as this book was being written.) In another wing of the Palace Hotel at that time were thirty Polish pilots, playing cards. All were killed.

All over the south coast then, RAF nurses were taking the force of the Luftwaffe's fury. Above them, a great slogging match was being waged between RAF and Luftwaffe fighters, whilst bombers pounded the airfields. WAAF nursing orderlies stuck to their posts amidst blackened shells of buildings.

Nursing Orderly Corporal Joan Daphne Pearson was asleep in her billet at Detling, Kent, when she heard a terrible noise of an aircraft crashing close to the WAAF quarters. She looked through her window at station headquarters and saw a twinkling light. An ambulance was on its way to the crash. Daphne immediately saw a problem. Before the ambulance could reach the aircraft it would need to pass through gates which were locked every night. She dressed quickly and dashed to the guard room. She shouted to the Guard Commander to open the gates and then ran to the fence, behind which lay the crashed aircraft. It was now beginning to catch fire. A policeman tried to block her way, but she side-stepped him and climbed the fence. Figures converged upon the blazing aircraft. Daphne saw a man dragging the pilot away from the fire. She took charge of the injured pilot and told his rescuer to break down the fence to let the ambulance through. She then dragged the pilot further from the blaze, took off his harness and found that touching his neck caused him to squirm in pain. She thought his neck might be dislocated. He was conscious and told her to get away, as the aircraft had a full load of bombs. But her nursing instincts would not let her leave him.

At that moment there was a tremendous flash and explosion as the aircraft's petrol tanks blew up. Again, Daphne's immediate concern was for the safety of her patient. She lay down alongside him to shield him from the blasts from any further explosions. A huge bomb then exploded, and Daphne had to hold the pilot's head still to prevent what might result in further dislocation. The ambulance had then arrived, and although further bombs were likely to explode, she got up and ran to the fence to help the medical officer with a stretcher for her patient. Together they got him aboard the ambulance as other bombs were exploding and then drove him back to the Sick Quarters.

For her gallantry and complete indifference to her own safety, Corporal Joan Daphne Pearson was awarded the George Cross.

No hazard daunted these young nursing orderlies on RAF stations targeted by the Luftwaffe. They 'carried on' at their vital tasks with a sang-froid that was truly amazing.

Betty Wragg, a WAAF nursing orderly at RAF Mepal, near Ely, Cambridgeshire, recalled how she was under no illusions about her new job.

> On my very first day I sensed what lay ahead of me and I realized I had never seen a dead person. There was a young airman who had been killed the night before and he was in a small ante-room waiting to be taken to Ely. I had to get used to the idea of seeing dead and badly wounded airmen, so I went to look at him. I'll always remember him. Although he had suffered injuries to the bottom half of his face, he just looked very peaceful – so young – and my heart bled for the mother who would soon know that her son had died.
>
> Even then we had bombers attacking Germany and I dreaded receiving the casualties that were carried in after each raid. They were nearly always facial injuries. So when a message was received for us to expect casualties I found myself praying, 'Please God, don't let it be another face.'
>
> We had one young lad brought in and the lower part of his face was all smashed in, an awful mess. We gave him morphia and did what we could before sending him off to hospital. I thought he'd never be able to do much for himself ever again. Yet months later he came back to thank us for what we'd done and he was all patched up and ready to go off on operations again. Burns were the most horrifying, though.

In the summer of 1940 the badly burnt airman was a problem confronting nurses all too frequently. Squadron Leader Tom Gleave's case was typical. His Hurricane was hit by German cannon-shells, and great spouts of flame engulfed him in his cockpit as if from a blowlamp nozzle. There was an explosion, another huge flash, and his whole body and face were wreathed in flames. The force of the explosion threw him clear of the cockpit. He pulled the parachute ripcord and lost consciousness.[2]

Tom Gleave's 'fried' body was delivered to Orpington Hospital, near Bromley, Kent. His eyelids and nose were burnt away, his legs and body horribly scarred. He woke up under a bed in the Orpington hospital. He had just had an emergency operation. The Luftwaffe were bombing the area, and patients had been slid under their beds for greater safety. He remembered how the floor rocked as bombs whistled down and nearby anti-aircraft guns opened up. His nurse knelt beside him and put her hand on his shoulder and the other over the cage on his burnt legs, sprawling herself protectingly across him. His mouth was dry with the effects of the anaesthetic. Vaguely amidst all the crashing of bombs he remembers asking his nurse for a drink. 'Nurse brought a bowl of ice cubes and a glass of iced water. Then she placed some ice in my mouth, repeating this every ten minutes. It was delicious.'

That raid went on for hours. Never once did that nurse leave Tom Gleave's side. She crouched beside him, adjusting the pillow beneath the charred skin of his head from time to time and placing cubes of ice in his mouth. Never once did she think of taking cover herself.

Badly burnt men were then being treated too by Royal Naval nursing sisters at the RNH Portland, Dorset. In the days following the evacuation of Dunkirk, air raids became more and more frequent. The Superintending Sister at Portland remembers clearly the horror she felt at receiving 150 blackened and badly burned men from HMS *Foylebank*, which had received a direct hit and was set on fire in the harbour.[3]

Sisters of Queen Alexandra's Royal Naval Nursing Service on duty in the RNH Haslar, overlooking the Solent in Portsmouth, worked right through dozens of air raids, evacuating some patients to the cellars and doing the rounds of others too ill to move when the hospital received a direct hit. Nurses tended their patients by torchlight in the blackout, and when there was such a rush of casualties they carried them up three flights of stairs to the third floor. As in other front-line hospitals, shattering glass was a great problem because it was so difficult to see and could easily sever an artery of a patient too ill to fend for himself.

An account of an air raid on the RNH Haslar in *A History of the Queen Alexandra's Royal Naval Nursing Service* throws an interesting light on the way nurses and doctors simply refused to be cowed by the bombing.

A raid had just started and the night sister had placed her case sheets on the table for the medical officer to complete, when the ward was filled with the roar of an aircraft's engines.

> 'Do we duck?' Sister inquired pleasantly.
> 'Certainly not!' replied the surgeon commander emphatically.
> It was sang-froid such as this which must surely have supported many of the medical teams working world wide through similar difficult situations.[4]

To the nurses in the RNH at Plymouth it seemed as though they had been singled out by the Luftwaffe for special attention. Situated close to the Devonport dockyard, it was not really surprising that during the height of the blitz, the hospital was hit on three consecutive nights. After that experience patients were not kept there any longer than necessary and were evacuated to nearby stately homes for longer term care. Sisters nevertheless continued to serve in the danger area in the resuscitation ward of the RNH. Nightly bombardments would begin at ten o'clock and continue until three or four in the morning. Operations would begin at 7.30 in the morning and continue throughout the day and evening.

All nurses were working very long hours. Dorothy Blackburn, then a 17-year-old probationer nurse at Queen Mary's Hospital for Children, Carshalton, never had a spare moment during raids.

> We moved as many children as we could to the re-inforced places in the hospital but we could not find places for the children in spinal carriages. They were mainly children with tubercular hips from poor families in the East End of London. Naturally, when the bombs were dropping they were terrified and cried out for their mothers. We just couldn't leave them to take cover ourselves so we stayed by their spinal frame carriages telling them about that nasty man Hitler who was making a lot of noise and he was going to get into trouble one of these days. And then when the 'All Clear' sounded we had to get a move on, making their breakfasts. You see their parents would bring food in for them and there would be a note saying this one had a kipper, the other one a fried egg and I had to cook it for them. When their parents came to visit them they would ask the children if they enjoyed their kipper or whatever it was. I don't know how we managed to keep going with all the jobs we had to do and with so little sleep due to air raids at night as well as those in the daytime.
>
> One day I was bustling round the ward trying to get through a thousand and one jobs when the Ward Sister flounced in saying, 'You silly goose! Don't you know there's an incendiary bomb on the roof? Deal with it!' Terrified, I had to climb a ladder with my bucket of sand and a shovel and throw sand on the blazing and crackling device until it went out. I wonder now how we managed all that sort of thing.

For Dorothy Blackburn and other nurses at Carshalton and London there would be greater terror to be faced four years later when Hitler's long-vaunted secret weapons – the V1 and V2 rocket-bombs – hit the hospitals there ...

By 17 September 1940 Hitler realized that he had failed to reduce RAF Fighter Command to that degree of impotence for his planned invasion to succeed. His battle for Britain had been lost. He announced that the invasion of Britain would be postponed 'until further notice', but the blitz would go on. He would force Britain to its knees by launching massive air raids against London and all the major cities.

In those raids, tales of brave acts by nurses in hospitals throughout Britain are legion. Many of them were never recorded owing to the confusion of the moment, but they live imperishably in the memories of those patients and nurses who were privileged to witness them and survive.

Some accounts did reach the newspapers. Newspapers of 16 October carried reports of 18-year-old probationer nurses ignoring falling bombs as they helped to rescue patients when their hospital in south-east England (the location not being revealed for security reasons) was twice attacked by the Luftwaffe. High-explosive bombs cut through part of the kitchen quarters, affecting wards on both sides. One nurse, Sister Hooker, was killed, five of the staff were injured and several elderly patients died from shock. The *Daily Telegraph* correspondent wrote: 'While they worked, German bombers were continuing to fly overhead and splinters from anti-aircraft shells were falling. On all sides I heard the remark: *"The nurses were wonderful"*.'

When high explosive bombs hit another London hospital, nurses attending a staff dance ran out in their evening dresses and worked through the night helping to rescue trapped patients.

In indescribably exacting conditions, rendered perilous by a hail of bombs, Red Cross VADs helped to fight two extensive fires. Doctors, nurses and auxiliary hospital workers vied with one another in the risks they took to succour the wounded. Ambulances with nurses accompanying patients raced through the streets, heedless of the dangers from overhead. Nothing daunted them.

Margaret Browne was training at St Thomas's Hospital during the blitz on London. She recalled the frightening as well as the comical times:

> The hospital was hit several times in raids between September '40 and May 1941. Nurses and medical staff were all busy moving patients or in rescue work. In one raid three of our staff were exceptionally brave. Dr Norman, a physician, a medical student called Maling and the Assistant Clerk of Works, a Mr Frewer, searched for patients, tunnelling under slabs of concrete and rubble whilst bombs exploded all around. They never thought of their own safety

but only the lives of those they were trying to rescue. All
three were awarded the civilian VC – the George Cross.

We trainees had to move to another hospital housed in
army huts. Some days we had to work in the operating
theatre helping with the smaller operations such as varicose
veins, haemorrhoids and tonsils. At about seven o'clock one
Monday evening the medical students were being allowed to
'get their hand in'. A young woman, already anaesthetized,
was heaved on to the operating table and into the usual
ungainly position to have her piles attended to. We took one
look inside her thigh and all fell about giggling and laughing.
There, right at the top, was tattooed a heart and arrow with
the words underneath, I LOVE CYRIL.

That operating theatre was a revelation; one surgeon
operated with only pyjama trousers under his gown, the chief
anaesthetist favoured rugger shorts and one surgeon secured
his sleeves with bicycle clips! Once a nurse in charge of his
case found the clips lying beside the sterile gloves and masks.
She swept the lot off wondering who'd put the dirty things on
her clean table, before we'd a chance to tell her they'd been
sterilised too.

And so life went on during the blitz, the tragic and comic woven
together in a sustaining blend.

In retrospect, what is particularly interesting about reports of the
bombing of hospitals is the way newspapers stressed the grandness of
the human element and the stoicism of patients and medical staff in
words that today seem hardly credible.

Of one particular raid on a London hospital a journalist on-the-spot
wrote, 'The last man to be brought out was a patient whose legs had
been pinned down by a heavy piece of masonry for several hours.
Although in severe pain, he laughed and joked with his rescuers all the
time. A doctor gave him morphia and another man gave him a
cigarette.'[5] Nowhere, it seems, was there anything but a heartening
story to tell of the bravery of those nurses now in Britain's front line.
Everywhere, people reacted defiantly, their spirit and resolution
toughened by it all.

Hospital beds had to be found for the thousands of casualties in
London. Special trains stood ready to take them north. Sister Simonites,
who had given up nursing in 1939 when she had a young baby,
responded to a call for volunteers to serve on hospital trains. But she
had not bargained for what it would entail.

We volunteers were asked to assemble one morning at York
railway sidings. Imagine our surprise when we were
introduced to our 'hospital'. There were 9 filthy wagons

smelling strongly of fish, with a gully down the centre – in fact they were just nine old fish wagons, reeking to high heaven. 'There you are,' they said. 'All yours!'

We were faced with the task of converting each wagon to a ward for 30 patients, a total for the train of 270 stretcher cases. We held a meeting. Decided to buy tins of white paint and distemper, Red Rud for the floors, and gallons of strong smelling disinfectant. Two men agreed to bolt brackets to the walls to hold 30 stretchers in two tiers.

Next morning we turned up at the siding in our working clothes and started scrubbing and cleaning the inside of the wagons. The men scrubbed too and then started painting the walls. We left two carriages for our own use; one for the ladies and one for the men. We were now all ready for our first call.

Similar preparations were then being made all over Britain. Margaret Pritchett, then a Red Cross nurse, was with Dr Louis Glass (later to become Lord Mayor of Birmingham). 'We had a very exciting time running the gauntlet of bombs collecting casualties from the London blitz and taking them to hospitals in the country,' Margaret recalled. 'After loading casualties, we had to feed them. We made them minced meat with mashed potatoes followed by rice pudding cooked on a coal burning Dixie stove on the train. We took about 300 patients each time. We slept on stretchers. I did this for two years during the time Britain was being bombed.'

All those trains did yeoman service. Thousands of casualties came by train to hospitals in the north of England. Schools were used as 'over-flow' hospitals. Nurse Goodman Platts (now Mungall), then a probationer, was sent to Bootham School, Clifton, York, where classrooms were converted into wards. 'I had to polish the brass door handles as they had never shone before!' 'Casualties from London arrived at all times. Stretchers filled the wards and corridors and even the chapel,' recalled Beryl Allinson, then at York County Hospital.

But Goering's fifty-seven nights of terror for London failed to break the capital's morale. Now he looked round for easier targets. The first great air raid outside London fell upon a city packed with armament factories and skilled artisans making weapons of war: Coventry.

On the bright moonlit night of 14 November 1940, Nazi bombers came with one intent – to reduce the whole city to a mass of rubble. And they almost succeeded. Great fires started round the cathedral itself. The fires were targeted again and again, with succeeding waves of bombers, spreading the fire in all directions.

The first shower of incendiaries started fires in the Coventry and Warwickshire Hospital itself. Then the Nurses' Home was hit with a high-explosive bomb seconds after the last nurse had left. Tales are now legendary of how nurses in Coventry that night ignored the shrapnel whizzing down upon them as they pushed patients on trolleys across the courtyard to safer areas, and how they tended to patients for eleven hours on end as bombs exploded around and on the building itself. They are told in graphic detail by eyewitnesses and nurses themselves in a companion volume to this – *Heroines of World War Two*, also published by Robert Hale Limited. It is sufficient here to once again make note of the brief appreciation of their efforts by the hospital registrar, Dr Winter, who said: 'The nurses stood firm. Their morale was stupefying!'

Four nights later it was Birmingham's turn to be blitzed. Beryl Allinson, then a second-year probationer at the Birmingham Hospital, got her baptism of fire when a land-mine dropped on the roof.

Six hundred fires were started, and again nurses had the problem of dressing very painful burns as they worked through a hail of bombs. They took pride in coping with the stream of casualties brought in by fifty ambulances, often driven by women. These drivers also aroused admiration. One rescue party leader, a veteran of the First World War, recalled finding a group of women drivers sitting filing their nails in the local ambulance depot before the blitz actually started and said to himself: 'You wait till the bombs start falling, girls, and it'll be a different story then.' A week later when the raids began he popped into the depot and there the girls were, sitting waiting for emergency calls doing their nails! 'They'd been in the midst of it all ferrying casualties through streets where houses were crashing down all around them, and dealing with death and mutilation in forms as horrible as any battlefield had ever seen, then they came back to wait for the next call and did their nails!' he said.[6]

And so the raids on the arms towns continued. Sheffield, one of the world's great arsenals, was devastated shortly before Christmas 1940. Fire and destruction of buildings made most streets almost impassable, and casualties were taken to hospitals on handcarts when ambulances could not get through. Merseyside was used to the raids by day and by night. Sister Sylvia Suthren saw Liverpool burning for eight nights. 'What sticks in my mind were the terrible burns men had on their buttocks when incendiaries had fallen on them whilst digging in rubble for survivors.' Next to Merseyside, perhaps the most intense and continuous attacks fell upon Plymouth, Clydebank, Belfast and Hull to put docks out of action. But inevitably hospitals were also hit.

It was not just in hospitals that nurses displayed conspicuous gallantry in Britain then. In Portsmouth, during one of the many massive air raids, two midwives attending women in childbirth distinguished themselves.[7] Mary Farr was with a young mother-to-be when the first bombs fell. Refusing to take cover herself, she protected the young woman with her own body when bombs were exploding all around. At one time the destruction of neighbouring buildings was so great that it seemed the house she was in, already bomb-damaged, was about to collapse on both of them. But Mary Farr attended to her job and delivered the baby before the 'All Clear' sounded.

Another midwife, Mrs Evelyn Lever of Manchester, had not practised her profession for more than twenty years, but when, at the height of a heavy raid on the city, a doctor called for a doctor and midwife, neither could be found, and so an appeal was made to Mrs Lever. Though the bombs were shaking the district, she answered the call without a second thought. As she approached the house where her patient was lying in labour, Evelyn Lever saw in her path a blazing gas main. She took a firm hold of her bag and dashed through the smoke and heat to the house itself. Inside she was confronted by a wrecked hall and staircase, down which water cascaded from fractured pipes. Evelyn Lever managed to get her patient down into the cellar and attended to her there.

For their courage the two midwives were awarded the medal of the civil division of the Order of the British Empire.

During the 1940–41 blitz years, 43,667 civilians were killed, and 50,387 seriously injured, but civil morale was not disturbed nor production appreciably reduced. To quote the well-known phrase of the time, '*Britain can take it!*' Nurses certainly could, and did. When in 1940–41 over five hundred hospitals were bomb-damaged yet never ceased to function, nurses did lose their own lives by disregarding their own safety for that of their patients. Fifteen nurses were awarded the George Medal for conspicuous bravery.

Whilst the blitz on Britain was petering out, a more distant danger was occupying the minds of the British War Cabinet and inevitably, towards that danger, nurses were already moving.

3 The Middle East

The Western Desert was a marvellous
battleground in which to retreat.

Fred Majdalany[1]

In the autumn of 1940 when nurses who had escaped from France with
the BEF were on extended leave in Britain, their future was being
decided by a hostile Italian army facing the British forces across the
frontier of Egypt. At any moment it might take the offensive. Mussolini
was so determined not to miss the opportunity of sitting at the peace
conference of a war he thought was about to end, that on 10 June 1940
he declared war on France and Britain. On 7 September, he ordered
Marshal Rodolfo Graziani to attack Egypt. On 13 September 1940,
fourteen Italian divisions advanced sixty miles into Egypt to Sidi
Barrani. The desert war, which would take Britain's front-line nurses on
a two-thousand mile chase across the Western Desert through Alamein,
Tripoli and on to Tunis, had begun. With surprising speed, troop
reinforcements, supported by contingents of nurses for casualty clearing
stations and field hospitals, were dispatched from Britain round the
Cape of Good Hope to the Suez Canal.

It was an exciting time for Marjorie Doyle (later Bennett).
Despite alarming experiences of nurses in France, she and her
colleagues were delighted to be on the way to where the action was.

> Although there were lectures to attend on board – such as
> those on tropical diseases and the sordid lectures on venereal
> diseases – we had plenty of time for relaxing socially.
>
> We were treated like royalty in Cape Town and when we
> eventually sailed, a lady in a white dress stood at the end of
> the quay and sang a farewell song to us. Very moving. It was
> then we felt as if we really were being sent off to war.

They soon discovered the reality of what going to war meant. 'We
went into a fly-ridden transit camp at Akaba in the middle of no-where,'
said Marjorie. 'We learnt how to live with flies, bugs, beetles, rats and

mice. We soon got into the way of eating with a fork or spoon and using the other hand to waft away the flies as we lifted food to our mouths.'

The desert flea, though, was the supreme torturer. He never rested. No matter what measures were taken, the flea was always there. Some nursing orderlies hit upon a highly recommended remedy which did not appeal much to the newly arrived nursing sisters, and that was to keep a cage of tame mice close to the bed. They believed that by humans sleeping close to the mice, the fleas would migrate from their bodies to those of the mice.

Nurses had their own remedy, as Margaret Jennings recalled:

> We waged a nightly onslaught against the little devils that inhabited our beds. Armed with a bar of moistened soap, two of us would stand at the ready on each side of the bed. On the command 'Now!' we'd whip back the sheet, flash our deadly blows, and count with satisfaction the fleas sticking to our soap at the end of each exercise.
>
> One other difficulty of desert life, which all nurses had to live with as they moved forward just behind the front line troops, was 'Gippy tummy', a form of dysentery, and the awful latrines. These were usually a long way from the tents [they needed to be] and comprised little more than long poles supporting a canvas screen. Inside were lengths of planking in which were holes, with buckets beneath. For obvious reasons the canvas did not reach the ground, as each morning the 'dung cart' drawn by a mule came round and the buckets were emptied into the cart.
>
> The Egyptians seemed fascinated by us women going behind the screen, and the canvas structure was open to the sky. Very disconcerting it was to find a brown arm reaching beneath your bottom to remove the bucket.

For those newly arrived nursing sisters it was the lull before the storm. At first their patients were mainly men stricken with dysentery, sand-fly fever, septic cactus wounds, heat exhaustion and desert sores.

All this changed on 9 December 1940. For six weeks the Italian army had sat at Sidi Barrani threatening the port of Alexandria, the Suez canal and the way to the rich oil fields of the Middle East. Meanwhile the British, deciphering Italian codes, made plans. Two British divisions secretly assembled and struck hard and fast. Totally surprised, seven ill-equipped Italian divisions broke and fled the field. Not all got away; 38,000 were taken to prison camps.

Italian wounded presented a problem for the nurses. Those carried into forward British hospitals were terrified. They clung to their beds when nurses tried to take them into the mobile showers. They had heard

about the 'showers' in German concentration camps – gas chambers. To
stiffen their resolve in the line, they had been fed propaganda about what
to expect if captured. They were convinced the British would either shoot
or gas them. Many refused to take their medication until the adminis-
tering nurse had taken a sip of the proffered draught herself. Eventually
trust was established, and special wards were set aside for Italian staff to
run themselves.

Once the British front moved forward, so too did the Army and RAF
nurses with their field hospitals and casualty clearing stations. Cases of
severe heat exhaustion increased alarmingly. Patients were cooled under
showers and then sent to a medical ward equipped with an oil-run
refrigerator producing ice to pack around their bodies, especially under
armpits and in the groin. An added complication was that twenty-four
hours later, most patients suffered bouts of acute diarrhoea.

In November 1940, however, many nurses in the Middle East suddenly
found themselves on a boat crossing from Alexandria to Greece, as is
discussed in chapter four.

The Eighth Army during this period was making bold advances over
hundreds of miles up the desert, followed by headlong flights back the
same way, and the nurses had to be on the move with them, pitching their
tented wards on the arid desert amongst rough yellow rocks and grey
earth. And at each new base, trenches had to be dug for protection
against air attacks. Red Cross markings offered little protection from
pilots seeking a target into which they could empty their guns.

To cope with a front line which was rarely the same from one day to the
next, mobile field hospitals close to the fighting were a boon. Most of the
Army nurses were experienced in manning mobile hospitals, but many of
the Princess Mary's RAF Nursing Service were rushed forward into the
Western Desert without so much as a course in field conditions. Needless
to say, they coped admirably nevertheless.

The German Air Force was ever active, engaging British fighters and
then dive-bombing and strafing columns of transport or tents. To be fair
to the German pilots, once a column was on the move the dust clouds
raised by their wheels made it impossible for anyone to discern whether
or not there was a red cross on the roofs of vehicles. All were in the front
line.

The well-respected war correspondent Ernie Pyle, who was with the
Eighth Army then, noted that although he had heard of German aircraft
firing upon ambulances, he had never seen evidence of it. In fact, he told
of examples of exactly the opposite, where, for instance, the Germans
who had been shelling a battlefield stopped doing so – and held fire for
eight hours – whilst a battalion surgeon took away the dead and wounded
in his ambulance. Pyle had also been told about British ambulances
obliviously passing German machine-gun nests and the Germans letting

them through once they saw the injured in the back.[2]

War took its toll on both sides. The fresh-faced soldiers who had set out from Britain had become lean with nut-brown skin often afflicted with desert sores – scratches which readily festered and never really healed, re-infected all the time by swarms of merciless, fat black flies, irritating them all day long. 'When I was dressing wounds on the ward I would be accompanied by two Italian POWs with fly swats waving over the wounds. Eugh! The smell of some of them when the dressings were removed. Revolting,' recalled Marjorie Doyle.

On 22 January 1941 the British Eighth Army captured the port of Tobruk, taking 25,000 Italian soldiers prisoner. Three weeks later, Hitler sent his 15th Armoured Division under General Erwin Rommel to help his ally Mussolini. The fresh troops of the German Afrika Korps swept past a depleted Eighth Army which had sent divisions to Greece, and by 10 April Tobruk was besieged.

A handful of British nurses serving with the Hadfield-Spears hospital unit were in Tobruk for seven long months until the siege was lifted in December 1941. These tough nurses and ambulance drivers had recently seen front-line service in Syria, where the Free French Foreign Legion fought against pro-Nazi Vichy French troops, and before that with the British Expeditionary Force in France. Their commanding officer was Lady Spears, wife of Major-General Sir Edward Spears, British Minister to Syria. The hundred-bed hospital was accredited to the Free French Forces. Nurses and drivers were fully trained professionals operating in battle areas. The hospital, financed by Sir Robert and Lady Hadfield and by funds collected in the USA for French Relief, had a well-equipped mobile operating theatre up with the forward troops.

Their ambulances had no doors at the sides so that the driver and nurse could eject sideways at the first sign of a dive-bombing attack. The windscreen had a top panel which hinged so that it could be swung forwards; this was always smeared with oil and sand to stop the tell-tale glint of reflected sunlight that might be spotted by hostile aircraft.

Throughout the long siege Hadfield-Spears ministered to a raw division of Australian infantry, a detachment of Northumberland machine-gunners and a few Rifle Brigade troops with nine British tanks. Those troops could not speak highly enough of their special nurses who were always on call. 'What we disliked most was going out in the ambulance at night to wherever wounded soldiers were lying in the rubble of a cave or building, fumbling around bloody, shattered limbs and applying dressings by sense of touch to deep abdominal wounds that you couldn't see properly,' recalled Louise Robinson.

> When we went out by day the ambulances would create a miniature sandstorm and then the next thing we saw would be fountains of sand leaping upwards as bombs landed

around our vehicles. One curious feature about the Stuka
dive bombers was that they were by no means as accurate as
we had been led to believe. They would scream down in a
terrifying dive and pull out having almost touched the
ground, yet their bombs were mostly wide of the mark.
Nevertheless they gave us a nasty feeling inside and we were
always so relieved to get back to the hospital Common Room
for a mug of hot sweet tea and a fag. All nurses smoked
them. We took deep drags of free 'Victory V' cigarettes,
soldiers claimed were made of Camel dung, but we smoked
them just as avidly. Dying from them now perhaps.

Some nurses never came back. They would set off with a grin and a
wave, and the ambulance would dwindle to a speck on the desert as it
went out to bring in casualties from one of the perimeter defence-boxes.
And that was that. Sometimes they'd be found later. The ambulance, a
bullet-riddled, burnt-out wreck with a pathetic, shrivelled bundle lying
beside it on the sand. The soldiers were hardened to it all. So too,
eventually, were the nurses. They learnt to accept the desert. But what
they never got used to was the smell of wounds and guts and death with
its horrible sweetness, wafting about the area.

At last, on 10 December 1941, the siege of Tobruk was lifted when
the Eighth Army linked up with the garrison after battles incurring
heavy casualties. More nurses were sent to the Tobruk front line.

Not all the hospital ships got safely through to port. Mavis Amery's
was torpedoed just off Tobruk itself. 'Ginger' Violet Bath, on the
well-travelled hospital ship *Aba*, made a swift turn-round after loading a
full complement of wounded for Alexandria. 'We just had to send our
life-boats onto the beach and take the wounded off from there as best
we could.'

Norma Whitehead and her nurses arrived safely in the port on the
Llandovery Castle. She recalled:

As the ship weaved its way slowly through sunken wrecks in
the harbour we could see what had been happening and
guess what was in store for us. The buildings were little more
than ruins, a mess of broken, tottering buildings, shells of
houses and small warehouses.

On the quayside trucks, ambulances and sweating,
sunburnt soldiers without shirts, waited for us to dock. What
a welcome they gave us. Whistles, cheers and cries of
amazement came from them all. Women! They carried our
kit into waiting trucks and drove us to the hospital. Or rather
the wreck of a hospital.

Early the next morning the crump of shells landing intermittently awoke the nurses. The port was in full view of enemy artillery observers and was being shelled constantly.

Apart from their medical skills, nurses were doing a great job for the garrison's morale. Their very presence was uplifting. Norma Whitehead said:

> There were times when we looked at young men brought in with abdominal wounds and we lifted the field dressings to look and then had to keep our faces expressionless. I remember one young chap who looked at me all the time I was putting a pad over holes round his navel and the torn mess of his back. And I knew there was nothing I could do for him really and he would be dead within an hour or two. But I managed to raise a reassuring smile. And he smiled back. And we just worked on methodically going from one young lad to another.
>
> Being together in the desert all working for a common aim, men and women alike irrespective of rank, forged bonds between us. Discipline such as we had formerly known, disappeared. In its place came a companionship. The custom of officers to address men as 'Driver' or 'Corporal' ceased. Everyone was known by his name, usually his first name. We were all part of a team. And no one took advantage of the new relationship. We were all a long way from home and a kind of affinity grew – a feeling that in our shared plight we had something precious in common with each other. It's something that people who have never been in similar situations will never be able to understand. We all respected one another.

It was not long, however, before Rommel attacked again. British casualties were heavy. Every morning whilst the battle raged around Tobruk, all patients who were fit to travel were transferred to the hospital ship and on to base hospital.

An amusing incident occurred when a German truck drove up to the wire in front of an Eighth Army defensive position. The soldiers naturally opened fire. Thereupon the truck stopped and a German doctor stepped out. He was most annoyed. 'Why do you shoot at me?' he demanded. 'I am a German doctor going into Tobruk to attend to our wounded.' He was, apparently, under the impression that Tobruk had been taken and was surprised when told who actually was still in possession of the port. He soon found himself attending to wounded Germans – as a POW himself.

Theatre Sister Henrietta Hallows recalled the unusual aspects of life in Tobruk when she and twelve other QAs were there:

I loved my job there because I was working with a German surgeon and German anaesthetist. The surgeon was highly skilled and worked fast. I admired his technique and learnt a lot from watching him operate. The anaesthetist was a different chap altogether. He was an ardent Nazi and gave the German wounded a Nazi pep talk before putting them under for the operation.

We often had to deal with Arabs requiring surgery. They all seemed to have this obsession of picking things up in the desert and taking them apart. More often than not, objects they picked up were highly dangerous. Children would be brought in with their eyes blown out, and limbs hanging off. We did what we could for them but they never learnt to leave things alone.

I recall one funny example of the Arab's habit of picking things up. We had just amputated a leg in theatre and the orderly had, for the moment, wrapped the severed limb in brown paper. He then propped it on an oil drum ready for taking to the incinerator but before then went to the lavatory. When he came back the parcel had gone. He looked outside and quickly called me over. 'Hurry or you'll miss it. Look at those two Arabs. They've pinched that brown paper parcel!' We watched as they ran over the sand until they felt far enough away to examine their prize. One of them unrolled the paper and then both jumped back when they saw the bloody leg they had been carrying. They flew from the scene.

When it came to Arabs, rank counted for nothing in the British hospitals. In Number 6 BGH, where the fiery redhead Sister 'Ginger' Violet Bath ruled the roost in the operating theatre, there was a scene one day which could have found a place in a Whitehall theatre farce.

A Lieutenant rushed down the corridor, flung back the fly screen door and shouted: 'Sister, Sister come quickly. There's been an accident. King Farouk's outside demanding treatment.'

'Tell that to your grandmother,' I said, not believing a word.

'It's true. It really is Farouk and he's demanding treatment.'

'Demanding indeed,' thought Sister Bath. She went to the door and saw three enormous limousines with an entourage of flustered, well-dressed Egyptians. The injured man was still in the centre car. 'Bring him in on the trolley,' said Sister Bath.

Then it all happened, as she recalls:

We had those old portable trolleys which were held together by butterfly nuts and bolts. When I put my hand on it, I felt it wobble. Then I saw those men heaving an enormously fat man out of the back of the car. It was the Egyptian king, Farouk, sure enough.

'What's the matter with you, young man? Get on the trolley.'

'I'm a very important man,' he said.

'I don't care if you're the King of England,' I said. 'There's only one kind of treatment here. The best we can provide.' He was not used to being ordered about. Especially by a woman!

With great difficulty his massive body was heaved onto the trolley. A slow tearing sound came from beneath his frame and almost in slow motion he collapsed through the trolley and lay partly supported, arms stretched out.

It took all our efforts to extricate him from a mess of twisted tubes and canvas. Then we got him wedged onto another trolley. I was walking alongside him to the theatre with his eunuchs trailing behind, when I felt his arm sliding up my arm higher and higher. The dirty devil.

'Get him undressed,' I said to the orderlies.

Two minutes later the orderly came back. 'He wouldn't let me undress him,' he said. I stormed into the room. 'Here, prop up his back,' I said to the orderly. And I debagged him, in no uncertain manner, the horrible man.

By this time his entourage had swelled to a mob of excited Egyptians braying outside the hospital. The next day two Egyptian planes dropped floral tributes over the tented wards.

It was no pleasure looking after King Farouk and his suspected fractured pelvis. He brought his own cooks who set up the kitchen outside the officers' ward. One of his eunuchs had to taste all the food first to make sure it was not poisoned.

That week-end we had a concert in a large tent. Halfway through a messenger came onto the stage and announced: 'Will the cook go back to the officers' ward. Farouki wants his dinner.' You can imagine the roar of laughter.

As it happened his wife, Farina, – a lovely woman in every way – was having her third child and so Farouk went back to his palace as soon as possible. He wanted to give us a medal of the Order of the Nile. I refused mine. I just couldn't bear to take anything from a man who would paw a woman as he did me.

At that time, whenever there was a lull in the fighting, even in Tobruk, nurses did manage to accept invitations to social evenings from officers' messes and reciprocated by inviting guests to the Sisters' mess. Sister Henrietta Hallows, serving in Tobruk, found this could lead to romantic involvement. One day she was in Casualty when a young RAF officer came in from a game of football with a broken wrist. Something of the chemistry of the Casualty Ward and Henrietta seemed to work upon him. He introduced himself as Denis Lee, and further meetings followed. They fell in love and very soon they were married to each other in front of a congregation packed into the Tobruk church. Her commanding officer gave her away and the unit padre officiated. The improvised wedding reception turned into a very good party, despite the supposed shortage of liquor. As it happened, some English Tommies had found a good way of getting free beer. When the air raid siren sounded, the NAAFI employees would all dash to the shelters, and the wily Tommies would stroll nonchalantly into the store and help themselves.

In May 1942 Rommel renewed his offensive. Stukas hammered the town day after day. The Eighth Army withdrew from Libya, leaving Tobruk isolated again. Orders were given for the evacuation by sea of as many casualties as possible, complete with all nurses. But one remarkable young English lady, Susan Travers, stayed behind.[3] The daughter of a retired English admiral, she had chosen a unique way of serving her country. She had joined the French Foreign Legion!

She served amongst men with silent pasts and non-existent futures; men on the run from the law; men with only their present duty, to fight and die for the honour of the Legion. Men of fifty nations, of all persuasions and beliefs, or none at all. It was said to be the toughest and most desperate fighting force ever raised. A strange Service indeed for the slim, well-mannered daughter of an English admiral! With these Legionnaires she had driven ambulances in Finland and Syria, given immediate first aid to the wounded, and then in the summer of 1942 joined the 13th Demi-Brigade of the Legion in the Bir Hacheim 'box' – one of the southern fortified strong points in the ring defending Tobruk.

There she was when Rommel was launching his all-out attack to reach the Suez Canal. Seventy tanks of the crack Italian Ariete Armoured Division went in against the 500 Legionnaires.

By day and night without cessation artillery barrages and dive-bombers preceded assaults by infantry, until eventually the defenders' ammunition and water was running out. So far, every attack was repulsed. A signal came from the British Corps commander: 'Well done! Hang on! Congratulations! Hang on! All will be well.'

All was not to be well. The Germans were now massing to take over the attack from the Italians. Rommel then sent the Legion's General Koenig a message: 'All further resistance on your part will only lead to useless spilling of blood. Show the white flag and lay down your arms.'

The fierce Free French commander refused. For another four days the pattern of bombardment and attack was kept up. By the night of 10 June 1942, Legionnaires had fired their last shells, and there was not a drop of water left in the men's water-bottles. Then it was that ambulance driver/nurse Susan Travers was told to stand by for a key role. General Koenig had decided his unit should break out by several routes to make their way as best they could to the British lines eight miles away. In his staff car he would lead, with Lieutenant Colonel Amilakvari, a small column of trucks carrying the wounded through the German positions. He chose as his driver the experienced English ambulance driver Susan Travers.

Preparations were made in utmost secrecy. Nobody knew what was going to happen, but the old 'sweats' in the Legion guessed a big show was looming. Their officers, true to tradition, were shaving and putting on their smartest uniforms.

On the night of 10 June, whispered orders were given. Silently assault troops assembled. At last, in the pitch-black before dawn, General Koenig climbed into his staff car. He stood up with his head through the sliding roof and gave the command: '*Foncez!*' ('Let's be moving!')

Figures scrambled into frenzied activity. Susan Travers gripped the wheel of the powerful Ford staff car and waited for the next signal. Sweat broke from her hairline and ran down her forehead. Koenig tapped her shoulder firmly. She gunned the engine, let in the clutch and swung the heavy car in a tight lock from under the camouflage net on to the sandy desert track. She roared eastwards into the dark night. Koenig tapped her shoulder again, this time with the side of his hammer-like fist, spurring her on to greater speed. The Ford kicked and bucked, wheels spinning for purchase in loose sand, and then bounded ahead with a force that threw Koenig backwards.

Suddenly sprays of red and green tracer bullets zipped overhead and flares soared in the sky and hung in a white glare. Bullets ricocheted, screaming off rocks, and mortar bombs burst amongst the column. Trucks blazed behind Susan as she zigzagged through the shifting, treacherous sand. As her feet danced over the steel pedals of clutch, brake and throttle, she might well have wondered how on earth an ambulance driver/nurse came to be driving like a demon through a maelstrom of fire for a brigade commander of the French Foreign Legion. But her main concern then was to keep that engine from stalling as she bucked her way over rocks and soft sand, leading her battered convoy from the Bir Hacheim garrison to the British lines.

It was not until 10.30 the next morning that a weary Susan Travers skidded her bullet-holed staff car to a halt in a billowing cloud of dust. She had driven her commander and two-thirds of his men to safety, though in that hectic drive through enemy defensive positions, eleven legionnaires were killed and thirty-two wounded.

They joined the British Eighth Army in retreat towards the Suez

Canal. Disaster seemed imminent. On 16 June 1942, German radio announced that Rommel had won the desert battle and that all British forces had been wiped out. The Afrika Korps was now massing 3,000 tanks close to the Egyptian border, ready for the final battle. Sister Marjorie Bennett, then back in Cairo, recalled how confident the Egyptians were of a victorious German entry into the city. They had torn down British flags flying from the tops of buildings and replaced them with Nazi and Italian ones.

On 29 June all Women's Royal Naval Service personnel were evacuated. At any moment it seemed that all nurses would receive instructions to embark and flee the city. Every woman had to have a bag packed ready to embark at a moment's notice. But the position of nurses was soon made clear by a letter to all units from the Director of Medical Services. He said nurses and women ambulance drivers were not to be evacuated. They were too valuable to be lost and they were also 'good for morale.'

In July 1942 the two desert armies faced each other at a point marked on the map by an insignificant little railway station whose name would go down in history: El Alamein. There, Rommel's last bid for Egypt was halted. Now Britain's Eighth Army had time to be reinforced and re-equipped under its new commander, Montgomery, ready for its victorious role at the same place three months later.

It was a time too when those nurses who had been in the forward areas were able to recuperate and take leave, sightseeing in Cairo, Alexandria or even further afield in the Holy Land. Once again they could have their white dresses and caps laundered by the 'dhoby' boys. 'Mine was an intriguing character,' recalled Sister Margaret Jennings. 'To finish off the white clothing, he would have a mouthful of starch, which he spewed through gaps in his teeth onto the garment, as he wielded the iron. I always tried not to think about it, when I put on my dress.'

> My escort on a memorable visit to Cairo was Tommy, an admirer who had first seen me when he had visited a patient in our hospital. He was a Canadian Air Force Lieutenant, tall, slim and dark with a twinkle in his eye and a voice that captivated me. He must have been equally smitten as he started to write to me and his letters led to our meeting in Cairo. Again and again we met joyously for the next few months. Tommy had a jeep so we were able to see more of ancient Egypt's heritage.

All too soon it was time for the battle that would turn the tide decidedly against the Germans: the battle at El Alamein. Nurses were moved forward close to the front line, to deal with the expected rush of casualties.

The battle of El Alamein began in bright moonlight on 23 October 1942 with a shattering bombardment by the entire Eighth Army artillery – 900 guns firing with maximum intensity for fifteen minutes. Then the infantry attacked. It took twelve days of terrible slogging before the breakthrough came.

It was a 'near run thing', with almost all the infantry reserves used before Montgomery could signal: 'The Axis forces are now in full retreat.' That day, on 6 November 1942, Montgomery emerged from his desert caravan to tell reporters the news. Christopher Buckley, special correspondent of the *Daily Telegraph*, was there: 'Montgomery, who was wearing a tank beret and a grey pullover, said: "It has been a fine battle. There is no doubt of the result. The enemy is completely smashed. We intend to hit this chap for six out of North Africa." '

And for those men who had fought so hard and survived to fight another day, there was good news too. Sir William Beveridge, in a report also published that week, guaranteed them provision for their future health, insurance to provide against sickness, unemployment, old age, and for families. It really did look as if those warriors would be coming home to a land fit for heroes. Or had their fathers heard something like that before?

However, in Britain it was a time for celebration.

But for those nurses in the Western Desert dealing with the immediate cost of that 'fine battle', there could be no feelings of joy. 'We had far too many mutilated young men in our care for us to feel like celebrating,' said Sister Margaret Jennings.

> The poor, wretched, dirt and blood-caked casualties were carried in, stretcher after stretcher of them. Some had been half roasted alive in their tanks. Others so badly mutilated that it was amazing they were still alive. Our training had scarcely prepared us for the horror of it all – some with parts of their face missing, others with deep abdominal wounds, legs hanging by threads of tissue with bones protruding. The urgency of the task lent skill to our fingers. Bleeding was stopped, transfusions given, plaster of paris [sic] applied over Thomas splints, and pain killing injections given. One by one we worked our way through them all, washing them, dressing their wounds and putting them between clean white sheets. The expressions of relief and gratitude on their faces as they sank incredulously between those sheets and saw they were being tended by female nurses, was unforgettable.
>
> I remember how one boy, he was still no more than a boy, called me hours after his arrival. 'I wonder', he asked, 'if you knew I haven't been washed yet, Sister.' I explained, 'Well, yes, we have to wash and attend to the most seriously wounded first, and we'll get round to you soon.' His humble

acceptance was touching: 'Oh, I see, well don't worry about me then.' This was the general attitude. We never heard any complaints.

As for us, we just snatched a meal and a rest whenever we could be spared for a few minutes. Our cat-naps would be shattered by calls of 'Convoy in. Convoy in' echoing round the compound. Time seemed to lose its meaning. The courage and fortitude of those lads was such an example and inspiration to us that we forgot our own weariness.

British casualties at El Alamein were indeed heavy: 13,500 killed, missing and wounded. But a resounding victory was achieved. It came just in time to precede General Eisenhower's landings at the other end of the Mediterranean, at Oran and Algiers.

The Eighth Army advanced to meet this new US and British force, and nurses advanced with them, as the *Egyptian Mail* reported on 9 February 1943:

BRITISH NURSES ARE IN THE FRONT LINE

Nurses are keeping up with the forward troops during their fifteen hundred miles chase from El Alamein to Tripoli. 'Blimey, nurses!' was the expression of amazement used by our wounded all the way along – amazement at finding nurses up with the most forward Casualty Clearing Stations, amazement at finding only a short ambulance ride from the front line, the gentle hands and soothing words of nursing sisters.

The Chief Principal Matron of the Middle East, Miss P. Sowter, said: 'We are very proud of the work our Sisters have done.' Sitting at her desk at Military Headquarters she told a military correspondent of some of the adventures of those nursing sisters in the Western Desert. 'One Matron wrote and told me that they were machine-gunned by German planes and had to burrow in the sand just after leaving Tobruk. Luckily we were not hit,' the letter continued, 'but what an awful job it was getting sand out of our hair.'

It was about this time that nursing sisters further to the west in North Africa were experiencing far more taxing problems than how to get the sand from their hair. Theirs was more a problem of salt water. They were being torpedoed in the Mediterranean itself *en route* to Algeria and Tunisia, where an undermanned First Army was fighting against the odds with a fresh German army in formidable defensive positions in the Tunisian mountains.

Casualties were terribly high, and more nurses were desperately needed.

4   Greece, Crete and Malta

Casualties were the worst I'd ever seen.
They'd been operated on in awful
conditions.

Violet Leather

Whilst so many nurses were engaged in the Western Desert campaign, a
small contingent was in the front line of the Balkans. It was in the
autumn of 1940 that nurses stationed in the Middle East suddenly found
themselves on a boat sailing from Alexandria to Athens, dodging
U-boats and the German Air Force. They were going to take part in one
of the most curious campaigns of the whole war.

Italy had invaded Greece from Albania. Britain was honouring a
secret agreement with Greece, signed in 1939, to come to her aid if she
were attacked. Amongst Britain's contribution to Greek aid was a
contingent of doctors and nurses of the 26th British General Hospital,
who would tend to the needs of wounded Greek personnel.

On 16 November, nursing sisters of 26th BGH disembarked from
their troop-ship at Piraeus, spent two nights in Athens and then were
driven out to the beautiful summer resort of Kifisia in the valley of the
marble mountain Pentelicon.[1] Their first job was to establish three small
hospitals in three different hotels: one for surgical, one for medical and
one for cases of venereal disease. At first 26th BGH was not busy, and
so they took on some patients from the overcrowded neighbouring
Greek hospital – mostly cases of soldiers from the Albanian front with
frostbite.

At first all went well for the Greeks. Their small army, supported by
RAF aircraft, launched savage counter-attacks which quickly drove the
Italians back into the desolate mountains of Albania. Their toughness,
training and knowledge of the mountainous terrain was more than a
match for the Italians' superior weaponry.

Casualties were heavy on both sides. Greek casualty clearing stations
and Greek hospitals close to the front line were so overcrowded, men
lay in the hallways and even on the steps; few of those on beds were able
to discard their mud-soaked uniforms because there were not enough

pyjamas or bedclothes to go round. American journalist Betty Wason, with the Columbia Broadcasting Corporation, visited one of those hospitals. She found that most of the nurses were young women who had chosen nursing, thinking it to be a pleasant social activity, never for a moment imagining how things could change if a war took place. Nevertheless, these young women proved themselves to be as courageous as the soldiers. Betty Wason was haunted by the memory of a nurse with whom she ate on one occasion. The young woman was extremely anxious about returning to duty. As she was about to leave she sighed and said, 'Sometimes I wonder how we keep it up, except that we are so busy we haven't time to think.' Then she had said, 'Our free days are worst of all, for then we cannot help but think about the horror of it ...'[2]

Joanna Stavridi, a London-born Red Cross nurse then serving in the operating theatre of a Greek front-line field ambulance unit at Arta, was horrified by what she saw happening. Surgery was primitive in the extreme. In all fairness to the Greek medical officers, it must be said they were overworked and without adequate supporting staff. The unit was also frequently at risk of being encircled. Consequently, when soldiers were brought in with legs and arms blasted by shell-fire, decisions had to be made on the spot and without much time for consideration. Fractures, which in a British general hospital might have been splinted to prevent further displacement of bone ends, were treated as crush injuries that might cause circulation to be impaired. Limbs were quickly cut off above the fracture. But that was not the end of the horror for Joanna. The way limbs were amputated was crude in the extreme. It was a quick 'chop', little better than in the days of the Crimean War.

These unfortunate amputees were then passed to 26th BGH at Kifisia – hotels converted into makeshift wards and operating theatres. There, surgeons had to operate again in order to provide the stump with a flap of skin and tissue so that it would heal better and later take an artificial limb. The tough Greek fighters could not understand why they had to have yet another operation.

Nurses of 26th BGH would never forget the experience of receiving those gallant men who had driven the Italian invader from their native land. They were in a dreadful state. Most of them were covered in lice, and their clothes were flea-ridden. Everyone had to go through a cleansing and disinfestation process, and all the contaminated and devitalized tissue had to be removed from the wound before corrective surgery could begin.

In addition to the Greek casualties, there were Italian POWs. They were in an even worse plight. In the long march through the mountain blizzards, many had lost their boots, and old clothes wrapped round their feet had frozen; so too had their rain-soaked clothes. Hands and feet were frost-bitten, and thousands already had gangrene. More amputations were required.

It was hard for everyone in the hospital. Yet there was still a little time

for relaxation, especially over the Christmas period. Greek civilians in
Kifisia showed their appreciation of what the hospital was doing and
showered them with invitations to share their sparse festival fare. It was in
fact a time when church bells rang almost every day to herald yet another
Greek victory.[3]

Then the bells ceased to ring.

The Greek army had outdistanced its supply lines. It paused to take
stock of the situation. The flow of casualties coming into the Greek field
ambulance units slowed to a trickle. Joanna Stavridi took time out to visit
her sister convalescing in Athens. She arrived there looking tired and
dishevelled, but after a hot bath was soon back to her best form. She was a
strong-looking girl with magnificent black hair tucked under her crisp,
white nurse's cap. Daughter of a London banker, she had taken her Red
Cross training in Britain and had come to Athens in 1940 to help nurse her
sister through an illness. Though now all were British, Joanna's family
had been Greek for three generations. It seemed natural for her to offer
her nursing services to Greece when the Italian invasion began. They
were snapped up eagerly by the field ambulance unit she had just left in
the north of Greece. Now back in Athens, she enjoyed being with her
sister, who had married a Greek man. But the conversation over the
dinner table inevitably drifted round to the question, 'What are you going
to do next?'

In 26th BGH, during that lull in the war, nursing sisters found
themselves debating similar questions. 'What are we going to do next?'
'Shall we be going back to the warm sunshine of Egypt?' They did not
know that they would soon be joining another British general hospital
now on its way from Suez.

Politicians sitting in the Greek cafés, sipping glasses of ouzo and noisily
munching black olives and calamari, were a little more specific in their
debates. They could see the danger and asked, 'What is Germany going
to do now? Hitler will not let his little friend Mussolini be disgraced.
Sooner or later we'll have his tanks thundering across our frontier.'

In 26th BGH, rumours were already in the air. By late February the
question 'When will the Germans strike?' was anxiously voiced.

On 6 April 1941 the German Army struck hard and decisively to save
Mussolini's face. Britain hurriedly sent a token force of 53,000 troops.
Nurses from Kifisia hospital watched Australians in their broad-brimmed
hats, and suntanned New Zealanders, driving north.

To no avail. Nazi tanks soon smashed their way across Macedonia.
Two days later Salonika fell.

For nurses it was now another Dunkirk. On 16 April the New Zealand
hospital, which had just been established at Larissa, left for the coast,
leaving all their equipment behind. German armour raced towards
Athens. Ahead of them, British troop-transporters were frantically
evacuating bemused soldiers back through Athens to ports they had left a
few days earlier.

In despair at this turn of events and the treachery of pro-Nazi members of the Greek government who had given false orders to Greek officers in strategic defensive posts, the newly appointed Greek premier, Alexander Korizis, offered his resignation to the King, George II, and went back to his flat. When he entered, his wife asked him, 'How's the news?' He smiled and said, 'Better'. Then he went into his bedroom, closed the door, and shot himself.

Now the entire front was in confusion. Hospitals began sending their older nurses back to the port to be evacuated. Others stayed behind at Kifisia, as the thud of bombs and the echoing spatter of machine-gun fire got nearer.

In the last days of April 1941, nurses did their final rounds of the tented wards, gave pain relieving morphia where needed and set off in whatever trucks were available. Some nurses were now heading for Piraeus harbour, others to Argos in the Peloponnese. In every port and on every road south, German bombers were waiting for them. For the nurses, darkness was their only salvation. Quietly, in the black of night, a large Greek fishing boat glided into the beach at Argos, picked up the nurses and took them to the Australian destroyer *Voyageur*.

It was now time for the walking wounded of 26th BGH at Kifisia to leave, as German infantry was getting too close for comfort. The first contingent left. On narrow roads they made slow progress in convoy, a column too tempting for the prowling Luftwaffe to ignore. The Stukas dived, bombed and machine-gunned trucks and ambulances alike. Those who survived were brought back to the hospital.

The wounded commanding officer, who had just boarded a ship, was brought off and given an emergency operation; he left on the next ship. Now nurses were getting out of the area the best way they could. Two of them managed to fly off in a Sunderland flying boat. Greek nurses came in to staff the hospital as the last of the British nurses and medical officers boarded trucks to leave. They set off in the dark and roared down the road.

As soon as daylight came they were attacked again from the air. Each time that dive-bombers swooped on the convoy, trucks braked and their occupants ran for cover into the fields as the whole area was raked with machine-gun fire. At one time they took cover in a graveyard, but this did not deter Luftwaffe pilots who, having knocked out the few RAF fighters sent over to Greece, were now having a field-day inflicting death and destruction unopposed.[4]

It was the same scene all over southern Greece then as trucks raced for the beaches and ports. At times they had to bypass road-blocks of pro-Nazi sympathizers anxious to curry favour with their new masters by taking matters into their own hands.

Sister Violet Bath (now Leather) arrived at Piraeus in the old warrior of a hospital ship, *Aba*.

As we drew alongside, the Transport Officer came aboard to bring on the wounded. He himself looked dreadful. I told him to go to our ward room and have a rest. The next time I saw him he was running along the quay shouting: 'Get the Hell out of here.' That was it. We took no more casualties from there. But there's one thing that niggles with me to this day. A stupid Australian Matron had a group of Nursing Sisters with her who could have scampered up that gang plank in no time at all but she insisted that the wounded get aboard first. It was too late then. They were left to become prisoners of war. Stupid woman wielding her authority like that.

Some of the nurses taken from the beaches of Greece went to Crete. Already there was Number 7 BGH, under the command of Lieutenant-Colonel C. Carlton, MC. The unit had been *en route* from Leeds since 1 January 1941. It had disembarked in Suda Bay on 19 April to set up camp at Lower Galatás, close to the sea-shore between Crete's major port, Canea, and Maleme airfield. Their tents were dug in to a depth of three feet and were soon receiving a steady flow of casualties. On 27 April the dreaded signal arrived: CROMWELL. It warned the hospital to assume second degree of readiness against enemy attack.[5]

With Number 7 BGH then were eighty-five sisters evacuated from Greece and also the English Red Cross nurse, Joanna Stavridi. She had sailed from Greece on a yacht together with Colonel Neil Hamilton-Fairley of the RAMC. On the way, their yacht had been dive-bombed and machine-gunned. Two of the crew were killed and six badly wounded. They managed to reach a small island, and within a few days another boat took them to Crete.[6]

Almost daily then, nurses saw German reconnaissance aircraft flying low over their camp and the whole island.

On 5 May signals ordered the hospital to begin evacuating patients to Egypt aboard the hospital ship *Aba*, anchored in Canea Bay. Sister Violet Bath had an unusual request there.

We were anchored close to the wreck of the battleship *York* which had been holed but rested in shallow water, and there were aboard still some civilian wounded. Most of them were able to scramble down the rope ladder to our lifeboat. The captain asked if we could send a Sister to help with a special case. I was still nimble enough to climb up those rope ladder things, so I volunteered. I found a woman there who was panting and obviously about to give birth to a baby. I had to try and remember all my training but everything went smoothly, thank goodness, and I felt very pleased at having delivered a baby in the midst of a German invasion, for by the time the baby did come the paratroops were landing.

When I got back to the *Aba* I found that 587 wounded soldiers had been put aboard and some of the nurses too. We set sail with all speed but not before the dive bombers had a go at us. We were hit and holed but made it safely to Alexandria and then had to go into dry dock at Haifa for repairs.

I was then sent on my way to Syria where on 8th June 1941, British and Free French Forces had landed to overthrow the French garrison loyal to Vichy France. It was a vicious war for five weeks. I was Sister-in-Charge of an operating theatre in a front line Mobile Field Hospital. The war seemed to be going on all around us but we had no time to think about how close were the shells or machine-gunning. We were just too busy. At the end of it all I was mentioned in despatches and given the award of ARRC.

In Suda Bay, Crete, just after Sister Bath had left in the hospital ship *Aba*, the Luftwaffe came again, dropping bombs all round the area of Number 7 BGH which was hit several times, killing Major J. E. Rouse, Major Wardrop and Privates Bastable and Fardoe. Captains Easton and Hardwick were seriously wounded. All nursing sisters then remaining in the hospital were told to make their way to the evacuation points on beaches to the south of the island.[7]

From 20 May onwards the Number 7 BGH war diary recorded that all ranks not on essential duty were taking cover in slit trenches under constant machine-gun fire. Bombs wrecked the hospital stores and dispensary.

A little to the south of the hospital, Captain Roy Farran of the 3rd Hussars was sitting at a deal table having breakfast, when suddenly overhead there was a throbbing of old Junkers 52 engines flying in slow formations of three. In the sky below them, hundreds of green, yellow and red parachute canopies were puffing open. A parachute army was landing. Thus began the biggest and bloodiest airborne operation of the whole war.[8]

At ten o'clock that morning German parachutists captured the hospital and took as prisoners one officer, a hundred other ranks and 300 walking wounded patients. They marched them off towards Galatas, using them as a screen. The swastika flag was raised above the hospital. An hour later it was hauled down by New Zealand troops who recaptured the hospital.[9]

Hurriedly, the last of the women nurses remaining with Number 7 BGH now ran to their trucks, carrying a few precious belongings on their backs. At speed they made for the old steamship *Iona*.

At eight o'clock that night, under cover of darkness, patients were moved from tented wards to caves nearer the sea-shore. The operating table was close to the mouth of the cave to make the most of the daylight, but the floor sloped, it was fouled with goat excrement and doctors slipped and stumbled amongst all the welter of blood and muck. British Red Cross nurse Joanna Stavridi, who had once written home saying she wondered whether the smell of ether and the sight of wounds would make her sick, found that she had no time to think about the conditions under which she was now working.

Nursing orderlies were detailed to be in charge of each cave section to make sure everyone stayed out of sight during the hours of daylight, for low-flying aircraft now came in, machine-gunning anything seen moving.

By 25 May it was clear that German troops would soon overrun the whole island. Personnel of the hospital unit were paraded. Captain Sherman and thirty nursing orderlies were detailed to stay behind with the 200 'lying' patients. The remainder were to make their way to the embarkation beach at Sphakia. They were evacuated on 31 May. In completing his account in the Number 7 BGH War Diary, Major James Driburg recorded that fifteen officers and 190 other ranks were missing. 'Also a prisoner of war was Miss J. A. Stavridi who was evacuated from Greece and was working at 7 GH as a VAD'.

What actually happened to Joanna Stavridi, according to Colonel Hamilton-Fairley, was that she insisted on staying with the wounded. 'She was desperately keen on her work and so completely fearless. Many times she risked her own life in dashing out of the cave to bring back medical stores for her patients.' She epitomized the true courage of all those nurses who, having already experienced the stress of being shelled, bombed and shot at, carried on determinedly doing their duty. In August 1941 she was awarded the highest honour of the Hellenic Red Cross for her gallantry.

As for those nurses who managed to sail away from the evacuation beaches, further tests were in store for them. They were almost continually bombed all the way to Alexandria. Their hospital, the Number 7 BGH, was disbanded on 31 July, and Sisters were posted for duty in hospitals preparing for the next phase of the Mediterranean conflict.

HM Hospital Ship *Aba*

Burial At Sea

As now the throbbing engine's beat, at last, is stilled
The swiftly moving stream of sparkling spray
That eddying swirled against our sides, and bubbling, spilled
Itself astern has slowly died away;
We wallow sluggishly like a log without control,
Inanimate upon an oily sea,
And chattering Diesels mute, we gently heave and roll,
A thing that lived and now has ceased to be.

Above, the cloud-flecked sky, assumes a gradual
    change,
From blue to gold, from gold to red to green,
And then to mauve; all hues throughout the rainbow's range,
Outline the clouds in every varying sheen.
The cooling breeze, that late with white, betopped the crest
Of every wave, by now has elsewhere sped.
The setting sun, in fire and gold, begilds the West;
Deep silence spreads; a day is past and dead.

In sorrow we assemble aft, beneath the Poop,
The few of us, whom for a little while you knew,
Who tried and failed, to bring you home; in saddened groups
We come to bid a last farewell to you.
And there, what once was you, Comrade, the empty husk
Neath flag, in canvas sewn, a plank for bed,
Awaits its journey's end, as silent in the dusk,
We wait until the last sad words are said.

'Into thy hands, Father of all, we now commend
Our Comrade's soul, his body to the Deep.
To those he loved and leaves behind, they comfort send.
His warrior's soul, with you, a while now keep.'
The Chaplain ends his prayer, we ponder o'er each word,
Questing the why and wherefore of it all.
From neath the flag, thy form's now gone, a splash is heard;
Silence, no volley here, no bugle call.

And so with sad salute, we say a last farewell,
And though the seas your mortal body claim,
We know your spirit lived to quit that empty shell.
And like the sun just set, to rise again,
To rise again, as sure as morrow's break of day,
As sure as now, with throb and beat, once more
The ship vibrates to life and slowly gathers way
And we return to what we did before.

Major A.D. Wall RAMC
Senior Medical Officer, HM Hospital Ship *Aba*

Amongst the nurses in the desert hospitals then were many, such as
Sister Marjorie Bennett, whose hospitals had been left behind when the
Eighth Army advanced. She preferred to be closer to the action.
Consequently, she volunteered for service with a general hospital in
Malta.
    Nurses on Malta had been enduring the holocaust that had engulfed

the island since Mussolini declared war on Britain in 1940. Fortunately, on 11 September 1940, an additional twenty nursing sisters had arrived for duty before the blockade began in earnest. Amongst them were two, Sister J. R. Palmer and Sister E. R. Palmer, who were to distinguish themselves and earn awards for gallantry. With these reinforcements, the hospital services were well prepared for the ordeal of siege conditions they were to face for three gruelling years.

The raids had started when Mussolini sent his bombers to Malta just a few hours after entering the war against Britain and France, and from then on, Britain's key link in the Mediterranean faced the combined wrath of Italian and German air forces.

First to be severely damaged by bombs was the Royal Naval Hospital at Bighi, when direct hits wrecked wards in the latter weeks of 1940. The Hospital Matron, Miss E. Campbell, and Sisters Chapman and Nockholds (who one day would both become Matrons-in-Chief QARNNS) and Sisters Mansell and Foster survived and joined the army hospital at Imtarfa, along with Surgeon-Commanders Crosfill and Gurd, RN. At that time any extra help was a boon, because not only were there many casualties from air raids and those from ships who managed to limp into harbour after having been attacked at sea, but also there was a disturbing number of patients coming in suffering from poliomyelitis, causing wards to be cleared.[10]

Malta's close proximity to Sicilian airfields made it extremely susceptible to aerial attack and naval blockade. Britain was determined to hold on to the island because it provided a base for operations against the Italian supply route to Libya and to Rommel's Afrika Korps.

In December 1941 Hitler appointed Field Marshal Albrecht Kesselring as Commander-in-Chief, South, with specific instructions to paralyze Allied shipping taking supplies to Malta. He almost succeeded. But Hitler's patience ran out. 'That miserable mound of dirt that's causing us so much trouble will have to be captured,' he said, and he ordered the Field Marshal to annihilate Malta's air defences. Then General Kurt Student's 30,000 parachutists would invade and take over the island.[11]

Hitler's last ominous words on the matter were: 'I want every installation on Malta pounded to dust; I want the people dazed and broken, cowering in their caves like animals, so that when we do come they will throw themselves at our feet and beg for mercy.'[12]

Imtarfa hospital felt the wrath of the Luftwaffe on 13 April 1941, when twenty-eight bombs fell on the buildings, wrecking wards completely and shattering windows in others. Bombs fell on the Barrack hospital, killing many patients and blowing the Night Sister off her feet, but she was at work again the next morning. In a raid at Easter, 1941, bombs fell on the whole hospital area from midnight until dawn. The Isolation Hospital and other buildings got direct hits but, miraculously, nurses suffered only minor wounds. Doors and windows of both hospitals were blown off, and both water supply and electricity were cut off for a short time.

In January 1942 the new Number 39 British General Hospital was opened, although its life was short. On 25 April a very heavy dive-bombing attack which started at 0700 hours demolished most of the hospital's hutments. Many patients and orderlies were killed or seriously injured.

The nearby Number 45 General Hospital took patients and nurses from the Number 39. Several nursing sisters remained with patients considered too ill to move. But then the hospital was attacked again and again. Nurses then showed tremendous fortitude. The unit war diary records that:

> Miss J.M. Pollock set a fine example of courage and devotion to duty while bombs were falling upon the hospital. She and the remaining Sisters supervised the work of removing helpless patients to the ground floor. Two Sisters in particular, were outstanding. Miss E. R. Palmer was on duty alone when bombs exploded on her ward killing one of the few remaining patients. Miss J. E. Palmer went to her aid clearing the ward, having previously cleared her own ward. The attack took place when the orderlies were at dinner and the nurses coped on their own. While the bombing was at its peak the nurses carried mattresses in to put over patients as a protective cover. At one time one of the Miss Palmers lay on top of a patient under a bed, shielding him with her body. They both remained in the hospital until the last patient had been taken away. In that last raid the hospital lost 8 staff and five patients killed with 9 badly wounded.

Fortunately that small island, measuring no more than seventeen miles by nine, possesses a honeycomb of natural caves and grottos which once had been used as granary stores, but when the air raids got worse thousands of civilians were housed below ground. It was into one of these caves that the Royal Engineers were tunnelling to make an additional surgical block.

They were not quite ready for occupation, but the hospital's commanding officer decided it was now too dangerous to wait for refinements. The whole of one hospital and the operating theatre of Number 39 BGH was moved below ground. Most of the patients went on stretchers, but the seriously wounded and helpless patients were manoeuvred down in their beds.

The onslaught now intensified. In nearby hospitals, nurses worked on when the air raid sirens sounded. Through the windows they could see gull-winged Stukas diving onto the docks and harbour of Valletta, and onto airfields, towns and villages, their engines howling stridently, accompanied by the rending screech of their underwing sirens. The walls of the mighty ramparts of Valletta captured the hellish din, echoing and amplifying it tenfold. Day after day the onslaught went on.

In April 1942 the American carrier *Wasp* brought forty-seven Spitfires into the Mediterranean. They then flew 700 miles to Malta. But once on the airfield – before they could be put into the safety of revetments – all but ten were destroyed by German bombers. One can imagine the terror of those times, for during this phase of the aerial bombardment more bombs fell on the island than on the whole of London during the height of the blitz. But Malta did not 'cower and cringe', as Hitler had expected. It carried on.

The commanding officer of Number 90 BGH Imtarfa hospital, Lieutenant-Colonel W. R. Hamilton, became a bombing raid casualty. On 13 July 1942 he and his wife were badly wounded when bombs fell on the roof of the hospital, the Sisters' Mess Shelter and the hospital married quarters. Mrs Hamilton died shortly afterwards.

In November 1942, a direct hit on the Sisters' Mess killed two sisters and injured several others – one of them severely when a large piece of flying masonry shattered four of her lumbar vertebrae. The wards were always overflowing. In the midst of this series of raids, an epidemic of enteritis in the Durham Light Infantry brought scores of patients into the hospital.

Bombs rained down daily. Buildings round the hospitals and harbour crumbled to rubble, blocking the streets. The dockyard became a mass of twisted cranes, and the harbour itself little more than a graveyard of sunken ships. Old towns were smashed to pieces, street by street.

Beleaguered, hungry, cold, dirty and dog-tired, the defenders stuck it out. For months no convoys got through. Starvation was a reality for everyone, from the governor, General Sir William Dobbie, down to the lowliest labourer. Rations were cut to 1,600 calories a day for men and 1,500 for women. (At home in Britain, rations never fell below 2,800). An orderly at one hospital confessed he had great difficulty in keeping his hands off the meals he was serving to patients. Consequently, the health of civilian and military personnel suffered through malnutrition, and there were outbreaks of typhoid and polio.

A remarkable feature about Malta at this time was that despite all the trauma of death and destruction around everybody, human nature showed its resilience. Cinemas remained open, romantic relationships developed, and unit concert parties burgeoned, with staff from hospitals even managing to take leading roles, as the RAF concert party officer, Roger Keys then Clerk of Works on the island, told the writer.

> Everyone was keen to help. Sometimes during emergencies there were of course problems. Amusing at times. We had for example a hospital dental surgeon playing the part of a German Luftwaffe pilot in full regalia. He was called back to

hospital for an emergency operation. Not thinking about what he was doing, he ran back through the streets in theatrical costume just as he had been onstage. Local civilians saw this figure in hated Luftwaffe uniform and gave chase. Thanks to the Military Police, he managed to get to the hospital by the skin of his teeth.

Nurses recognized the need for a change of scene, and a little relaxation and amateur dramatics for some was one way of relieving stress.

The realities of war weighed heavily upon nerves stretched thin by constant pressure of the bombing, a feeling of isolation, and worry about whether the island would be able to hold out or not. And if not ...? By 7 August 1942 it was estimated that food and fuel would be completely exhausted in three or four weeks. If help were not received there would be no alternative but to surrender. Then nurses would be faced with that question others had faced elsewhere, of whether to stay with their patients and become prisoners or risk leaving the island by air or sea.

Their worries eased somewhat when, on 15 August 1942 they heard the news of a desperate 'do-or-die' attempt to relieve Malta. Thirteen freighters and the tanker *Ohio*, supported by every available warship, ran the gauntlet through 'Bomb Alley' to the island. With them was the old aircraft carrier *Furious*, ready to fly off thirty-eight desperately needed Spitfires. On the airfields around Sicily and southern Italy, the enemy had massed 800 aircraft, and twenty submarines. All lay in wait.

Only five merchantmen reached Malta, yet the supplies they carried were enough to sustain the island for three vital months. But the best news of all came from the airfields, where joyful RAF ground crews greeted the Spitfires touching down in the darkness between flares and hastened them to safety. The news put renewed life into everyone. After that, Malta revived. Spitfires kept the bombers away, and once again nurses could carry out their duties without one ear cocked for the air raid sirens. And convoys could come through again.

Malta was unconquered, but the losses had been appalling. Impressed with the courage of everyone on that defiant island fortress, King George VI awarded it the George Cross, the civilian equivalent of the Victoria Cross.

Now the nurses could nurse casualties in more normal conditions. They could clear the backlog of wounded and empty the wards for those coming in from the next phase of the North African campaign.

5 Tunisia – Springboard to Europe

> We have arrived straight into plenty of
> work and the Sisters are thrilled to be
> really in it at last.
>> Principal Matron Miss Lucy Wane
>> In a letter to Matron-in-Chief

British and American troops landed on the French coastlines of Morocco and Algeria in November 1942 with a twofold objective of completing the destruction of the German and Italian forces in North Africa, which the British Eighth Army were pursuing with such success across the desert, and also of providing a possible springboard for an attack on the European mainland of Italy.

But the campaign did not quite go according to plan.

Things began to go wrong at dawn on the day of the landings. The French were not co-operative. Their Navy, remembering how the British had sunk their ships at Oran, was vengeful and organized stubborn resistance from Vichy French troops, inflicting over a thousand casualties upon the first wave of Allied assault troops.

British nurses, fortunately, were right there in the action with their hospital ships. Casualties from the harbour and beaches were carried to them for immediate surgical treatment and then taken to a hospital in Gibraltar. It was particularly fortunate, too, that sisters from the Royal Naval Nursing Service were there to deal with the compression injuries suffered by sailors who were in the water when depth-charges from their sinking ship, HMS *Partridge*, exploded.

When the French opposition in the Algiers naval base had been overcome, British and American armies expected to be driving forward at top speed through Tunisia to close the back door to Rommel's Afrika Korps now retreating through Libya with the Eighth Army in Victorious pursuit. But Allied planners had not reckoned on the speed with which their enemy could land forces by air across the sixty-mile straight from Sicily into Tunisia.

Consequently, with superiority in numbers, the Germans defending Tunis gave the Allied fighting men a terrible mauling. Virtually every infantry battalion which had landed with the invasion was down to half-strength. They came to a halt at Tébourba. Hospitals were full to overflowing. Nurses with the tented Number 97 BGH at Guelma had great difficulty in finding beds and even space for stretchers for the 2,000 casualties from the fierce Tébourba battles. Evacuation of the wounded from the battlefield was extremely difficult because of the exposed nature of the hill positions and the mud.

Working as far forward as possible were nurses of Princess Mary's RAF Nursing Service, flying casualties back to base hospitals. On some days they would fly as many as 700 wounded men 400 miles from the front. During April 1943, 7,000 were evacuated by air, and during the whole campaign 18,000 were evacuated usually to Algiers or Oran, or sometimes to Gibraltar, America or England.

With such ferocious fighting, frequently hand-to-hand, it was not surprising that another kind of casualty came for the nurses. One for which they had little specialist support.

The medical planning for the North African campaign had made no provision at all for psychiatry, and when British troops came up against such fierce resistance in the hills of the 'bloody Djebels', many instances of mental breakdowns came to light, bringing chaos to the front-line medical units which had no provision for their treatment of 'bomb-happy' soldiers – to use their own vernacular. Patients had to be evacuated hundreds of miles back to Algiers; hospitals became clogged with cases which, had they been treated at once locally, could have been returned to their units in the line.

The situation was partly saved by the work of military psychiatrist Stephen MacKeith. He had long foreseen that psychiatric as well as physical casualties were an inevitable component of battle conditions and put his ideas into practice, often against opposition from conservative medical officers in the forces who scoffed at his theories as modish and unnecessary. Their view was simple: a man either fought or was a coward.

Undeterred, MacKeith arranged for two psychiatrists to establish psychiatric treatment centres for the First Army in Tunisia early in 1943. One of them went to a field hospital close to the front line at Thibar. It was a strange-looking location, the hospital in the white buildings of a monastic seminary in a green valley into which led one road, churned by trucks into an almost impassable morass of clogging clay and red-brown mud which sucked the boots off those who had to walk through it.

Sister Yvonne Hunter Lander had only just disembarked when she heard about her posting there. 'Some kind of SOS came to our matron for nine nursing sisters to go to a front line unit. I don't think I was very popular with the matron so it was a case of 'You, you and you, will go to the 71st tented Field Hospital'. We arrived late one night and when we got up the next morning the hospital had miraculously broken camp and gone.'

   The psychiatrist there and his colleague at another front-line unit
restored some kind of order with the cases of psychoneurosis by
establishing a three-tier system of treatment and rehabilitation. In this
way almost a third of the patients were soon returned to their units, a
third given non-combatant duties in the theatre and a third sent home.
Colonel Stephen MacKeith favoured this routine, even though it did
involve a conflict of loyalties between the clinical needs of the individual
front-line soldier and the manpower demands of the military machine.
The bottom line for psychiatrists and nurses involved was to reduce
'wastage'. This was the way it was to work for the next two years for
doctors and nurses in Africa and Italy. It was no easy task for nurses,
who often had to offer an opinion on patients in their care.
   Meanwhile, during those last few weeks of the campaign in Tunisia,
casualties poured into casualty clearing stations and field hospitals which
were often close to the front line. Occasionally the evacuation
procedure did not work without a hitch or two, as was recalled by the
well-known singer and comedian, Sir Harry Secombe, in his book *Arias
and Raspberries*. He was then a lowly Lance Bombardier in a 78th
Division Field Artillery regiment.
   His glasses were shattered when he was riding his motor cycle to join
his unit in support of the Number 36 Brigade attacking Green Hill. He
managed to make the rendezvous, but his eyesight was so bad without
his glasses he was useless for any duties other than carrying ammunition
boxes. Consequently, he was sent back to the rear to get a new pair. For
some curious administrative reason he was officially classified for the
journey as 'walking wounded'. He was then in the system, issued with a
brown label tied to his jacket, put on a train to Souk Ahras and told to
report to the general hospital.
   He tells in his book how he arrived at the hospital in the middle of an
air raid; bombs were falling and things were a bit chaotic. An orderly
gave each of the walking wounded a pair of pyjamas and told them to
get into bed. 'This is the way the British Army looks after its lads',
thought Harry and promptly pulled the clothes over his head and went
fast asleep. He remembered nothing more until a doctor in a white coat
shook him awake, as he was later to write:

        'How are you now Brown?' he asked.
        'Pardon, sir?' I tried to bring him into sharper focus by
     narrowing my eyes.
        He repeated the question.
        'My name is Secombe, sir. Lance-Bombardier 924378.' I
     knew that much.
        The doctor looked at something tied to the foot of the bed.
     'Aren't you Fusilier Brown?'
        'No, sir.'

'Have you got dysentery, then?' The doctor was getting irritable by this time.

'No, sir. I've broken my glasses,' I stammered.

'Get out of that bloody bed, man.' The MO was furious. 'Give him his uniform and send the bugger to the optician,' he said to the orderly with him.

As I dressed I learned that there had been a monumental mistake and that some poor fusilier had been up all night filling sandbags in between rushing to the latrines. Then, to cap it all he'd been given an eye test, which must have seemed a strange treatment for what ailed him.

I was given short shrift, and was provided with two new pairs of spectacles in no time at all. Secretly I had banked on having to wait a couple of days while they tried to fix me up with the strong lenses I required, but I had to be content with just one night's bed and board. I don't know what was in the drink they gave me that night but it was nearly a week before I had a bowel movement – and it took a mortar attack to move me.[1]

Whilst young Secombe was being rushed back to his unit, nurses were rushing about too. Hundreds more of them, as well as infantry reinforcements, were needed in Tunisia. But at least the nurses were already on their way.

From various parts of Britain they travelled to Greenock and boarded the SS *Strathallen*, an old vessel that had been converted into a troop-ship. But whoever had been in charge of the conversion had given little thought to comfort. Three women were crammed into cabins designed for one, which meant that dressing and undressing had to be organized so that only one body at a time stood on the floor. One morning before they sailed, nurses in Sister Beatrice Hownam's cabin were jolted awake by a frightening banshee-like noise, which, after recovering their wits, they recognized as the lifeboat drill-alarm. The captain wanted to have at least one practice in calm waters before having to do it in the rough weather of the Atlantic. As they sailed away from the dull green shores of Scotland in convoy and out into the grey Atlantic, those nurses naturally hoped they would not be in for a very long voyage. Their destination was shrouded in secrecy.

Kay Summersby, of the First Aid Nursing Yeomanry, recalled the miseries of that crowded voyage as a discomfiting catalogue of hasty meals, endless queuing for toilets and persistent seasickness. During the first few days on board, personnel were frequently reminded to have 'torpedo bags' ready: bags to be grabbed should the ship be torpedoed. Suggested contents of each bag were items such as official papers, posting orders, medication and warm clothing. Many of the womens' bags contained 'more important' items such as make-up, jewellery and nylons. Kay Summersby, an Anglo-Irish divorcee with red hair and green eyes who had been a fashion model for the House of Worth, Paris, before becoming a member of the First Aid Nursing Yeomanry, recalled packing her own bag with her grandmother's earrings and other small items of cosmetics and underwear. Well, after all, she was going to meet the most important man in the Mediterranean theatre of operations then: General Dwight D. Eisenhower, her boss and a man who would soon mean much more to her. Her close romantic relationship with the man who was to be Supreme Allied Commander in Europe and future President of the USA had begun in May 1942, when, as a driver in the FANY, she was detailed to pick up a VIP passenger from London's Paddington Railway Station – a certain major-general with a German-sounding name. From then on, the 'nursing' side of her duties disappeared. She became his personal driver and, as she was to tell later in her book *Past Forgetting*, something a little more personal than that.'[2]

The *Strathallen* met heavy seas, and passengers had a very rough passage for more than two weeks. Then one night the sea appeared to be much calmer, and when nurses went on deck to take the fresh air, they saw something that they had not seen for the past three years because of blackout restrictions in Britain – a town on the starboard side brightly lit up.

It was on the North African coast, and they had sailed through the Straits of Gibraltar. The significance came with the dawn and the bright blue sky with its blazing sun beaming down upon them. They felt the trip was virtually at an end. And they relaxed happily, thinking of soon setting foot on dry land.

Sailors, however, soon put a damper on the nurses' feelings of exhilaration. They told them to take care. Hitler had sent U-boats into the Mediterranean to protect Rommel's supply routes. Now they were prowling in the area with magnetic torpedoes, ready to strike at every available target. As if to emphasize the seriousness of the situation, great booms and spouts of water broke the idyllic Mediterranean scene. Escorting destroyers were dropping depth-charges. Then everything became quiet. Everyone was told to prepare for disembarkation within twenty-four hours. Bags were packed. Optimistic passengers unpacked their 'torpedo bags'.

That night, impromptu parties erupted. But revellers returning to their bunks after one o'clock in the morning ready for a good night's sleep were rudely deprived. A tremendous explosion shattered the silence of the night. The ship rocked violently, as a torpedo slammed into the ship's engine-room. The sea flooded in, and the ship listed ten degrees to starboard. Passengers clutched at stanchions as the floor sloped alarmingly. Smoke billowed into the passageways, and steam belched from ruptured boilers. Nurses who still had 'torpedo bags' grabbed them with their Mae West life-jackets. Sister Beatrice Hownam remembers staggering to the lifeboat station and seeing the sea, normally 10 ft below the rails then surging barely 2 ft below them.

With the order to abandon ship, a frantic crew began to launch lifeboats. Despite all the boat drills, things went wrong. Boats got tangled, and some immediately filled with water and capsized. Panic-stricken men and women, fearful of going down with the ship before their lifeboat was launched, slithered down into the thick oil welling from under the ship and coating the sea. Men and women were everywhere in the foaming water, splashing furiously and propelling floats with their hands. All were desperate to put space between themselves and the sinking ship, and the veteran sailors recalled that the suction of a sinking ship would drag them down until their lungs seemed to burst. They had one thought in their minds – to get as far away from the ship as possible.

The ship, though, seemed to have stabilized itself in a listing position, and incredibly there were still nursing sisters on board working in the sick bay: Olive Stewardson and Julie Kerr. Already they had dispatched stretcher-cases to safety but delayed their own departure to look after badly burnt engine-room crew just brought in. When more burnt crew members were carried into the sick bay, three American Army Corps women went to help.

Others in the lifeboats found themselves adrift on a moonlit sea. FANY ambulance driver Kay Summersby remembered it well: 'The sea around us was filled with drowning men and women. We pulled some of them into our boat and there the nurses were soon at work.'[3] Applying dressings was no easy task when all the time the boat was rolling and pitching madly as depth charges exploded below.

When dawn came, all those still on board the badly listing *Strathallen* were taken off – including those sisters who had stayed behind in the sick bay. Sadly, though, five British nurses had already lost their lives.

For the way in which they had disregarded their own safety whilst tending to the wounded, Sister Stewardson and Sister Kerr were recommended for the award for gallantry of the RRC.

Later that morning destroyers began picking up survivors. Those who were fit enough had to climb a rope-ladder, while the wounded were hoisted aboard. Kay Summersby and many others were taken to Oran.

Their immediate problem then was getting a completely new outfit to replace torn and sodden uniforms which would never again be the same. As far as Kay was concerned, everything was made easy for her. With one telephone call to Eisenhower's office, transport was provided and an advance of money and accommodation arranged. Many of his staff knew of their close relationship, which had for months prompted fruity speculations. Eisenhower sent his B17 aircraft for her the next day to bring her to his headquarters in Algiers. There she went on a shopping spree to replace what she had lost. Although her greatest loss was that of her 'woollies', she ended up buying underwear designed for women 'of a certain calling': black mesh panties and brassieres which were 'cut out at the nipples ... not for nursing mothers!'[4]

General Eisenhower was not the only VIP interested in the fate of those shipwrecked young nurses. So too was his Chief of Staff, General Walter Bedell Smith. A note in the diary of General Everett Hughes throws some light on what happened to them when rescued. He told how General Walter Bedell Smith, Chief of Staff to Eisenhower, flew to Oran to meet the women survivors – five members of the US Women's Army Corps, thirty US navy nurses, and two hundred English nurses. He promoted all five WAACs to captains, and 'got some personal entanglement with Nurse Wilbur, who returned a Chief Nurse' but the English nurses got nothing except a new battledress.[5]

So it was that Beatrice Hownam and other survivors, in their ill-fitting battledresses had to wait a little longer for their flight to Algiers. Amongst them was the new Principal Matron, Miss Lucy Wane, who had typically managed to come through the shipwreck still immaculately turned out in her neatly ironed white blouse. The first thing she did was to march into the army ordnance stores in Algiers to arrange for her nursing sisters to be re-equipped. She found the Ordnance Officer had no stocks whatever of women's clothing but she did arrange for an issue of men's underclothing and toilet items such as brush and comb. She wired to the War Office, asking them to get suppliers to send out half-made tunics and skirts to be fitted in Algiers by local tailors. In addition, she ordered hats, shoes, ties, underwear and stockings but did not expect to get them through ordnance for a few weeks.

Her short stay in Algiers had taught her something else: that the present Army Nurse's uniform was quite inappropriate for North Africa. She asked for permission to wear khaki because of the working conditions of nurses in field hospitals. In a later letter Lucy Wane wrote of another big problem for nursing sisters – elastic. 'Elastic is almost unheard of in the shops and so is soap. Worst of all is watches.'

An amusing postscript to an earlier letter written by her to the Matron-in-Chief was that of using her charm on an American officer who had made her a present of cold cream, powder, rouge, shampoo and other items which he had bought on board the ship, 'in case there were any ladies short of these things'. Obviously he was an officer living up to the Boy Scout's motto: 'Be prepared'!

Lucy Wane would soon learn that cosmetics could be bought in Algiers along with many other luxury articles not to be found in Britain. Apparently some army staff officers had discovered that such items could be dispatched to the UK at a handsome profit, if you knew the right people and were doing well out of it.

Lucy Wane's new domain in Algiers was the magnificent Number 98 General Hospital which stood high above the city on a hilltop and was set in the most beautiful residential area at the end of the rue Michelet.

When wounded soldiers saw that hospital they thought it was heaven. Fusilier John Cooper of the Lancashire Fusiliers certainly did, as he told this writer.

> I was wounded in both knees fighting in the 'Bloody Djebels' and was taken by stretcher to a point where I was loaded onto a mule of 574 Pack Transport Company. They had special saddles with panniers which held a stretcher each side. I'd never before seen such whopping great mules. I must say it was an experience I never wish to repeat as we came stepping and slithering down the mountainside, swaying rhythmically to the steady pace set by the troop of mules. The going was awful. One thing I shall never forget about North Africa was the mud. Wherever we went there was this thick, clinging mud. I had always thought Africa was a place of hot sunshine. But it wasn't then. At last we were off-loaded to a Casualty Clearing Station still within shell-fire range and I was amazed to find nurses there. They were superb, for that Clearing Station had all the attributes of a butcher's shop. I was a butcher myself and should know. From there I was taken to a hospital at Souk-el Khemis where two broken legs were diagnosed and both legs put into plaster from thigh to toes.
>
> From there we moved to a tented hospital at Bone before finally arriving at the 98th General Hospital in Algiers. Little did I know then that I was in the company of such a great man as Sir Alexander Fleming and maybe one of the first of many to benefit from his wonderful discovery – Penicillin.
>
> I owe a lot also to all those nurses who looked after me on the way down from the Djebels to the base hospital itself. I cannot say enough about them. When I had my plasters removed, a big Irish Guardsman taught me how to walk again. He used to walk me down to the main gate where we'd sit under the palm trees eating dates and grapes and watching the gas powered buses coming up from Algiers fully laden. Paddy used to tell me that after the war he was going to buy a light-house off the coast of Cork and wave to all the troopships that went by. I often wonder what happened to him. Strangely enough all I could think about was to get back up the line with the lads. It somehow didn't seen right to be enjoying oneself whilst all your mates were up in the line.

It was indeed at this stage of the war, in the autumn of 1942 and spring of 1943, that nurses dealing with casualties from the front line had the satisfaction of seeing for themselves the tremendous effect this new drug, penicillin, had on the death and disability rate of their critically wounded patients. It was a real boost to morale in those overcrowded hospitals of North Africa. However, the boost to morale which the front-line soldier appreciated more than anything else was the sight of those nurses so close to the front.

Here mention must be made of those men who brought those wounded men down from the mud of those 'bloody Djebels' – the stretcher-bearers. By day and night they were out, crawling forward across machine-gun-swept no man's land to bring in their bleeding comrades. Some of them made an agonizing passage scores of times in the course of a battle. For them there was no rest, no time when they could scramble into a slit trench and escape the inferno for a few moments. They had to come and go in the path of terror.

When those wounded men found their own women nurses ready to look after them in field hospitals, it really did have an impact upon them. They went back to the front not only with wounds healed but also with a new determination, an inflexibility of purpose to see the thing through to victory.

At the end of April 1943 nurses in forward hospitals were quietly put on a state of special readiness. The final breakthrough was about to be mounted, and the doctors had budgeted for 6,000 casualties.

At dawn on 6 May the First British Army launched its assault on Tunis. To the south and north, American and French troops joined in the attack.

Three days later, on 9 May, the German Commander-in-Chief, Sixt von Arnim, drove from his rear headquarters along the dusty road toward Allied headquarters, all the while seeing thousands of his own men handing in their weapons. A quarter of a million German prisoners walked into the camps. It was an amazing spectacle which war correspondent Alan Moorehead witnessed. 'Their attitude was, "Well, it's finished for me now. I don't have to fight anymore. I can relax a bit." They did not have to worry about the future. They were simply going off to another place.'

So too were the nurses. But, as usual, they did not yet know where. Meanwhile, they got on with nursing the 2,000 pain-ridden, disabled and mutilated soldiers who were casualties of the final breakthrough. They lay in hospital wards along the north coast of Africa, from Casablanca to Cairo. In comforting and caring for these men the nurses had little time for pondering the question: 'Where do we go from here?'

They would be told where soon enough.

Plans had already been made. Wards were being steadily emptied, to be ready for the next campaign. Hospital ships were gathering. Reinforcements were making up deficiencies in front-line units, and long-awaited equipment for hospitals was coming through in plentiful supply. Calculations had been made. The quantity of that equipment did not augur well for those who would be making that next assault on what Churchill had described – so erroneously, as it turned out – 'the soft underbelly of Europe' – Italy.

But in that brief interlude between the African victories and the launching of the next phase of the campaign against Nazi Germany, both US and British commanders were concerned about morale. It was not going to be easy to motivate those veterans of the Western Desert and the bloody Tunisian Djebels. They knew what to expect from war now.

War correspondent Ernie Pyle, who later would be killed in action himself, painted a vivid picture in words of how he, and the soldiers he marched with, saw the never-ending condition of being at war:

> I only know war consists of tired and dirty soldiers who are alive and don't want to die: of shocked silent men wandering back ... from battle; ... of dead mules and hospital tents,... and graves, and graves, and graves.
>
> That is our war, and we will carry it with us as we go on from one battleground to another until it is all over, leaving some of us behind on every beach, in every field. We are just beginning with the ones back of us here in Tunisia. I don't know whether it was their good fortune or their misfortune to get out of it so early in the game. I guess it doesn't make any difference, once a man has gone. Medals and speeches and victories are nothing to them any more. They died and others lived and nobody knows why it is so. They died and thereby the rest of us can go on and on. When we leave here for the next shore, there is nothing we can do for the ones beneath the wooden crosses, except perhaps to pause and murmur, 'Thanks, pal'.[6]

No doubt Pyle had assessed correctly the mood of the soldiers going on to the next battlefield. They were going to need all the motivation that could be given to them and no doubt too the sight of nurses sailing with them in the same convoy would help a lot. But a far more serious problem than the motivation of disillusioned and exhausted soldiers occupied the minds at Allied Command Headquarters. It was the possibility of something more frightening – casualties from poison gas.

Ominous reports were reaching Washington and London indicating that Hitler was planning to resort to the use of poison gas to repel any attempted invasion of southern Europe. Allied agents had verified that the Germans had a quarter of a million tons of toxic munitions in readiness. Amongst these chemical warfare weapons was a new nerve gas, called Tabun. It was colourless, almost odourless and attacked the nervous system through the lungs and eyes, causing death within five minutes. And there was also mustard gas.

The headquarters North African Theatre of Operations was alerted, and contingency plans were put in operation. But no one thought of alerting the nurses.

Within a year, nurses in Italy would be caring for thousands of military personnel and civilians suffering and dying from the effects of poison gas.

All, of course, was hushed up.

Everyone was busy with the immediate task. The biggest invasion force of all time was gathering. On the plains of Kairouan two airborne divisions were assembling. From ports all along the North African coast 2,000 ships were emerging; one Canadian division was sailing directly from the United Kingdom. Amongst those ships linking up with that formidable armada were hospital ships and carriers. Some of these, sadly, would be lost with their nurses aboard. But others would go on to land on the shell-battered beaches of Italy. For now, the assault on Sicily was about to begin.

6   Sicily and Salerno

If the planning and conduct of the
campaign in Sicily were bad, the preparations for the invasion of Italy, and
subsequent conduct of the campaign in that
country, were worse still
Field Marshal The Viscount Montgomery
of Alamein, KG[1]

On the morning of 10 July 1943, Sister Marjorie Bennett was on the
hospital ship off the coast of Sicily, waiting to sail into the bay at
Augusta. She and her QA colleagues wondered what was holding things
up. In the noisome fug of the troop-decks many men still swung in their
hammocks retching their guts out. Those sitting dressed with their
webbing strapped ready for disembarking slid helplessly up and down
the benches, their feet in a broth of their vomit. From time to time the
loudspeaker crackled and called officers to assemble in the mess room.
Men jumped up excitedly and then trooped back and plonked
themselves onto chairs. The message eventually percolated through to
the 'lesser beings' that 'things were not going quite according to plan'.
The news was greeted by those nurses pulling hard on their cigarettes,
who had been that way before, with a shrug of the shoulders and a wry
comment of 'Do they ever?'

On the North African airfield of Kairouan then, planes were beginning
to limp back to base with their cargoes of dead and dying airborne men.
They were rushed off to hospital, and survivors told nurses horrific tales
of the calamitous assault on Sicily.

Eisenhower's prime concern was to hush up the scandal. It would not
have done for the public to have heard how the lives of young British
and American volunteers in the airborne divisions had been squandered
off the coast of Sicily. How allied anti-aircraft guns had fired on the
airborne armada; how some pilots towing gliders broke their tows miles
out to sea; how many of those gliders, including that of the First
Airborne Division's commander, General Hopkinson, hit the water two

miles off shore; how some landed miles inland, and one even in Malta. No mention could be made of the fact that of the 147 gliders which had so proudly set off from North Africa that evening, nearly half of them, sixty-nine in all, had crashed into the sea, killing 252 highly trained men.

Instead, the public heard a different story, a splendid one telling of an outstanding victory. So whilst nurses were comforting the wounded from the fiasco of the airborne assault on Sicily, the public opened their morning newspapers and read: 'The Allied invasion of Europe has begun. A powerful force of Canadian, British and American troops landed at 3 a.m. along a 100-mile stretch of the south eastern coast of Sicily.' Things, indeed, were not going according to plan. Nor were they going to get much better. The nurses were not spared either.

During the first few days of those air and seaborne landings, the hospital ships and hospital carriers off shore received a terrifying hammering from the air. Fighter-bombers swooped down from behind the hills, dropped their bombs and then machine-gunned along the line of shipping and zoomed off again before the fighters from Malta could reach them.

As dusk approached, the hospital ships which had been loading both Allied and enemy wounded all afternoon turned on their lights, as well as the electrically illuminated red crosses on their sides and decks, as required by international law. Nevertheless, a flight of German planes turned their attention to the 8,000-ton hospital ship *Talamba* two miles off the coast of Syracuse.

The *Daily Telegraph* war correspondent watched in horror as the ship received a direct hit. 'I saw the *Talamba* go down, her nursing sisters, her wounded and her crew crying out in the night for help. She and two other hospital ships had spent the afternoon picking up wounded without regard to nationality.' He told how the hospital ships had 'stayed well clear of merchantmen and warships, but at about ten p.m. a new formation of German planes came over. Thwarted by concentrated fire from a cruiser and other vessels they made straight for the *Talamba*, dived and released their bombs.'[2]

As the ship began to sink, stern first, nurses, orderlies and doctors did everything possible to get the wounded off in lifeboats. In some cases drastic action was needed. One surgeon who had just amputated a soldier's leg hastily bound up the stump tightly, strapped the man to a stretcher and slid it over the side, hoping it would float. It did, and the man survived.

A destroyer and other craft went to *Talamba*'s help. The cruiser kept up a covering barrage against the planes closing in. Other hospital ships escaped by prudently extinguishing their lights. A nursing sister with a broken leg managed to keep herself afloat for over half an hour before she was rescued. One of her colleagues, Sister Maud Johnson, was not so fortunate and was never seen again. Within fifteen minutes of the first bomb landing, the ill-fated *Talamba* reared out of the water by the bows and slid to the bottom.

* * *

Right from the first hour that the assault troops landed, flat-bottomed water-ambulances, which could get close up to the beach, plied between the carrier and the shore bringing casualties almost straight from the scene of the battle, often under fire themselves. When the carrier had a full load, it took the wounded to the hospital ship a little further out in the bay.

Casualties were so high that an urgent signal was sent to Malta for more nurses. Noelle Starr was wakened at midnight, taken to a motor torpedo-boat with seven other nurses and rushed across a choppy sea to Augusta. 'Germans were fighting nearby and we took cover in caves until they were driven back,' she said. When Sister Marjorie Bennett and her colleagues landed on those beaches of Sicily they were driven slowly along dusty tracks and were shocked by the debris of battle lying around them. 'Here and there alongside a glider smashed to matchwood, were rows of crosses with a British or German helmet on top. Bloated corpses lay stinking in the burnt-out wreckage of tanks and armoured cars. What a relief it was to reach Syracuse and take over the hospital from the Italians there. German as well as British wounded were brought in and treated just the same. They were no different to our boys and I could see they were amazed to see women nursing so near to the front. I couldn't help wondering what an awful waste war was and how just a handful of men could lead millions of ordinary men to fight each other when, out of battle, German soldiers and British shared their few possessions and chatted amicably together.' So mused Marjorie Bennett some fifty years later.

Pauline Greenway, nursing amidst the slaughter that was Sicily then, put those same thoughts more strongly. 'I came to the conclusion it was not a war with the British fighting Germans and Italians but soldiers fighting politicians. The ordinary soldiers got on well as they lay, chatting in a mixture of German and English often in adjacent beds and sometimes under fire from German planes.'

Sister Marjorie Bennett, a devout Catholic, recalled how some soldiers knew that they were about to die. 'One young man who had lost both legs and had abdominal injuries too, said to me one afternoon when soldiers on each side of him were dozing in their beds: "Sister, will you say a prayer for me, please? I'll feel better then." I sat down on the edge of his bed, took his hands in mine and we said the Act of Contrition together.'

As the 'poor bloody infantry' advanced through the plains and foothills of Sicily, the grapes were just beginning to swell, though they were not quite ripe enough for eating. This did not deter thirsty Tommies. They blundered into the rows of vines, plucked a handful of green grapes, and then there would be a bang and a call for 'stretcher-bearer', which troops soon began to recognize as the signal that another poor beggar had lost his foot. The mines in the vineyards brought in a crop of casualties that could have been avoided, had the warnings been heeded. Often, too, a mate of the soldier or the stretcher-bearer would run the risk of having his foot blown off by going in to rescue the first victim.

Apart from these surgical cases, nurses were kept busy with cases of malaria and dysentery. All troops had been issued with mepacrine tablets to prevent them catching malaria, but not all men took them. Some were suspicious about what was in those tablets – just as they always suspected that tea back in the UK had been spiced with a bromide sedative to depress the sexual urge. Anyway, some soldiers, not knowing what the sickness of malaria was really like, did not care if they caught it. 'Better than catching a burst from a Spandau, eh?' some would declare, hoping it would keep them out of the firing-line for a few weeks. Others would sell the tablets to gullible Sicilian girls as 'anti-baby pills'.

On the other hand, despite taking all the precautions – taking their tablets, rolling down their sleeves and wearing long trousers instead of shorts in the evenings – conscientious soldiers still came down with malaria, and sometimes with a particularly virulent form like that which decimated men of the Green Howards on the Catania plain. One of them, Maurice Pinkney, said, 'I was told that the malaria we had contracted was from a vicious kind of mosquito which had been specially bred in the laboratory of the Italian Malaria Research Establishment just outside Catania and that when the island had been "softened up" by Naval guns and RAF bombers prior to the invasion, the whole Research Establishment had been wrecked and the virulent mosquitoes had escaped. Anyway it laid me low then and again just before D-Day in Normandy.'

Another kind of casualty began to filter through in greater numbers to hospitals after the first month of the Sicilian campaign. They were men suffering from 'battle fatigue'. Often they would be soldiers with a previously good record who had been pushed just too far. One corporal, who had served right through the North African campaign with the First Army, explained to Pauline Greenway how it happened: 'It was those Moaning Minnies that finally did it,' he said, his hands shaking and rubbing his cheeks as if trying to wash away the memory of it all. Pauline was at a loss to understand who those moaning minnies in his platoon were. Later, she discovered they were indeed terrifying.

They were a new form of German rocket artillery, code-named NEBELWERFER for some unknown reason, for they were not a smoke-thrower but a kind of six-barrelled mortar which could fling salvo after salvo of high-explosive shells screaming into defensive positions at a rapid rate. It was not just the effect of the shells bursting around the troops that filled them with undiluted terror but the fearful noise they made like a chorus of gigantic mules suddenly braying from just over the ridge ahead. After a few such bombardments, some soldiers eventually lost their nerve completely and went to pieces.

One of the important aspects of the jobs for nurses and doctors then was to achieve the physical and mental rehabilitation of the front-line soldier. It took a lot of courage for the wounded to go back into the line from the safety of a hospital bed. Farley Mowat, in action with the Canadians on the Catania plain, overcame his dread and went back to serve right through the Italian campaign.[3] Others sometimes just could not make it at first and needed further treatment by nurses and doctors in wings of special hospitals set aside for such casualties.

Nurses indeed had to be more than a dispenser of medication, something of a psychiatrist and a counsellor at times too. And they learnt by experience. Sister Marjorie Bennett remembered one awful experience which she learnt to avoid in the future. She was putting the dressing on a soldier who had lost both his eyes when a cigarette lighter he was making from a rifle bullet had exploded in his face. Whilst Sister Bennett was applying the bandages over his eyes, the soldier groped about the top of the box by his bed which served as a bedside locker and took hold of a letter. 'This came for me this morning, nurse. Would you read it for me, please?'

In her haste to please him and also get on with all the other dressings on her round, Marjorie took the folded paper and started to read aloud straight away. Then she faltered and stopped halfway through a sentence which had begun, 'I feel you ought to know that your wife ...' She knew what would be coming next but did not know how to avoid reading it. The soldier insisted. '... that your wife has been having an affair with an American and says she is going to go back with him to the States after the war.'

That night the man tried to kill himself. After that, Marjorie Bennett always put such letters in her pocket and said she would read them later when she had finished her round. 'It was safer that way.'

In contrast with the battle and surgical cases facing nurses were those of the self-inflicted wound. It had not taken soldiers in the rear echelons many weeks in Sicily to discover the bargaining power a tin of bully beef had with attractive young women and their mothers. Unfortunately there was often a further price to be paid for the favours these young ladies dispensed – venereal disease.

Unlike the German Army, neither the Canadian nor British ones provided clean, mobile brothels in which men could make the most of any respite from the miserable business of killing and being killed. Inevitably then, VD was an ever-present problem for hospitals which had barely enough beds for the battle casualties.

In Marjorie Bennett's hospital at Syracuse they had a special VD ward set aside for the victims of such dangerous liaisons. 'I used to think what a waste it was for us to be using such a precious medication as penicillin on such men when there were so many others who had been

fighting at the front needing it and blitz victims at home,' recalled
Marjorie Bennett.

Indeed, penicillin could then only be spared for troops overseas.
Margaret Browne, nursing soldiers at Chertsey and Basingstoke, recalls
having to rely mainly upon M and B 693 until just before D-Day 1944.

Sister Bennett, however, was not averse to a little romance herself,
for when the fighting had once again left her hospital some way behind
the firing-line, she too had time for social activities after duty, as she
recalled:

> We went to the magnificent opera house in Catania and to
> concerts. Gracie Fields came over to entertain the troops and
> we went to parties in different officers' messes and the
> officers' club. Sometimes we'd have a super meal at the
> Albergo San Giorgio which was run by the British as an
> Officers Transit hotel. Then, one night our Sisters' Mess gave
> a special dance to repay all those officers who had invited us
> to their own functions. After one such evening my own life
> was never the same again. I wonder if I had known what I
> was letting myself in for would I have gone to that dance?
> Yes, I would. That was the evening I met a handsome RAF
> officer stationed in Malta. He'd flown to Sicily on a liaison
> visit to Catania airfield. From that moment on whenever
> things got tough I would turn my thoughts to Bill. Like a
> teenage girl I'd wonder if we'd get married, where we might
> live and what we might do. It was a great feeling. Well, being
> in love is, isn't it?

Marjorie Bennett would get the answer to some of those questions very
soon.

On 17 August, the Americans entered Messina. After thirty-eight
days the campaign, which had started so catastrophically, was over. It
had cost the Allies some 30,000 dead, wounded and missing.

Now there was a short period for 'rest and recuperation'. The hospital
wards in Syracuse and Catania were emptying slowly, and nurses had a
little more time off duty. Marjorie Bennett made the most of it. So did
her boyfriend, Bill. He made frequent excuses for liaison visits to Malta.
But towards the end of August he could see the time rapidly
approaching when everybody would again be on the move. So, no
doubt, would Marjorie. 'He proposed marriage to me one night. I told
him I could not cook. He said we could live out of tins. I said I couldn't
clean windows. He said he'd do that. He said he was not a Catholic. I
said we'd write to the Pope. The Padre wrote to the War Office and we
got married in Syracuse church.'

It was at this time that nurses from all parts of the Mediterranean theatre of operations were on the move. Some of them, sadly for the last time in their short lives.

At 0300 hours on 3 September 1943 – four years to the day since war broke out – 600 guns fired a barrage onto the quiet beaches of Reggio Calabria from across the Straits of Messina. The only casualty was an Italian battery commander hit by a brick thrown in rage by one of his own men. With the Germans gone, the Italians were in no mood to play the hero.

War Correspondent Christopher Buckley wondered if there had ever been such a scene in history of 'an invading army being met by its opponents on the shores of their native land with a touching of caps and requests to "Carry your bag, sir?" '[4]

It was a memorably happy day for the assault troops. Memorable indeed because it was probably the last really happy one for those warriors who would fight their way 800 miles northwards for the next two years of a campaign. They would be thrown into battle against appalling odds resulting in horrendous casualties. River lines and their dominating mountain peaks would be taken, lost and retaken by units who would then face yet more stubbornly held crests beyond.

No wonder nurses such as Margaret Jennings and Diana Sugden, who had to tend to the tragic casualties of that long bloody march northwards in Italy, often wondered if the generals knew what they were doing – over 313,495 young men suffered death or disablement.

However, whilst Montgomery's Eighth Army was making its way painfully northwards from Reggio Calabria, nurses were being warned to get ready for their part in the next Allied offensive. And they were not told what a bloody one it would be either.

Back in Egypt, at Kantara hospital, Sister Jennings and her colleagues were suddenly given four hours notice to be on the move. 'We packed, entrained for Alexandria, embarked on the *Neuralia*, and resigned ourselves to the prospect of a long voyage to an unknown destination.' They sailed through the Straits of Messina and then were told their destination and task: to assault the beaches of Salerno and move on to capture the vital port of Naples. The nurses would be in close support on the beaches.

On the next night, however, aboard all those ships carrying 100,000 British and 69,000 Americans for the assault landing, a carnival atmosphere prevailed. NAAFI beer and bottles of wine were swigged, and the old favourites of the 'Roll Out the Barrel' vintage were being sung with gusto. The once tense faces of men who had braced themselves for the ordeal ahead with the philosophy of 'When you gotta go ... you gotta go' were now relaxed and happy. And so too were those of the nurses. Now there would be no casualties, certainly not after the latest news. Straight from the ship's tannoy. Italy had surrendered!

Unconditionally laid down her arms! There would be no bloody battles for the beaches.

Those celebrations of 8 September 1943 were short-lived. German infantry were already in their slit trenches, waiting. One of the bloodiest battles of the Second World War was about to begin, and nurses would be right in the midst of it.

At 0300 hours on 9 September, the deceptive quiet of those beaches was rent by the noise of an avalanche of bombs and shells, as assault craft set off for the beach.

The German artillery waited. Dawn was breaking. Now every German weapon around the bay opened fire. Enemy dive-bombers flew over, dropping chandelier flares which hung in the sky illuminating the whole ghastly scene. Heavy-calibre high-explosive shells ploughed up the beach; wounded and dying lay everywhere. Nurses were in it straight away. 'As we had suddenly and unexpectedly become front line nurses instead of a base hospital unit, we were split into CCSs [Casualty Clearing Stations] and FDSs [Field Dressing Stations] and we went forward with 5th Army troops,' recalled Sister Margaret Jennings.

Everyone was in the front line. Nurses, clerks, cooks and even the generals. The shallow-draft hospital carriers which nosed ashore to take off wounded from the casualty clearing stations were under constant shell-fire. The beaches were now so packed with men and material that medical officers and nursing sisters could hardly find a place for their field hospital. 'Most of our hospital equipment was blown all over the beach by shelling,' said Flora Whyte Urquhart. 'We set up three operating theatres in bombed buildings using whatever equipment we could beg or borrow. Convoys of wounded came in continuously and surgeons worked non-stop.'

On 13 September, four days after the landings, the British hospital ship *Newfoundland* sailed from Bizerte carrying a hundred American nurses bound for the beaches, along with more British nurses too. The captain of the *Leinster* recorded what then happened. 'The *Newfoundland* was amongst five hospital ships cruising off shore having full recognition lights as per Geneva Convention. German bombers made a most deliberate bombing attack, setting *Newfoundland* on fire.'[5] They scored direct hits on the *Newfoundland*, just behind the bridge. The ship's British matron and five of her nurses, plus all the ship's doctors, were killed outright. Fire raged right through the ship, flames flickered from every porthole and she began to sink. Horrified wireless interceptors heard a German pilot shouting exultantly into his microphone: 'I've hit a hospital ship! She's on fire. Sure to sink.'[6]

When the bomb hit the *Newfoundland* nurses were asleep below deck. Passageways were blocked with debris. Some nurses managed to scramble through on to the deck. RAMC orderlies carried the wounded to lifeboat stations. Michael Aston, then a Cadet, recalled that in the starboard alleyway RAMC nursing orderlies lay dead.[7] A fire burnt fiercely, and they could not get near to them. They could hear someone screaming in the fire. The ship's QA staff nurses were in cabins on the port side. Sister Lee was at a porthole, and they tried to pull her through but didn't succeed. The ship lurched and listed heavily to one side. The order was given to abandon ship. They simply had to leave her. She was lost in the fire.

The hospital carrier *Leinster* moved closer to the stricken hospital ship *Newfoundland*, sailing through burning oil and tongues of flame spurting upwards. It was a bizarre scene in the garish light of the blazing *Newfoundland*, as one after another of the sixty-two survivors, some with blood and oil-soaked wound dressings, were hauled aboard and taken below by nurses and orderlies.[8]

Fully laden with wounded on board, the *Leinster* made for Bizerte. An unusual incident was then recorded in the ship's war diary. One of the patients was a German Lieutenant prisoner of war. At 0300 hours, after the ship had sailed from the Gulf of Salerno, a nurse found him hanging from the rail of the bed above his bunk by a pyjama cord tied round his neck. He was unconscious. She quickly cut him down and applied artificial respiration, and he recovered. Three hours later he became violent and had to be given morphia and hyoscine. Later in the day he was given paraldehyde. His condition deteriorated, and he developed hypostatic pneumonia. He died at 2205 hours and was buried at sea.[9]

'What had happened to him?' the nurses asked themselves. The story pieced together was that he believed that as a prisoner of war he was going to be tried by court martial as a spy and then shot. Panic and fear led to his attempt to kill himself.

Back in the Gulf of Salerno that night, the hospital ship *St Andrew* finished rescuing all the American nurses and landed them on the shore, where the enemy was now so close that the hospitals themselves were under direct artillery-fire. A salvo from a German battery fell upon and around the operating tent of Number 14 British CCS, killing the surgeon, his patient and several of the theatre orderlies.

The situation on the beachhead was critical. At one time, German tanks got within 400 yds of the shore as German infantry units threw in counter-attack after counter-attack. But General Mark Clark refused to be budged from that beachhead. 'The only way they're going to get us off this beach is to push us step by step, into the water', he told divisional commanders.[10]

The situation was grim, and nurses saw it all happening around them. Margaret Jennings remembered how it was as they moved forward to be close to the front. 'As we passed soldiers waiting to go forward it was a great treat to see grins spreading from ear to ear on their faces, and to be greeted with rousing hails and cheers. We were told later we sent up morale one hundred per cent of those troops waiting to go into battle. We were all in need of support for our morale then.'

At that time morale had plummeted to the point where soldiers were ready to mutiny. When a draft of 1,500 infantrymen, many of them from North African hospitals who thought they were on their way to rejoin their own divisions – numbers 50 and 51 in the UK for the invasion of France – were landed on Salerno beach instead, 700 of them just sat down and refused to fight. Corps commander Lieutenant General Richard McCreery talked to the men. Most of them agreed to go forward to Number 46 Division, but 192 still refused. They were disarmed and put in prison compounds next to Germans who booed and called them cowards. In the end they were court-martialled and sentenced to seven years' penal servitude, except for the sergeants who were ordered to be shot. At the last minute they accepted a reprieve on the condition they went into the line.

Many a soldier who saw nurses going to the front said to themselves, 'If she can go, so can I,' as one infantry officer later confessed to Sister Iris Ogilvie Bower. Nurses were such a tonic for morale.

Sister Jennings' Field Dressing Station was in a bomb-battered building with no running water.

> We brought water from a stream and boiled it and lived off bully beef and a breakfast made by crushing hard tack biscuits mixed with dried milk to make a kind of porridge.
>
> With hardly any equipment we struggled on sometimes by candlelight. One day I removed a young soldier's field dressing from his leg and saw the lower half hanging on by a bit of skin and tissue. An amputation was urgent. But there was no blood for a transfusion. One of the doctors whose blood matched knelt beside him and gave a direct infusion. A successful operation was performed in the hastily erected operation theatre, and the lad lived to tell the tale. I heard he received his artificial limb at a later date. We did wonder how they all got on but they moved on so quickly.

Stretchers lay side by side with grey-faced, shocked soldiers lying in blood-soaked clothing. One afternoon, an orderly gently pulled her sleeve and directed her to another young man. She has never forgotten the moment she removed the dressing from his foot. 'My stomach gave a violent lurch, the smell was bad enough. And though I had never seen a case like it before I remembered my lectures. Gangrene. I knew what that would mean. His leg would have to come off. The soldier was so young and had no idea of the severity of his wound. Carefully I covered the foot with the old dressing, trying to hide my feelings. The orderly with me asked, "Aren't you going to dress the wound?" I quietly explained there was no point and no time to be lost. And I walked quickly over to the medical officer.' Margaret Jennings braced herself. Who was going to tell the soldier his leg would have to be amputated?

Who was going to answer the inevitable question of, 'Will my girlfriend still like me?'

No one liked that job.

But by then Sister Jennings knew the problem all too well. Soldiers faced with being permanently disabled sometimes became depressed to the extent of feeling that life was no longer worth living. They lost interest in themselves and their treatment. The nurse's job was then critical, for the will to live was essential to recovery. They had to convince patients that in spite of physical handicaps they were still needed by those who loved them and they could still be useful in the community.

Those last days on the Salerno beachhead were depressing days for everyone in the Field Dressing Station – medical staff and patients alike. The turning-point came on 23 September, when British Ten Corps forced a passage from Salerno to Naples. The cost of three weeks fighting was 12,000 casualties – almost 7,000 British and 5,000 American.

Nurses now found themselves in Naples, the strangest of the cities they had experienced so far. And the bombs would still be falling upon them.

7 Naples and Bari

Certainly there were some breath-holding
moments when we were stuck in the midst
of fighting vessels engaged in the battles off
Sicily and Italy.
                Winifred Barnfather Reid TANS,
                            aboard hospital ships
                            Somersetshire and *Aba*

The air-raid siren screamed yet again. After a day full of alarms, nurses
and patients in Number 92 BGH in Naples were plunged into deeper
despair. Would they never end? Bombs rained down on the port area
and also around the hospital itself.

'Each raid seemed to be worse than the one before,' said Pauline
Greenway. 'I suppose after a few days we became even more sensitive
to the different noises; first the sound of the bombs whistling down, then
the crash of the explosion itself, the tinkling of shrapnel falling, then the
long slow rumble of neighbouring buildings falling down.'

The city was a wreck. Piles of masonry blocked the roads, and
crumbling tenement blocks looked as though they would tumble down
at any moment. There was a smell of charred wood everywhere,
mingling with the foul odour of shattered sewers seeping through the
flagstones. There were bomb-craters where German demolition squads
had blown up everything that still functioned. Water supplies and
electricity mains were off.

But it was not just the air raids that strained the nerves during those
early days when the hospital was settling into its new quarters.
Enormous explosions could be heard coming from various parts of the
city without any warning whatsoever and without any aircraft overhead.

Then, one day, a great furore of noise came from the streets around
the hospital. Military trucks were driving round with loudspeakers
blaring out urgent warnings in Italian to civilians. At first no one in the
hospital grasped what was going on. Then they too got the message.
Panic stations. 'All patients and personnel were to evacaute the hospital
at once. Immediately!'[1] Every ward was packed with casualties: Allied

and German military and a few civilians too. The bedridden, the dying
and all the war-wounded had to be moved right outside the city limits.
Everyone in the city was ordered out, away from imminent danger. A
great trek had already begun. A million and a half people were on the
streets.

A German agent had given himself up after the first few mines had
exploded, and he told the authorities that before leaving the city
German engineers had laid thousands of delayed-action mines, timed to
explode when the city's mains electricity was switched on at two
o'clock that day.

Norman Lewis, a Field Security Officer in Naples then, recalled how
it was:

> The agent had specifically mentioned that 5,000 mines had
> been laid under the enormous building housing the 92nd
> General Hospital, packed at this time with war casualties, all
> of whom had to be moved to a place of safety. Our own move
> took place shortly before midday when streets were
> beginning to clear of the desperate crowds. I saw men
> carrying their old parents on their backs, and at one moment
> a single small explosion set off a panic with women and
> children running screaming in all directions, leaving trails of
> urine.[2]

The great exodus was by no means anywhere near completion when new
orders came: 'Everyone could go home. The danger was passed.'

Nurses could now try to get used to the totally strange surroundings of
the palatial hospital building which they shared with an American
hospital unit. 'To be honest I felt a strange nostalgia for my little tent of
Salerno days,' said Sister Jennings.

> In our quarters we had real furniture and marvellous beds.
> The floors were marble with enormous pillars and seemingly
> thousands of stairs. From our windows we had a wonderful
> view of Naples harbour. Whilst the water and electricity was
> off the orderlies had the unenviable task of carrying up
> buckets of water, two at a time to distribute for use in all the
> wards.
>
> As the battle front moved slowly towards Rome the
> casualties streamed into our hospital. I was in charge of two
> wards; one with twenty men with serious chest wounds and
> the other with a similar number of patients with amputations.
> Night duty was for me the worst time. All of these patients
> needed constant observation and care. Thank heaven for the
> assistance of conscientious orderlies.
>
> The saddest, coldest and loneliest task was dealing with a

dying soldier, in those darkest hours. What could be done,
we did. In the near nightmare conditions, there were
faint-hearted and weary moments, when one would wonder,
'How much longer?' and 'Would the war ever come to an
end?' The only people for whom the war was over, were
these poor lads, maimed and scarred for life.

Our armies had been pressing towards Rome for a long
time, suffering terrible casualties on both the Eighth and
Fifth army fronts. Churchill was reported as saying it was no
time for sorrow! It wasn't what *we* felt, seeing all these lads
who had been blown to pieces. But thus life was to continue
for us, more wounded, more air raids, more sickness and
more destitution for the Italians. No time for sorrow?

Some of these badly wounded young lads had an awful
bumpy journey before they reached us and the proper
facilities for treatment. In the heat of the battle, field
dressings were applied on the spot and then they'd be
brought down the mountain on stretchers each side of a mule
pack saddle, by jeep ambulance over terrible mountain
tracks and then ambulance to us. It was a tragedy we could
not get to some of them earlier to save their limbs from
amputation.

Such was the state of the campaign in Italy then, often 7,000 ft up in
the rugged Apennines. Recovering the wounded from the battlefield
required the courage that often merited awards for conspicuous
gallantry, like that to the Revd Ronald Edwards, chaplain to the
Hampshire regiment. When told that forty men were lying wounded on
the other side of the River Gari near Cassino and no assault boats were
available to bring them back, he immediately stripped off his clothes,
tied a signal-cable around his waist and swam through the turbulent
water which was being raked by machine-gun and mortar fire. He then
hauled a doctor across with a supply of splints and dressings. After that,
he swam back to the other side of the river to look for a boat. He found
one entangled in ropes in mid-stream. Again he swam out with a line
tied around him, and undaunted by mortar bombs landing in water
alongside the boat, he fumbled with the ropes and at last freed the boat.
He hauled it to the opposite bank, from where it was used to evacuate
the wounded. 'On one of the trips across the river with two wounded
infantrymen we were fired on by a Spandau,' he recalled. 'I stood up
and waved the Red Cross flag. Here let me say a word for the Hun, he
observed faithfully the Red Cross flag.'[3]

The citation for the immediate award of the DSO said that his action
not only saved valuable time for the wounded but was also an
inspiration to everyone.

Time was such an important factor in a wounded man's chances of recovery that surgeons decided to move their field dressing stations much closer to the action so that emergency operations could be carried out as soon as possible. Nurses went forward with them to the lower slopes of Monte Cassino, and through their postoperative care, many men survived who would not have done.

'The pressure of work weighed heavily upon all of us then,' said Sister Jennings. 'To make matters worse there was a terrible outbreak of malaria – the locals seemed to accept it as a matter of course. The orderlies took their mepacrine until the whites of their eyes and skin began to turn yellow and we somehow managed to keep going.'

Outbreaks of typhus and typhoid scourged parts of the city of Naples and outlying area, but the worst epidemic amongst Allied troops was that of venereal disease. It was something peculiar to men of the Allied armies. In Italy before the Allied invasion, the incidence was low, for it was a criminal offence for an Italian to infect another person with syphilis. And the German army maintained a rigorous supervision over brothels in which prophylactic precautions were taken. British soldiers were left to fend for themselves and take pot luck. Brothels, in the minds of 'do-gooders' back home, were still quaintly defined by law as 'disorderly houses'. No matter how many posters and pamphlets were printed about the prevention of venereal disease, precious bed space and nurses' time in hospitals were being taken up by men with VD. By November 1943, as many beds in the Naples hospitals were occupied by VD patients as with the wounded in battle and other sicknesses combined.

Throughout the autumn of that year in Naples, German air raids persisted in their efforts to bring the city to a standstill. Margaret Jennings recalled:

> We just kept going. My ward was on the top floor, flares dropped around the building, bombs landed close to us, windows were shattered and tracers, like streaks of red flame, shot across the sky like a malevolent fireworks display, particularly when the red, green and yellow flares floated down.
>
> Raids apart, our great moment came at 11 p.m. one night when the water came back on. With great glee a crowd of us in our quarters rushed around turning on the taps. The sheer joy of running water was such a delight to us. The trouble was we couldn't turn the taps off again! Water flowed and turned into floods down the corridors. We ran for help and found some Americans in their part of the hospital. Gladly they came to our aid whilst we watched with our girlish giggles. The Matron heard the commotion and was not equally amused to see American uniforms disappearing through the door.

Towards Christmas 1943, nurses in Number 92 BGH were given a little more freedom with their off-duty hours, as Sister Jennings recalled:

> One afternoon, my previous tent-mates from Salerno and I went into Naples, shopping. Shops displayed the most elegant underwear in pure silk and delicate lace, we had ever seen. We went inside, drawing pictures of bras and pants to indicate what we wanted, and asking 'Quanto costa'. Our visit to Naples, though, was brief. One glance into the back streets revealed such pathetic poverty, horrible squalor, and filth as to be fearsome. Thin-faced women were offering themselves to soldiers for tins of bully beef or cigarettes. We hurried away, glad to be back in the safety of the hospital.
>
> We sometimes had invitations to dinner at neighbouring officers' messes but Matron would not allow us out after seven p.m. There was still sniping going on around and booby-traps about.
>
> The air raids continued and one night we were wakened by the sound of planes diving overhead and the crack of anti-aircraft guns. Suddenly there was a terrific crash and splintering glass flew across the room. Jennie and I shot out of our beds, pulled on dressing gowns and ran for the shelter outside. Several hours later when we emerged, we found the hospital had been hit, though only one ward was severely damaged, two patients had been killed.
>
> We were so saddened to learn that one of our nurses had been killed too and another seriously injured. They hadn't got out quickly enough. The Americans had offered us the use of their operating theatre as it was nearer to the scene.

The work of British front-line nurses did not go unnoticed in the USA. A piece written in October 1943 by Newbold Noyes, jun., son of the *Washington Star* owner, read:

SHE BLUSHED FASTER THAN ANYONE I KNEW
SALUTE THE SISTER

> We stood with hats off and thought about Sister Mac. We had not seen her for a couple of months but the days she took care of us in Ward 4D East in the British General Hospital in Naples seemed very close this afternoon.
>
> A pale slender girl with dark hair and eyes, she was very conscious of the two pips upon her shoulder. The British call their nurses 'sister' but it is not a term of familiarity.
>
> Miss Mac liked discipline and order. That was why she had

such a hard time with Ward 4 where American field service volunteer ambulance drivers stayed when they were sick.

We were unruly, untidy and sometimes a little impolite, which she could not understand at all. Some of us were there long enough to get to know her pretty well.

On Christmas Eve, I remember, somebody got hold of a bottle of brandy. We made milk punch in a hospital bucket and lured her in for a party.

One of the boys had received a Christmas stocking from home and on Christmas Day we turned it into a present for Sister Mac. We put in some cigarettes, candy and a cake of toilet soap and a little jar of cleansing cream which somebody had been carrying around. Wally put in one of his cigars and we filled up the rest with oranges and nuts.

That day when she opened her drawer there it was, bulging and red with a card saying 'Merry Christmas Miss Mac'. She picked it up and turned slowly to face us, the blood rushing to the roots of her hair. She opened her mouth just once but nothing came out and then she ran from the room. But when she came back her hand was specially gentle as she took our pulses and tucked us in the sheets.

That was about three months ago.

SALUTE

The day before yesterday the Germans raided Naples and bombs fell on the hospital. So this afternoon, those of us who could get there, stood with our hats off and thought about Miss Mac. The coffin was incredibly small as it was lowered into the ground.And the tears rolled down our cheeks.[4]

Despite all the raids, the nurses of Number 92 were determined to celebrate Christmas 1943 in the appropriate style. Decorations were improvised. Italian toilet-rolls were painted with stripes of red and blue ink and hung across the wards as streamers, Christmas trees were dug from the hospital grounds to put in wards, and for Christmas Day itself those sometimes strict nurses dared to doff their Sister's caps in favour of frilly waitress-type ones made from crêpe paper and tinsel to serve the traditional British dinner of turkey and Christmas pudding. 'It all added to the atmosphere and was truly remarkable,' said Sister Jennings fifty years later. 'We Sisters too had our own festive dance. I met Ralph, a handsome young lieutenant from the RASC and so started a serious involvement.'

A hundred and fifty miles due east of Naples, on 2 December 1943, whilst nurses of the newly arrived Numbers 54 and 98 British General Hospitals were settling into their quarters at Bari, the citizens of that comparatively peaceful port were already in a festive mood. Many were setting out for a special concert at the Chiesa San Domenico opera house, whilst others strolled towards the restaurants and bars around Piazza Libertà. American and British soldiers swarmed through the narrow streets ready for a Thursday-night 'beano'. In that pre-Christmas build-up, night life in Bari was throbbing as never before. One side of the main boulevard was fringed with suitcases and portable stands, with Italians offering scarves and jewellery, and with arms bared to display rows of watches. Along the highway, jeeps, three-tonners, six-by-sixes and a variety of special rigs smoothly pulsed along.

Tied up on the east jetty amongst a mass of cargo ships waiting to unload was the Liberty ship *John Harvey*. Aboard, Captain Elwin Knowles, its master, was terribly worried; his army weapons specialist Lieutenant Thomas Richardson was a bundle of nerves. They were the only two men who knew what lay below decks: *2,000 100-lb mustard-gas bombs*.

For five days Richardson had rushed from one port office to another, trying to get the deadly cargo unloaded and away from the crowded port and city. It was a sitting target for Nazi bombers. Port officials laughed at his fears: 'You'll be as safe here as in the States. The whole area is ringed with anti-aircraft guns.'

Most sailors were already ashore, mingling with the army-base wallahs, many of whom had already earned millions of lire from one racket or another, flogging petrol, food and even penicillin. In the bars and trattorias money flowed freely.

Suddenly, in those busy streets, people stopped in their tracks. Heads swung upwards as a barrage from anti-aircraft guns shattered the night air. Then came the roar of engines. Junkers 88 bombers dived in low over the harbour and town. Disaster was only seconds away.

Ships in the congested harbour and buildings in the crowded streets of the via Abate and via Sparano seemed to explode almost simultaneously of their own accord, and front walls collapsed onto men, women and children fleeing to the air-raid shelters. 'It was more terrifying than any raid I'd experienced in Sicily or anywhere else,' said Diana Sugden O'Brien, then an Army Sister at Number 98 GH.

Great flashes of light leapt right through the doorways of shelters, catching everyone in a photographic instance cringing against each other. Smoke and flames belched through cellar hatchways, as bombs crashed down over the harbour and surrounding residential areas. Then there was a gigantic eruption, louder than anything ever heard before. An ammunition ship exploded.

In the shelters, crowded with Italian civilians and Allied soldiers, people were beginning to notice a smell predominating above all the other smells of singed hair, charred wood and debris. A familiar but strange smell. A strong smell of garlic. Reeking far more than the residual smell of cooking. Babies were crying, and old men and women too were wailing in paroxysms of coughing.

At last, after an eternity of cowering in the shelters, there came the last powerful 'crump' of high-explosive bombs, followed by the sharp clear bark of anti-aircraft guns hurling final defiance at the raiders. Faintly in the distance the deep growl of aero-engines faded into nothingness. Gradually the stunned citizens of Bari emerged from their shelters, thankful it was all over.

But all was not over. Another horror was in store for them.

Men, women and children were being brought into hospitals in Bari with symptoms which left both doctors and nurses puzzled.

Number 3 New Zealand hospital, which had only just arrived from North Africa, soon had to turn patients away because its wards had been filled with wounded from the Eighth Army's attack on the Sangro River. They were brought straight from the front to the Piazza Roma railway station. Thus, the air-raid casualties had to lie on stretchers in the corridors.

The hospital ship *Leinster* with its nine QAIMNS nursing sisters, moored just outside the harbour when the heavy raid began, packed its wards with wounded and returned for more.[5] Nurses of Numbers 54 and 98 British Hospitals in Bari were swamped with casualties from the raid. Number 98 coped only by 'borrowing' some New Zealand Sisters and nurses. Here, too, the medical staff receiving the rush of patients was only able to give emergency treatment at first, but nothing else.[6]

'Those casualties were unlike anything we'd seen before. They looked awful,' recalled Diana Sugden O'Brien, who had tended all sorts of casualties in her service in Africa and Sicily.

They came in such numbers that normal admission procedure was suspended. Patients were put to bed sometimes in the clothes they were wearing. For those patients fished out of the harbour, swimming amongst burning oil, there was not even time for nurses to remove their oil-soaked clothes in order to wash away the scum clinging to their bodies.

It was the same story at the American Number 26 General Hospital, which had recently taken over the Italian Ospedale Militare. Never before had any of them seen, from battlefields or air raids, such a complex range of symptoms as these patients now showed. Many complained of a gritty feeling and a burning pain in their eyes and streaming tears. They were all pale, weak, exhausted, cold and clammy, with perspiration pouring from them. Their pulses were rapid, breathing was shallow and blood pressure abnormally low. Most of them had extensive burns. Men's genitals were affected too, the penis often swollen to three times its normal size and the scrotum greatly enlarged. Most of them were treated for shock and burns. The very badly burned were given plasma, and all were wrapped in blankets as they lay on stretchers which were then raised at the feet to halt the possible loss of blood to the brain.

Despite all these measures, too many patients were dying – suddenly and unexpectedly. Doctors would be talking to a patient who would sit up in bed and respond to their questions and the next minute lie down and die. Doctors in all hospitals could not understand what was causing such sudden deaths.

Added to all the unusual symptoms was another puzzling one: the strange smell of garlic pervading the wards and corridors where men still lay in their oil- and water-soaked clothes.

Ophthalmic specialists took up the cases of the patients with tearful eyes that became so painful that they went blind. Bathing the eyes gave little relief, and eye problems continued to increase in severity. All hospitals were now full to overflowing, and still more military and civilian cases were brought in. A local gymnasium used as a clearing station was soon filled with patients lying side by side shivering on blankets. Nurses asked each other, 'What is happening?'. 'We couldn't understand why they were dying,' recalled Diana Sugden O'Brien. 'It was pitiful to see them suffering,' recalled Anne Watt Pfister, who was so horrified she took up their case forty years later (see below). Doctors asked each other, 'What are we going to do about all these patients dying on our hands?'

They called at the Royal Navy headquarters to ask if the shipping manifests showed any cargoes of toxic chemicals. Naval officers were evasive, saying that shipping manifests were top secret. Doctors persisted. 'Men and women are dying here because we don't know what we are treating. We must know!' Poker-faced navy officers said they would inquire from Admiralty in the UK. 'And for heaven's sake, how long will that take?' shouted frustrated doctors. The answer was even more infuriating: 'Oh, quite a few days.'

The two men who could have told them quite specifically what was happening, Captain Knowles and Lieutenant Richardson, had gone down with their ship, the *John Harvey*, and its lethal load.

But now some cover-up was going on.

Hundreds were being admitted to hospitals each day. The commanding officer of Number 98 British General Hospital, Lieutenant-Colonel W. J. Laird, soon had no doubts about what was causing the deaths of those servicemen. But he had been ordered to keep quiet about it. So had the nurses. Nevertheless, in his daily war diary he wrote: '331 casualties admitted today suffering from Mustard Gas burns which are being diagnosed as "Dermatitis NYD" pending further orders from HQ Number 2 District.'[7]

As if to convince doctors further, the German radio newsreader in Italy, Axis Sally, sarcastically announced one night: 'I see you boys are getting gassed by your own poison gas.'

Doctors in Bari then took matters into their own hands and sent a signal direct to General Eisenhower at Allied Force Headquarters in Algiers. But Eisenhower was already aware of the disaster at Bari. His response was to send for Colonel Stewart Alexander, an expert consultant on chemical warfare medicine.

Alexander was a stocky, bespectacled, 29-year-old who believed in giving straight answers and kowtowed to no one, irrespective of rank, when it came to his speciality. He was just the man to bludgeon his way through red tape.

Before he flew to Bari from Algiers, his brief from Eisenhower was oddly, and perhaps even purposely, vague. 'There seems to be some concern over the number of unexplained deaths at Bari as a result of an air strike. There is a possibility that a toxic agent is involved.'

Colonel Alexander lost no time. As soon as his plane landed at Bari, he drove directly to Number 98 British General Hospital. His reactions were instantaneous. As he stepped inside the building his senses rang alarm bells. He turned to the British commanding officer, Colonel Laird, and asked, 'What is that odour?' Laird replied: 'It's from the oil most survivors picked out of the harbour had on their bodies when they were brought here. We haven't had time to disinfect the wards yet.'

The pugnacious Colonel Alexander was not satisfied with that. The smell had triggered memories of his days in the laboratories of the Edgeware Arsenal in Maryland where he had worked with mustard gas. The air of the hospital in Bari was so reminiscent of that which permeated his laboratory! He said nothing, but walked on examining and questioning patients in the wards. He looked at arms and bodies where skin was flaking and peeling off in layers. He questioned doctors: 'When did blisters appear? How long did it take for the skin to peel? Were skin irritations always this reddish-brown colour?' Alexander nodded at each reply from Colonel Laird, who had studied the case histories of all patients many times but had the ward Sister always with him to confirm his response. Alexander looked at the patients' diagnosis – 'Dermatitis NYD' (Not Yet Diagnosed).

A post-mortem was hurriedly carried out on some of the dead. Alexander then took Colonel Laird to one side, and they agreed the men were in fact suffering from the effects of mustard gas. Alexander then asked: 'Have you checked with the port authorities whether the ships in the harbour might have been carrying mustard gas?' Colonel Laird replied: 'I have and they tell me that no such information is available.'

A conspiracy of silence had already begun. Prime Minister Winston Churchill had ordered all references to mustard gas purged from the records. But at least nurses and doctors in Bari now knew what they were treating and what had been making their own eyes run and chests heave with coughing by breathing the gas coming off the patients' sodden clothing.

Sister Anne Watt (later Pfister) was appalled by it all. And especially by the way they had been ordered not to say anything about the mustard gas patients to anyone. However, the memory of the way those patients suffered stayed with her for the next forty years, and then a strange event happened which brought a measure of consolation to some of those patients.

Quite by chance one evening she was watching television and saw an interview with a former Royal Navy seaman, Bertram Stevens, who said that he never had a proper war disablement pension for injuries to his eyes and his lungs incurred in the Bari raid of 1943. This kind of injustice roused her ire. Straight away, on that evening of 21 January 1986, she wrote to Prime Minister Margaret Thatcher and said that she had nursed so many men like Bertram Stevens and it surely was time that his suffering over the years be properly recognized by the award of an appropriate pension.

At last, the cat was well and truly amongst the pigeons. The Prime Minister passed the letter to the Policy and Finance department of the Ministry of Defence and also to the Department of Health and Social Security. In the House of Commons, the Secretary of State for Social Services, Norman Fowler, was then 'bombarded' by questions from Members of Parliament, Michael Mates and Dr Oonagh McDonald. The crux of Bertram Stevens' case was that he would have claimed sooner *had he been aware of the precise nature of the substance with which he had been contaminated*. (Author's italics)[8]

Clearly, the national press was going to make the most of the government's discomfort. Here was something which had been swept under the carpet for far too long. And Sister Anne Watt Pfister and others who had nursed those men in Number 98 GH in Bari were not going to be kept silent any longer.

There was no alternative for the government but to accept the situation as graciously as possible. On 13 March 1986 the Department of Health and Social Security wrote to Anne Watt Pfister saying:

> Ministers have looked again at Mr Stevens' case. They sought the advice of the Department's senior doctors and reconsidered all the points very carefully. You will be pleased to know that in the special circumstances of Mr Stevens' case it has been decided that this war pension should be backdated so as to take effect from the date when his symptoms first manifested themselves after his discharge from the Royal Navy. *You may also be interested to know that we are taking steps to investigate the other 600 or so casualties who were contaminated by mustard gas at Bari in 1943 to see whether similar action is appropriate.* [author's italics][9]

True to their word, the appropriate government departments made strenuous efforts to trace survivors of that disastrous raid. A special investigation was mounted in 1986–7. Its report showed that of the 693 casualties known to have arisen from the Bari harbour mustard gas disaster in 1943, 161 were killed or declared missing, and a further 185 claims were examined of which 106 were successful. As a result of Anne

Watt Pfister's effort 106 veterans had their pensions increased, sometimes backdated, or they received a lump sum in recognition of their disablement.[10]

In 1943 the immediate and worrying problem for Prime Minister Winston Churchill was not mustard gas but how to get the Allied armies in Italy advancing again. He felt it had been nothing better than 'snail's progress' after Naples had been taken. As far as he could judge, from the luxury of the Flower Villa at Marrakesh where he was convalescing from a recent illness, a plan would have to be hatched to restore the offensive spirit to both the Fifth and Eighth armies. They had spent Christmas 1943 shivering in their slit trenches high in the Apennines, where they were held up by the formidable German defences of the Gustav Line. In Morocco, looking at the map of Italy, the solution might have seemed simple to Churchill. An amphibious operation could outflank the Germans. He came to a decision. Landings would be made on the beaches of Anzio, twenty miles south of Rome, and the city would be captured shortly afterwards.

It was a decision which would take nurses right into the front line for many desperate months of fighting.

8 The Bloody Road to Rome

I feel like a lamb being led to the slaughter.
US Major-General John Lucas
before Anzio

To attempt a landing at Anzio with only
two divisions was to send a boy on a man's
errand.
US Official History's comment
on the Anzio operation

In the cold, dark, pre-dawn of 21 January 1944, nursing sisters of the hospital carrier *Leinster* went aboard and within a few hours set sail for the small Italian port of Anzio.

In that same convoy were 242 other ships of various shapes and sizes, including five Royal Navy cruisers and twenty-four destroyers. It was an impressive sight later that day as they steamed out from the Bay of Naples in line-ahead formation with silver barrage balloons glistening in the winter sunshine as far as the eye could see. Their objective, Anzio, so popular with the Romans as a holiday resort, was a mere thirty-five miles south of the Italian capital and nearly one hundred miles north-west of Naples. The plan was to bypass the formidable German defences of the Gustav Line around Monte Cassino, sixty miles to the south-east, which had held up the Allies for months, and from a beachhead at Anzio push inland to cut off and capture the entire German Tenth Army and open the way to Rome.

The plan, like so many in the Italian campaign, was doomed to failure from the start by uncertain leadership and disagreements at the highest level, which resulted in Allied soldiers and their nurses being forced to fight for their lives for four dreadful months on the beaches of Anzio.

At first, though, the news could not have been better. The commandos got ashore and moved inland without firing a shot. The news filtered back to the nurses on the hospital carriers. Hopes were raised, as slowly it began to dawn upon everyone that this was not going to be another Salerno after all. Or was it?

Anne Watt (later Pfister), who was ordered to keep quiet about the mustard gas casualties she nursed in Bari, Italy. Forty years later, after writing to Margaret Thatcher, she eventually succeeded in securing pensions for 600 of those casualties

Eileen Hawkin (now Haynes) used the Winnett Orr treatment on casualties with great success. Flies were allowed to settle on open wounds and when the plaster and maggots were removed some time later the affected area was absolutely clean

Violet Bath (now Leather) delivered a baby – aboard the damaged battleship *York* resting in Canea Bay, Crete – in the midst of a German invasion. The paratroops were landing as the baby arrived

Betty Wragg had never seen a dead person before she took up her new nursing job at FAR Mepal, Cambridgeshire. She decided to take a look at the body of a young airman who had been killed the previous night. Her heart went out to his mother who would soon hear the devastating news

Joy Wilson (now Hobley), after being inspired by Edwina Mountbatten's appeal for nurses in the Far East, found the bamboo-built hospital at Comilla, India, a real culture shock with its canvas beds and, at night, hurricane lanterns which simply intensified the already unbearable heat

After being ordered by her ward sister to 'deal with' an incendiary bomb on the hospital roof, the terrified probationary nurse, Dorothy Blackburn (now Waines), climbed a ladder and threw some sand on the crackling device

Iris Jones (later Ogilvie and now Bower) who received the award of Associate of the Royal Red Cross in recognition of her efforts in helping patients after high-explosive bombs hit her hospital at St Athan, near Cardigan. And at the RAF Club, 1996

Beatrice Hownam was aboard the ss Strathallen with staff of a general hospital when it was torpedoed off the North African coast in 1942. She survived the fire but five of her colleagues lost their lives

Marie Sedman (later Sedman Floyd-Norris) on her wedding day. Photograph was taken with a home-made cardboard camera with X-ray film! And Marie, today, holding photograph showing the later blessing of her marriage

Rosemary Gannon (now Hearn), sworn to secrecy about her work at Number 1 Casualty Clearing Station, RAF Wroughton, was on duty to receive the first of the D-Day casualties evacuated from the Normandy invasion beaches by air

rgaret Jennings (now Boyce) frequently faced the nizing task of telling young soldiers that their limbs ld have to be amputated. She had to convince the n severely depressed men that their lives were still worth living. And Margaret Boyce today

Susan Travers who, in May 1996, at the age of eighty-six was awarded the coveted Legion d'honneur for her bravery in the battle of Bir Hakeim of 10 June 1942

Winifred Barnfather (now Reid) as shown on her British Forces Identification Card. She was often in the midst of fighting vessels engaged in battles off Sicily and Italy when she worked aboard the hospital ships, *Somersetshire* and *Aba*

Joanna Stavridi, a former debutante and society girl, was disillusioned with the high life and frustrated by the confines of her sex. She travelled to Greece where she underwent her training, and then worked in areas of the fiercest fighting during the war. In 1941 she was awarded the highest honour for valour of the Hellenic Red Cross

Winifred Beaumont. Whilst she was in Imphal, India, a colonel recommended that every nurse be given a revolver loaded with at least one bullet so that she could shoot herself rather than fall into Japanese hands

left **Marjorie Doyle** (now Bennett) on her wedding day. She often accompanied a French count to officers' mess parties, and was once mistaken for a spy by the French police and spent the night in a police cell! And Marjorie Bennett today

above **Myra Jones** (née Roberts) at a reunion at the Imperial War Museum in 1995. *Left* Lydia Alford, Myra Roberts and Edna Morris (later Birkbeck) setting off on their first air evacuation flight to the Normandy beaches

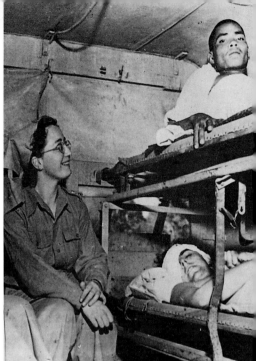

Mary Pinkney (née Webb) and her husband, Maurice, today after fifty happy years of marriage. They met at the Royal Hampshire Hospital where Mary nursed Maurice through his second bout of malaria. *Right* **Sheila McDermott** (now Bambridge) on the Arakan front in Burma tending to wounded soldiers waiting to be taken by air to a hospital in the rear

A hospital train bringing back wounded from the front

A hospital train in Britain moving patients from bombed cities

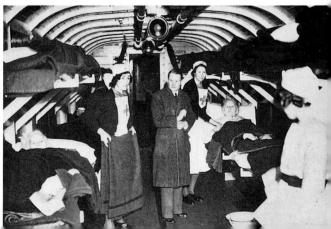

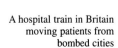

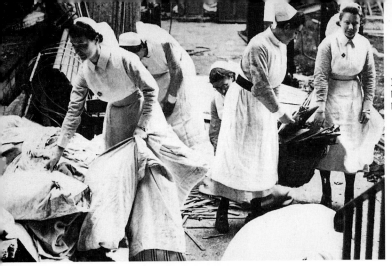

Nurses salvaging
bedding after Luftwaffe
bombs hit their hospital

The hospital ship, *Aba*,
on which Violet Bath
and Winifred Barnfather
served and which was
bomb-damaged in the
evacuation of wounded
from Crete

Eighth Army Desert Ambulance convoy under fire. Wounded driver being helped by comrades

Molly Budge (now Jennings) washing up
outside Tahag desert camp *(centre)* with
Vicki Shennon *(right)* and Jane Hitchcock
(with washbowl on ground)

Three army nursing sisters – the first women nurses
of the front-line casualty service to reach Benghazi,
Western Desert, 1942

Four of the heroic 'Hadfield Spears'
nurses who served in Tobruk during
the seven-month siege

Christmas Day in the desert. Note the
sandbags and protective earthworks round
the tented ward

Operating vehicle of Number 14 Casualty
Clearing Station, Western Desert, 1943

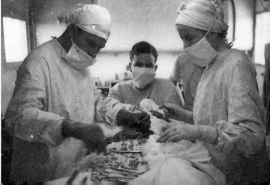

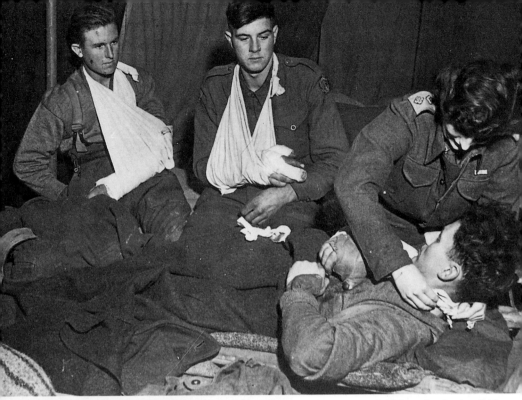

Applying a dressing in a field
hospital in Italy. Nurse wearing the
Africa Star ribbon

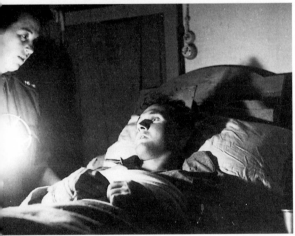

Lady with a lamp. Front-line nurse
with Eighth Army in Italy

Bringing in a casualty to a front-line
hospital

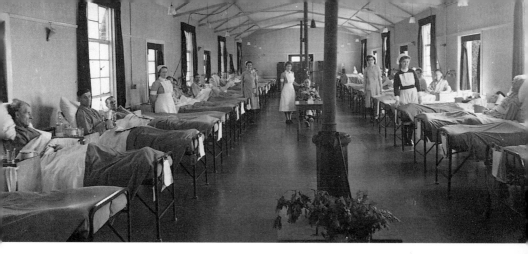

above Royal Hampshire County hospital ward where Mary Webb (now Pinkney) worked
receiving the D-Day wounded *below* Corporal Myra Roberts with wounded in air evacuation
Dakota returning from beachhead landing strip, Normandy

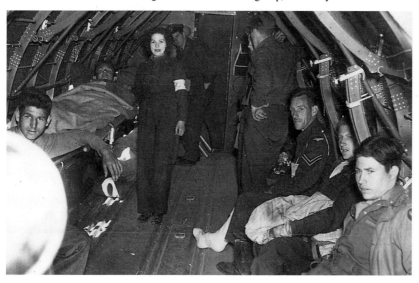

below RAF mobile field hospital with PMRAFNS staff tending wounded prior to evacuation

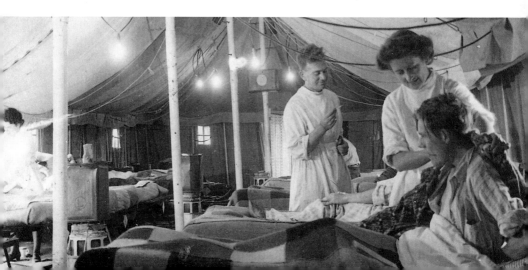

Brewing up on the beachhead.
Nurses of QAIMNS using a
'Tommy cooker' and mess tins

Army Sisters Morrison and Rogers pitching
tents for the 79th BGH, Normandy

Monica Carhart-Harris *(far left)* and siste
of 121 BGH, France 1944.   Note tl
nursing   outfit: wellington   boo
and battledress!

RAF nursing sisters, Iris Ogilvie (now
Bower) and Billie Bilson about to cross the
Rhine by pontoon bridge, March 1945

Pat Bradley (now Stephens) with colleague in Belsen concentration camp watching the disease-ridden huts being burnt

Pat Bradley (now Stephens), second from left, and colleagues of 74th BGH

Lord Haw Haw, William Joyce, the traitor who broadcast from Hamburg to England nightly, was brought in to 74th BGH with a bullet in his buttock in 1945. Pat Stephens (née Bradley) dressed the wound. Joyce was taken to Britain, tried for treason and hanged

Pat Stephens (née Bradley) with the lock of SS Chief Heinrich Himmler's hair, cut from him whilst on the post-mortem slab in 74th BGH by Dr John Glyn. She is holding a letter of affirmation by Dr Glyn

Nursing sisters released from Sumatra POW camp 27 September 1945. In February 1942 sixty-five nursing sisters left Singapore on *ss Viner Brooke* which was bombed and sunk by Japanese on the Banka Straits. Twelve nurses drowned. The survivors got to Banka Island where twenty-one of them were deliberately shot by the Japanese. Now only thirty-two sisters survived out of the original sixty-five. In the POW camp a further eight died of malnutrition and maltreatment

Miss Franklin who survived the horrors of Hong Kong, talking with Admiral C. Harcourt at Stanley POW camp when Hong Kong was reoccupied 30 August 1945

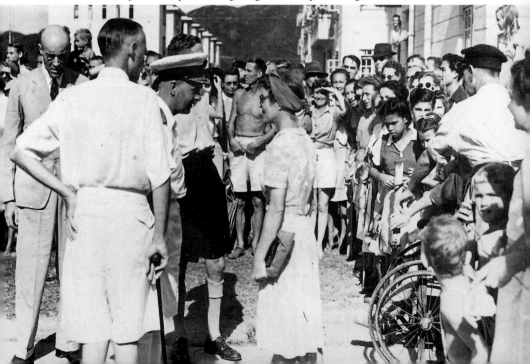

Wish *you* were here!
On the beach at Anzio.
British and American
nurses take a break

Typical care and treatment in a
forward area tent

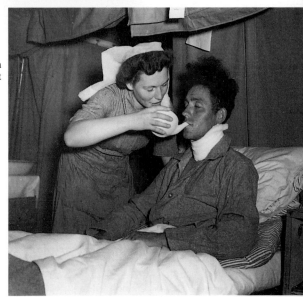

Coming down the mountain.
Wounded brought down from the
7,000 foot positions in the
Appenines by mule on tracks
impassable to jeeps

Two South Wales nursing sisters, Mollie Giles *(second from left)* and Iris Ogilvie, now Bower *(far right)*, enjoy their day out shopping in Bayeaux – away from the front line

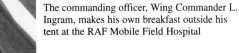

The commanding officer, Wing Commander L. Ingram, makes his own breakfast outside his tent at the RAF Mobile Field Hospital

The long and short of it! RAF nursing sister, Iris Ogilvie (now Bower) with the RAF's tallest pilot at the officer's hospital in Torquay after it was bombed

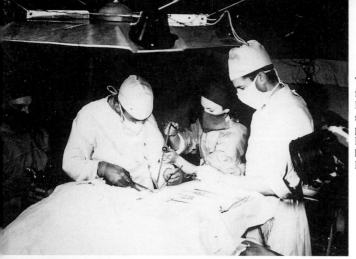

Tented operating theatre close to the front line with RAF nursing sister Iris Ogilvie (now Bower) assisting surgeons. Less than hours after his plane was hit over Caen, Sergeant Patrick McDevitt was operated on here in the RAF Mobile Field Hospital

A change from tents!
RAF nursing sister Mollie Giles in St Joseph's Hospital, Eindhoven during the battle for Arnhem, September 1944

Primitive but effective sterilization and treatment under canvas

On the beach itself, commanding officers were amazed. 'It was strangely peaceful,' said Colonel Webb-Carter, the CO of the Duke of Wellington's Regiment. He drove inland from the beach in his jeep along roads on which troops marched and was impressed with what he saw. The environs of Anzio looked attractive. Handsome villas and bright little farms mingled with plentiful trees to vary the landscape.[1]

It was a happy peaceful scene indeed to meet the eyes of those nurses of numbers 2, 14 and 15 Casualty Clearing Stations stumbling ashore with heavy kit that morning under the direction of the Beachmaster Major Denis Healey's sonorous voice, which one day would rumble round the British House of Commons as that of Chancellor of the Exchequer.

Equipment and vehicles poured ashore whilst the US commander, Major-General John Lucas, fearing a strong German counter-attack, kept in mind advice given to him by General Mark Clark before he sailed: 'Don't stick your neck out as I did at Salerno.' Advice which caused Lucas to be too cautious and to be sacked.

So it was that as the nurses from three British casualty clearing stations were setting up their tents on the beachhead, the forward assault troops were digging in, consolidating the ground they had gained – seven miles in depth and sixteen miles wide – in readiness for a counter-attack. The British Guards Brigade, which had anticipated a bold dash inland, was kept in reserve doing nothing, playing cards and brewing endless mugs of char, as the veterans of Indian service called their tea. Meanwhile, German troops, tanks and guns rushed down from northern Italy and ringed the beachhead.

Nurses and staff of the casualty clearing stations made good use of those three days of grace by digging their tents two feet deep into the beach and throwing up the sand and gravel into a protective wall round the canvas outside. Space was so cramped there was little room for all three units, plus the Number 93 US Evacuating Hospital there as well, but somehow they managed to get organized.

On the evening of the fourth day, German dive-bombers hurtled out of the clear January sky, their demoralizing sirens howling as they circled the invasion fleet off shore looking for easy targets away from the main body. Their first victim was the destroyer HMS *Janus*, which sank in twenty minutes. The second one to be picked off was an easy one, but clearly not a legitimate military one – the hospital carrier *St David*, then sailing near to the hospital carriers *Leinster* and *St Andrew* fully illuminated as ordered. A direct hit holed the *St David* seriously, and it began to sink. Nurses and doctors worked desperately to get patients up on to the tilting deck and lower them into rafts and lifeboats or directly into the freezing water with life-jackets strapped to their bandaged bodies. But all the while the stricken ship's bow was rising slowly out of the water. She was going down, stern first. From the bridge the captain shouted down to the lifeboats: '*Wait for the Sisters!*' But so quickly did

the ship sink that two nurses, several doctors and men of the Royal
Army Medical Corps, as well as the ship's captain, went down with her.

The hospital carrier *Leinster* was next to be attacked. Having seen
distress-signals from the *St David*, it was on its way to help rescue
survivors when bombs hit the forward davits and started a fire which the
crew eventually got under control. In the midst of all the bombing, the
Leinster launched all available water ambulances, and Sisters Edge,
Butler, Fraser, Johnson, Mansley, Owen, Tocker and Neilson RRCS,
who had joined the ship in June 1943 and had already had their baptism
of fire at Salerno and Bari, were again heaving sodden casualties aboard
whilst all around them bombs were exploding and shrapnel from
ack-ack guns was whizzing through the air. Everything seemed to
happen so quickly, but yet they picked up over a hundred casualties
from the stricken *St David*.[2]

The incident created a problem for the ship's captain. Should he or
should he not sail with all recognition lights of the Red Cross
illuminated? The experience so far suggested they might just be serving
as a target for Luftwaffe bomber crews who could not or would not
discriminate between targets. His problem became more acute when
members of the crew formally protested against the practice of sailing
with lights. In fairness to them, it must be said that they had been
through rough times. There was still more for them to endure, with
regular trips to the beaches in February and March 1944. On 7 February
they had a particularly hazardous time embarking wounded in water
ambulances from the beaches whilst the Luftwaffe made three heavy
raids aimed at ships in the harbour. Another terrible day for them all
was that of 2 March, when the water ambulances at the water's edge
came under intense shell-fire.

Living conditions for the nurses and all crew aboard the hospital
carriers could be grim, though they were better on some ships than
others. Food on some was terrible, yet on others quite good. When the
captain of the *Leinster* investigated complaints and inspected the
food-stores, he was confronted by a revolting sight, as he subsequently
recorded in the unit war diary: 'The food shelves were black with steam
flies, they were everywhere and into everything. Rats had multiplied
and were into everything that was not in metal containers.'[3]

But on the Anzio beachhead as the days went by, conditions were
very much worse. Everyone was in the front line. There was no escaping
sudden death, even when a soldier thought he had got a coveted
'Blighty' wound which would take him back to Naples and then to the
UK. Indeed, the Americans called their evacuation hospital, pitched
next to the British casualty clearing stations, 'Hell's Half-Acre' because
it was subject to shell-fire and bombing throughout the whole Anzio
campaign.

One might ask: 'Why were the women nurses not evacuated?' They
were far too valuable there on the beaches. Just as in June 1942, when

Rommel massed 3,000 tanks on the Egyptian border and women of the WRNS had already been evacuated, the Director of Medical Services made his policy clear – the women nurses were far too valuable there for the morale of the wounded. On the beaches of Anzio they more than demonstrated their worth in that respect.

Nurses slept – as much as they could – in slit trenches with bedsprings placed across the top on which were piled protective sandbags. Trench sides were covered in blankets to prevent the sandy walls sliding on top of them. Once they were down there for the night, no one got out. They all had their own makeshift urinal cans which they emptied next morning in field latrines built right in the middle of the camps. They were roofless and constructed with men in mind and surrounded by shoulder-high strips of hessian sacking. With so many more important hazards to face, they soon got used to 'sitting it out' as brazenly as did the men in theirs.

Until the breakout in May 1944 conditions at Anzio for the nurses resembled the trenches in the First World War. Yet, as then, everyone – nurses and soldiers – tried to create some kind of normalcy in that crazy existence. For soldiers, beetle-racing spread like wildfire, and bookmakers handled the betting. Beetles had their backs painted in a variety of colours, and they were paraded around the ring under jamjars. Just before the 'off', all bettles were placed under one big jamjar in the centre of the 'course' – a circle about six feet in diameter. At the 'off' the jar was raised, and the first beetle out of the ring was the winner.

The imaginative staff of Number 5 Division organized a pigeon-race. Amongst the pre-race publicity in the local army newspaper were the following instructions: 'Pigeons will carry two days reserve rations. AA Gunners will take notice that all Pigeons will be regarded as friendly. Spectators are warmly welcomed at the Starting Point but all are advised to wear hats.' Then followed the competition instructions.

Units had barbecues with Scottish pipers in attendance, to which nurses were naturally invited. Crude brandy was distilled using copper tubing from shot-down German planes. A slug of this dubious spirit gave many of those besieged on the beaches a better night's sleep and the courage to face the anguish waiting them the next day. And there was a never-ending supply of that.

Two monster long-range guns, 'Anzio Annie' and 'Anzio Express', with a range of over thirty miles, plagued nurses and soldiers on the beachhead. And in addition to these was a battery of 210-mm guns kept in a tunnel west of Albano, near the Pope's summer palace at Castel Gandolfo. All of these guns outranged the best guns the Allies had – the 155-mm 'Long Tom'. Constant shelling made life a misery.

Add to all that the cold wet winter of January–March 1944. The trouble was that the invasion forces were making no headway at all against the German ring of armour, anti-tank guns supported by fresh and determined infantry divisions secure on the high ground. Battered Allied infantry units pulled back to the beaches. And they knew what to expect there.

For months the Germans sent in attack after attack, preceded by barrages from their long-range artillery. German infantry attacked, not counting the cost and determined to throw the Allies back into the sea. In the first six weeks German casualties numbered at least 16,000 dead, wounded and missing, whilst the Allies admitted to 21,000 casualties.

Splashing their way through the mud and howling wind, orderlies brought their terrible loads to the CCSs where they were sorted in the triage system determining who should be treated first. A British medical officer, Major J. A. Ross of the King's Shropshire Light Infantry, described what it was like at their casualty clearing station pre-operative ward. It was in a big tent in which nurses, ignoring the shells crashing around them, stumbled amongst the stretchers from one shivering and shuddering patient to the next. The soldiers lay just as they had been left by panting stretcher-bearers, deathly pale, wearing bloodied and mud-soiled clothes and with wounds roughly covered with shell-dressings. Some – the head cases – lay open-mouthed, their breath coming in loud frightening snores. Major Ross was appalled. 'Some ... were carried in dying, with gross combinations of shattered limbs, protrusions of intestines and brains, with great holes in their poor frames. All were exhausted after being under continuous fire and after lying in the mud for hours or days.'[4]

Life for the nurses on those beaches could not have been worse. Week after week, bitterly cold rain poured down on their tents near the via Anziate, the floors became a sea of mud and icy winds whipped open tent-flaps where terribly wounded men lay dying. And all the while the shelling and bombing went on. Doctors, nurses and orderlies all worked frantically, trying to clear beds and keep up with the never-ending flow of wounded. Accounts show that it was quite usual for surgeons to be operating all night, taking a few hours' sleep before bending over the operating table for another eight-hour shift. It is hard to comprehend how they all managed. One surgeon, for example, carried out fourteen operations during the night and then another twelve the following day.[5]

So vulnerable were those casualty clearing stations to shell-fire that some wounded refused to be taken back to them. They felt safer in the gullies, where they lay with field dressings on their wounds. Derek Ball, then with the 2nd Northamptons of 5th Division vividly recalled the way those nurses stuck it out under fire.

> I wasn't wounded but went down with jaundice and was told that a lot of soldiers had it due to the tinned bacon which was so fatty. It came out of the tin wrapped in a kind of greasy paper and you could hardly see the lean for thick fat covering everything.

I was able to get about more and could see just what those nurses were doing when the shelling was on. They certainly weren't sitting cowering in the slit trenches, they were going from one tent to another making sure patients on stretchers were far enough down in the ground. They'd stopped using trestle beds because it was safer to have the patients lower on the ground to gain some cover from the walls of gravel and sand dug out to lower the floor of the tents themselves for greater protection. I had the greatest admiration for those nurses.

Shell-fire was not the only hazard nurses faced. Luftwaffe dive-bombers seemed to know when new drafts of infantry were arriving and came in to bomb them in the reinforcement camp which was alongside the casualty clearing stations. Dive-bombers attacked in force on 14 March, shortly after Derek Ball arrived with 5th Division. The whole area was plastered with bombs. Sand and rocks flew through the air, shrapnel from anti-aircraft guns cut through canvas, and the wounded lay screaming. Amidst them all ran three doctors and Sister Sheila Greaves from Number 15 Casualty Clearing station. Together they dragged the wounded out of their tattered tents, carried them back to the CCS and went back for more, whilst all the time the bombs and shrapnel fell whistling and sizzling around them. Sister Greaves well deserved the George Medal she was awarded for her gallantry under fire that day.

From those shell-battered beaches the water ambulances worked incessantly, loading casualties and ferrying them to the hospital carriers. The experience of Bill Dilworth shows how well stretcher-bearers, medical officers and nursing sisters catered for their charges.

I was blown up on a mine. My right foot, left leg, left side of my body and my back were badly lacerated. They took me to a casualty clearing station on the beach where a surgeon operated on me – the first of nine subsequent operations on my back. When I came to my senses again I was lying on a stretcher alongside the hospital tents which were sunk into the ground. Within a few hours we were taken on to a water ambulance which took us out into the bay where two or three hospital ships were moored. I remember being placed on the open deck but was still rather dozy with the injections. Suddenly bombs started exploding round us. A nurse immediately came to us to see if we had been hit. Another hospital ship, she said, had been hit and set on fire. She was wonderful, reassuring us that we would be all right and with that I fell into a doze again.

Reinforcements arriving at Anzio were shocked by the sights which met their eyes on the beaches. More so if they happened to be landing whilst wounded were being embarked on to the landing-craft they were leaving. The scene was imprinted forever on one observer's mind: 'There were bandaged heads and bodies with crusty red stains showing through, missing arms with flapping sleeves pinned over, chopped-off legs with blankets lying horribly flat, and stark staring shock cases.'[6]

During the next weeks at Anzio, whilst nurses were coping with the trauma of receiving such pathetic cases, General Eberhard von Mackenson of the German forces launched a succession of massive assaults aimed at driving the Allies into the sea. It was then that one of the most controversial actions of the war was about to be played out sixty miles south of the beachhead, at the once peaceful Abbey of Monte Cassino.

The ancient abbey, begun by St Benedict in AD 529, sat like a magnificent crown upon a 518-mile hill that overlooked the approaches to the Liri Valley. Because of its historical significance, its magnificent collection of priceless works of art, and the fact it was home to some 2,500 monks, nuns and civilian refugees, Eisenhower had forbidden Allied bombers to bomb it. But, because Allied generals were sure that the Germans were using the abbey as an observation post, permission was given for it to be bombed. On the morning of 15 February 1944, waves of Allied bombers unleashed their destructive cargoes upon the abbey itself, until it was a heap of rubble.

Ironically, the resulting ruins provided ideal cover for the German infantry, who then repulsed one attack after another. The Indian division attempted to capture the snow-streaked feature of Monte Cassino, but failed. Assaults made by the French, Americans, British and New Zealanders also failed.

But now a formidable force was being built up on that blood-soaked battlefield of the Liri Valley. It was to be a massive operation, with half a dozen nationalities involved. Its aim was the destruction of all German troops south of Rome.

Before it started, field dressings stations moved further up the slopes of Monte Cassino, and two nursing sisters volunteered to go with them to care for those too seriously wounded to be moved. Receiving those who could be moved, and as close to the front as possible to minimize delay, were the hospital trains equipped to carry 300 wounded. Sister Anne Watt (later Pfister), who had survived the bombing of Bari, was on one of them with other nurses and medical orderlies working feverishly to clear as many casualties as possible from all forward casualty clearing stations before the great attack on Cassino began.

Now, as they waited for this massive operation to begin, nurses were apprehensive. Yet more convoys of wounded would be overwhelming medical facilities. But preparations had been made. There was even a newly commissioned 500-bed hospital ship, the *Empire Clyde*, provided and staffed by Ellerman Line, already on its way to Naples. Sister Kitty Jones (later Hutchinson) recalled its splendour: 'It had cost half a million in those days to convert from a cruise liner to a 500-bed hospital ship. It even had special accommodation for mental patients.'

Infantrymen were understandably apprehensive about the forthcoming big attack. But there were some new troops on that front who were really eager for the fight. They were the Poles of General Wladyslaw Anders' Second Corps who had trekked all the way from Russian Gulag camps, through Persia to get to the Italian front. They were itching to have a go at the Germans who had invaded their homeland. Now, at last, they were in position and had been given the toughest objective of all – to capture the peak of Monte Cassino itself.

On 11 May 1944 Allied guns thundered out to begin the battle for Rome. The Germans were taken by surprise. Monte Cassino was captured on 18 May, and Allied troops advanced rapidly forward to link up with 150,000 soldiers breaking out of the Anzio beachhead perimeter behind which they had been trapped for long months. On 5 June 1944, Allied troops entered Rome to be welcomed by wildly excited crowds.

In Naples in the days following the fall of Rome, the *Empire Clyde* took on its full complement of wounded. 'They were mainly Poles from Monte Cassino,' recalled Kitty Hutchinson. 'The captain told us he had taken on 50 more than he should and they were lying on mattresses on the floor. They caused problems later when the ship pitched and rolled through rough seas. The mattresses slithered back and forward across the lower deck. The Poles had their own hospital in Scotland but we dropped them at Southampton. Our next load were Canadians; their hospital was close to Southampton. We were told to take them to Scotland. They were all long-term wounded likely to be out of action for three months or more.'

Perhaps it didn't really matter to those managing the war then, where they went. It mattered to the Poles, but they had already lost so much – their homeland – and were unlikely ever to get it back. And 3,784 of their comrades now lay dead on the dreary slopes of Monte Cassino. Covering the lower slopes then, where nurses with the forward field ambulances had been working, were masses of poppies, their red flowers weirdly appropriate to the scene.

Back in 'The Hatbox of Hell' at that time, as the Americans had called Anzio, the nurses were still dealing with the cost of the battles there. And in that lonely British cemetery on the hill by the road to Rome, rows of white crosses told their own stories.

Those nurses who took part in the year-long struggle to reach Rome still have memories of young men in pain and fear. Sister Margaret Jennings remembered a young man who cried out to her from his bed: 'Don't let them put me to sleep, Sister, or I'll come back without a leg.'

And what of the glory of capturing the Eternal City? It made front-page news for only one day in Britain. The next day's momentous news swept the Italian campaign from the headlines – another D-Day landing. This time it was the really big one, the decisive one in Normandy. And the nurses again were there on the beaches and under fire.

9 Into the Normandy Bridgehead

> Their bodies were black, their appearance
> horrific. We gave them morphia and more
> morphia and watched helplessly as they
> died. We moved the dead out of the ward
> and got on with trying to save the living.
> They were all so young and frightened.
>
> Mary Mulrey QAIMNS[1]

Dawn. The storm had abated. To the east the sky was beginning to be
tinted a faint pink. The nurses of Number 50 Mobile Field Hospital now
waited tensely. Sister Iris Ogilvie (now Bower) of the Princess Mary's
RAF Nursing Service sat in silence in the front seat of her ambulance. In
battledress, tin hat, a Red Cross armband prominently displayed on her
left arm, she gazed through the windscreen at the long column of
ambulances, jeeps, and trucks threading its way slowly down the road
towards the docks. She recalled: 'I couldn't believe it was happening. In
spite of the familiar sound of engines, everything seemed incredibly still,
almost unreal that early morning of 5th June 1944. I was setting out on
what was to be the greatest adventure of my life.'

As the convoy lurched inexorably forward in low gear, her mind
drifted back over the last four years: to the bombs falling on the two
hospitals where she had served and earned an award for gallantry; to her
whirlwind love affair with bomber pilot Donald Ogilvie; to her
wonderfully happy fifteen months of marriage; to feelings of such relief
and joy when her husband finished his tour of thirty missions over
Germany, and his award of the Distinguished Flying Cross. And finally
to the awful moment when the dreaded buff-coloured telegram arrived,
followed immediately by the letter from his commanding officer telling
her that Squadron Leader Donald Ogilvie's aircraft had been shot down
in a low-flying raid on Flushing (Vlissingen), Holland, and there had
been no survivors.

It was that news, she recalled, which caused her to be where she was
now, in a convoy bound for the invasion beaches of Normandy. In her
desperation to fight back and make her own contribution to Hitler's

defeat, she had volunteered for service with the RAF's Mobile Field Hospital.

The training, at Chichester's Fontwell Race Course, had been hard; no special allowances were made for her sex. In fact, as she learnt later, the view men took of her even being with the unit was voiced in terms such as: 'We don't want any bloody women in this outfit.' Fortunately then, Iris was unaware of this hostility towards her posting and that of her colleague, Sister Mollie Giles. Nor was she aware that the course was designed partly to test their physical and mental fitness as well as their professional expertise. She learnt all that later.

All understandable, for the unit was due to land on the Normandy beach and advance close behind the front-line troops. It was an entirely self-supporting unit, with its own transport, electric power, field telephone system, water supplies, cooking facilities and signals unit. The vehicles had all been 'water-proofed' so they could drive down the ramp of the landing-craft into the sea and on to the shore. 'We lacked nothing in the way of medical supplies available at the time; operating theatre, X-Ray department and so on. We even had our own Dental Unit,' recalled Iris.

Now they were on their way.

'They'll have a shock when they see you and the other Sister in this lot,' said the ambulance driver as he jumped down from the cab at Fareham assembly area. He was right. The moment Iris and her friend Mollie Giles climbed from their cabs to stretch their legs, all eyes were turned on them. Near by, their commanding officer was talking to the Fareham camp commander who took one look at the slim Iris Ogilvie, standing at a mere five foot two inches and with golden curls creeping out from her tin hat, and the slightly taller auburn-haired Mollie Giles, and exclaimed with astonishment in his voice: 'They're not going over, are they?'

They were, and like everyone else then in that camp they were now sealed off from the rest of the world. It was one of hundreds of tightly guarded camps covering most of England's southern counties, where soldiers were fenced off from the outside world by barbed wire and patrolled by armed military police. They were to wait there until called forward to hit the French beaches. Tight security regulations even forbade soldiers from approaching the barbed wire to talk to anyone outside.

Amongst those soldiers was Maurice Pinkney, a tall, sun-tanned sergeant wearing the Africa Star on his tunic. He had only just arrived from the nearby hospital where he had been recovering from a second bout of malaria originally contracted in Sicily with the Green Howards. Now he was afflicted by another very serious condition, contracted this time in the Royal Hampshire Hospital itself. In the vernacular of those days, he had been 'bitten by the love-bug'. He was quite seriously and incurably in love with the pretty young nurse who had mopped the sweat from his feverish brow and made him feel so much better.

And that nurse, Mary Webb, was equally afflicted, inexplicably drawn to the soldier who had already seen so much of the fighting in the Middle East and yet always had such a ready smile. The love virus had worked quickly on both Maurice and Mary during those few weeks they had been together in the Royal Hampshire Hospital.

Suddenly, though, wards had been cleared and Maurice was discharged to his unit already waiting in the nearby assembly camp. But Maurice was not going to be thwarted. He would get out and see Mary just once again before ... well ... before the balloon went up. So, at dusk that same day, when men were strolling towards the camp cinema and NAAFI canteens, he wandered, apparently aimlessly, towards a point where the wire gave way to a high wall overhung by branches of trees and bushes. Then he broke into a sprint, put one foot high on to the wall in the fashion taught at 'battle schools' and in one swinging movement was up and over the wall. Without pausing, he ran straight across the fields for six miles to Lainston House where nurses of the Royal Hampshire Hospital had their rooms. He scribbled a note on a piece of toilet paper that 'old' soldiers always carried in their pocket, and asked a nurse to give it to Mary Webb.

Within no time at all she was with him. Time was short, but long enough for Maurice to ask her: 'Would she wait for him?' The answer was never in doubt. She would. And the strength of her embrace emphatically sealed her promise. Now he had to go. This time it was at a much slower trot, and he had only gone a few yards when he stopped, turned to Mary and called out softly: 'Watch out for my birthday!' And with that he made off towards his camp.

Mary watched him steadily running away until he disappeared over the brow of a small hill. Then she walked slowly back to her room, excited and sad at the same time. Excited as any 20-year-old girl would have been when her boyfriend had risked court martial just to see her once again before going into battle. Sad when she thought of the empty wards cleared for the casualties expected any day now from the long-awaited Allied invasion of Europe. And she wondered if those last few words of Maurice's – 'Watch out for my birthday' – could carry a clue to when that invasion day would be. His birthday was 4 June. Mary's mind was swimming with all kinds of emotions stirred by the thought of Maurice rejoining his unit. She shuddered. Might even he soon be occupying one of those empty beds? It was then she realized just how much she cared for that young Green Howards sergeant, now behind the wire in the secure military camp. She was, indeed, in love!

At that time all over Britain hospitals of the Emergency Medical Service were in a maximum state of readiness to take casualties evacuated from the front line. Margaret Jackson Browne was at Park Prewett (Mental)

Hospital in Basingstoke which had been taken over by St Thomas's
Hospital in London. One mystery for her still remains unsolved, as she
light-heartedly said, using the 'hospital speak' of long-gone days:

> Where did they put all the loonies when the mental hospitals
> were cleared for the EMS? Some of them stayed, such as
> George. He brought in the coal and did other odd jobs for us.
> He always wore a cap and a thick grey suit. In confidence he
> would bring out his pocket watch and say he was never going
> home as his family wanted it. If he went home they'd take it
> off him.
>
> We'd had orders to empty all beds for the last two weeks in
> May 1944. Empty beds were spread with a grey blanket to
> take a soldier in a dirty, bloody uniform. A large trolley set
> with piles of towels, soap, flannels, razors, pyjamas was
> ready for men with no possessions.

All military hospitals too were ready and waiting. Everyone knew the
time was near. No one knew exactly when.

In another of those closely guarded camps, Sister Marie Sedman of the
QAIMNS, serving in the Number 75 British Hospital, was wondering
just when they would be called. They had moved in stages down from
Peebles in Scotland to their place of readiness now in Angmering, where
they were issued with a strange assortment of items for emergencies
once they hit the invasion beaches: a thick slab of vitaminized chocolate,
a flat airtight tin as an emergency ration, seasickness pills and, curiously
enough, a booklet of useful phrases in French!

They were all kitted out with the most unsightly of uniforms –
soldiers' battledress trousers and jacket impregnated with a solution
which some claimed was anti-gas solution whilst others maintained it
was anti-vermin. Whichever it was, it was universally disliked by both
men and women, for it left the material stiff and uncomfortable. For
nurses, the issue was absurd. The whole cut of the soldiers' battledress
was unsuitable for women. 'Those metal buttons on the flies broke your
nails,' laughed Hilary Lewis. 'When the waistband fitted, the seat of the
trousers was far too small!'

And Marie Sedman recalled: 'We were in fits of laughter looking at
ourselves but by dint of ingenuity and some help from those handy with
a needle and thread, trousers were made to fit. They were certainly
more serviceable than our scarlet and grey outfits for what we were
going to be doing. There was one more opportunity for us to wear our
best scarlet and grey uniform before we set off for France. The Royal
Engineers invited us to a dance at Rustington Lido. We had a late pass

until midnight. The next morning the Engineers were all gone. The invasion had started!'

'Get cracking, girls!' The voice of Flight Lieutenant Martin roused Iris Ogilvie and Mollie Giles from a fitful sleep. At last the waiting was over. The RAF's Mobile Field Hospital was on the move again. Gosport for embarkation. The advance party had already gone ahead, and sadly one of their doctors, Squadron Leader Grant, had been killed on the beach.

We put packs on our backs [recalled Iris] donned our tin hats and walked out into the darkness. We saw shadowy shapes and men darting about everywhere. What struck me was how silent it was considering the incredible activity. I found my ambulance and we sat in the darkness for a while before the convoy moved off. We reached the outskirts of Gosport at the crack of dawn. We stopped in a suburban street. I was astonished to find the inhabitants up and about. They waved to us from front doors and gardens. They came out with cups of tea and bowls of water for the soldiers trying to shave. One woman gave me a treasured tin of peaches. I sat on the kerbstone and ate it out of the tin. Morale was tremendous. The generosity and kindness of the women there did so much. The men remembered and talked about it in the grim days that followed.

A whistle shrilled. Orders echoed down the line. Everyone scrambled into their vehicles. Engines revved and we were on the move again. We drew alongside a Landing Ship Tank. It seemed enormous to me. Tanks were already on board, lighter vehicles were slung on to a higher deck. Hundreds of soldiers were already crowding by the rails. The next thing I knew I was embarking. I seemed to go through all the motions automatically. I didn't utter a word. Neither did anyone else. Tanks, vehicles and men poured on to the craft at a tremendous pace and in no time at all the fully laden LCT sailed and we joined a vast Normandy-bound convoy.

It was an incredible sight. Overhead, twenty RAF fighter planes roared. A reassuring noise as they patrolled above us for all the hours of daylight.

I sat on deck near some sacks of potatoes and helped the cooks with endless peeling. I was rewarded with a continuous flow of hot tea. When the call of 'grub's up' came, we were all ready for it: hot meat and vegetable stew and tinned rice pudding.

Mollie and I managed to get a few hours sleep and woke at daybreak to see, on the Normandy coast, smoke and clouds of red dust. It was a grim reminder of the fight being waged so near the shore, where our Field Hospital was soon to land. A cruiser close to our ship began to pound enemy shore positions with its six-inch guns. We just had to sit waiting until the tide was right to land. After what seemed an eternity our CO – 'Sunshine' – gave us the order to move. I still wasn't feeling frightened – the adrenalin was certainly flowing quickly.

The first truck to drive down the ramp almost disappeared into a hole in the shingle. Now he had to wait for the next tide to re-beach. By then it was dark. Suddenly the order came: 'Go!' We scrambled down the ramp and the next thing I remember feeling was the sand under my feet. I had landed on Juno/Red Beach near Courseulles-sur-Mer in the pitch darkness of June 12th, 1944.

In the darkness they followed shadowy figures up the sloping beach, hoping to find their assembly area. No one knew where it was. The beachmaster put them in a jeep, but they had only gone a few metres when the noise of shells and firing was so deafening the drivers stopped and shouted: 'Get out! Take cover!' From then on they walked and crawled, as bullets and shells cracked and whistled in the air around them.

'I found myself crouching by a bush,' said Iris Ogilvie. 'I felt very much alone. Great red balls seemed to be coming straight at me. "They're flaming onions," a soldier said. I was sure I'd be killed before I'd even attended to one casualty. Suddenly there was a lull and a soldier took us to the assembly area of our Mobile Field Hospital.'

Very soon they were fully operational, receiving casualties and arranging for their evacuation by air. Amongst them were many from the Green Howards. They had been in the fierce fighting in which one of their combat veterans, Sergeant-Major Stan Hollis, had won the Victoria Cross. The carnage was appalling, the casualties unimaginable and the beaches strewn with men cut down in the crazy rush up the sloping sand.

The wounded from the front, which had now moved on from the beaches, were brought into tents of the mobile field hospital. Their faces were grey with fear and fatigue. Iris Ogilvie recalled: 'Many of the wounded were a very sorry sight. We all worked non-stop, seeing to field dressings, intravenous infusions, giving injections, mainly of morphia and penicillin. I must have handed out gallons of hot tea and fed those who could eat. Apart from the medical care we spent as much time as possible talking to them and lighting the odd "fag" for those who were "dying for a smoke". My reward was to see smiles on their faces and in their eyes. Next morning the ambulances arrived to take the serious casualties away for evacuation to the UK.'

Receiving many of those patients in the Royal Hampshire Hospital was nurse Mary Webb (now Pinkney), anxiously scanning the lists of wounded from the Green Howards. Would the name of Maurice Pinkney be amongst them?

At about the same time as Number 50 Mobile Field Hospital RAF was setting off for Normandy, nurses of Number 75 British General Hospital were on the move too. 'We were cheered through the streets and we all felt proud to be part of the great adventure,' said Marie Sedman.

As they entered the dock area at Portsmouth they could not only smell the sea – they could feel it. Spray, whipped up from the waves over the quayside, fell on them like a light drizzle. The nurses, burdened with kit and steel helmets upsetting their balance, found that walking up the swaying gangway of the former Channel ferry HMS *Invicta* was a gymnastic feat in itself, made no easier by the chorus of wolf-whistles from waiting soldiers.

Once aboard, and below deck, most of the nurses were surprised to find they had been allocated hammocks in a most dismal and smelly part of what had been a mess deck. Fortunately for their morale then, no one had any idea of what a long and memorable voyage across the Channel it was going to be.

By now nurses had got used to the words: 'Things have not gone according to plan'. They had not. Assault troops had not reached their first objectives. Time shedules had to be altered. The site for Number 75 BGH had not yet been taken. They could not go back to the crowded port and they could not cross to France. Instead, their ship zigzagged along the south coast, always on the lookout for enemy torpedo-boats.

The food was dire. Bread and water were soon in short supply. The staple meal was cold porridge. Very few felt like eating. Everyone, it seemed, was seasick. Down below, men and women swung in their hammocks; others huddled and crouched, choking in the stench of boiled vegetables, the stink of oil and vomit. Their one thought was to get to land and escape from their misery, whatever those beaches might be like.

It was three-and-a-half days after leaving Southampton before HMS *Invicta* drew alongside the quay of Mulberry, the secret artificial harbour towed across the Channel days earlier. Dusk was falling as nurses reached the shore, and appetites were beginning to return. But the promised transport still had not come to take them to their destination. They huddled on the beach waiting, whilst around them small groups of soldiers were cooking an evening meal on 'Tommy cookers', lethal little objects that used petrol as their fuel. Eventually, an ambulance car arrived to take eight nursing sisters who were urgently needed at Number 2 Field Dressing Station at Courseulles-sur-Mer, where the wounded were overwhelming the casualty evacuation centre.

After waiting hours on the beach, the rest of Number 75 BGH were taken to Number 81 BGH, a tented field hospital just outside the village of Rys. They arrived at dusk, just when a seemingly endless process of ambulances drove up to the reception tent, offloaded their casualties and drove off again quickly. A more dramatic introduction could not have been imagined for Number 75 BGH as a foretaste of what their lot was to be like.

Nothing, however, could have adequately prepared the nurses for the shock of suddenly being amidst a bloodbath. Nothing, that is, except the years of hard training, the strict discipline of the hierarchy from Matron down through her Sisters and staff nurses, and the ingrained habit of getting on with the job and responding to an order and to a situation without further thought. Nothing except the nursing tradition that required that patients in their hands be given the finest professional care. And they rose to the occasion, giving more than generously. But it was still difficult.

'We just had to get on with it, no matter what we felt,' recalled Sister Marie Sedman (now Floyd-Norris). 'I was in the 3rd Ambulance Clearing Station and 75th BGH. No one ever came to see how we were coping with all the stress then and no one ever came to see us later. But we were young, though sensitive nevertheless. We were so near to the front line that I remember one day waving to the boys standing up in the turrets of their tanks. They were so glad to see us and so cheery. I was still on duty shortly afterwards when those same young lads were brought into Reception, half their faces blown away. Bodies burnt to a frazzle, some lay quietly dying, others screaming with pain.'

One day merged into the next, with the frenetic activity in wards packed tightly with stretchers of wounded soldiers, bloody and ashen-faced, some of whom were hardly breathing while others were making awful sounds to the crump of artillery shells. There was no end to it all. Surgeons worked continuously on eight-hour shifts. Heavy rain added to the problems. 'The hospital was in a field of grass a foot high. Pathways were just squelchy mud. Whenever we did manage a night in bed, the worst part was getting up. I sat on the end of the camp bed, reached for one shoe and then the other before moving on to the wet duckboards,' said Marie Sedman.

Conditions on the wards were primitive too. Boxes balanced one on top of the other served as shelves and cupboards. Hilary Lewis, who had served in a Birmingham hospital with all the latest equipment during the blitz, was appalled. 'It came as a shock to find we had to make do with old fashioned fish kettles to sterilize hypodermic syringes. Feeding the head cases through tubes was difficult too. There were no liquidizers then and it took time to push food through a sieve until it was soft enough to be fed to the patient through a tube.'

Field hospitals were worked to their absolute limits whilst the push past Caen was taking place. 'We are rapidly reaching saturation point,' wrote the CO of Number 75 BGH, Colonel M. G. Wells, in the unit war diary. 'Every bed space is occupied.'[2]

To relieve the pressure, Number 121 BGH arrived and pitched their tents nearby on the road between Bayeux and Caen. Sister Monica Dixon (now Carhart-Harris) recalled: 'We called it Harley Street. Some magnificent organization had put up huge marquees full of beds to cope with the convoys of wounded. We junior Sisters washed in a stream in the open, having been warned of snipers. Our Matron amused us. When she went to the latrines she held her umbrella up to warn the men it was ladies' turn.'

Casualties were horrendous as they filled hospital beds. Number 75 BGH, for example, admitted 394 in the two days between 1800 hours on 16 July until the same time on 18 July.[3] Nurses were rushed off their feet. 'I often had only an hour or two's sleep in 24 hours and then it was broken sleep with anti-aircraft guns cracking away in the field next to our wards and shrapnel falling through the tent roof when German bombers passed overhead. We had tin hats but the patients did not. Not many, if any, of us wore them when we were working on the wards. It didn't seem right somehow,' said Marie Sedman.

Such stress took its toll on the staff. Most of them bottled it up and employed various means to keep going. One matron's advice to Sisters who felt they had reached the end of their tether was to occupy their minds with any trivial job they could find, and to do it well until they felt in control again. 'Post-traumatic stress had not been invented. It's still double Dutch to me. You damn well just got on with your job,' said Hilary Lewis, formerly of Number 101 BGH.

Most nurses seemed to be able to do just that. Others, nurses and doctors, had problems. A medical officer of a Durham Light Infantry battalion had to be relieved by the MO of Number 149 Field Ambulance Station owing to extreme fatigue, after the battalion had suffered heavy casualties in an exposed salient.[4]

And by mid-July, the flood of mutilated bodies and the dead and dying brought into Number 75 BGH through the mud was beyond the endurance of one doctor. At 0700 hours on 21 July, with the rain battering on to the tent-roof, he got up, seized a scalpel, cut his brachial artery and shot himself. Enough was enough. In cold, official words the subsequent court of enquiry found that he 'expired in five minutes' and that he took his life when the balance of his mind was disturbed on account of both physical and mental fatigue following extreme pressure of work under Active Service conditions.[5]

He was replaced by a woman physician.

Casualties continued to fill all the beds and spaces for stretchers in Number 75 BGH. In eleven days the hospital received 2,400 admissions. Sister Marie Sedman recalled:

We were turning over 600 patients every 12 hours. They were in and out so quickly we didn't get to know many of them. There was, however, an exception with a young corporal

who was accidentally shot in the back whilst on parade. He
had a big hole in his body but somehow managed to lie in bed
embroidering his unit cap badge on to a piece of linen. I
wrote to his mother.

One day I said to him, 'Is there someone nice you are
going to give that to?'

'I have a favourite sister,' he replied.

A few days later, just before he left for England, he gave
me that beautifully embroidered cap badge. I must have
been that favourite sister. He died, we heard, that same
week. I still have that embroidery.

Hospital admission books recorded the awful toll. In the four weeks
that Number 75 BGH had been open, they dealt with 4,063 casualties.
Ambulances arrived, unloaded very quickly and were away again for
another load within ten minutes.

Such casualties inevitably seriously affected morale. The infantry had
been through hell. Many were already feeling they had seen too many of
their pals killed or horribly maimed, especially those who had been in
the thick of the fighting in Africa and Sicily as well as on the beaches of
Normandy and beyond. The problem of stress affected all ranks of all
branches of the services in the front line as well as the infantry soldier
from D-Day onwards. The condition was cloaked in various guises –
'battle fatigue' and 'exhaustion' and NYDN (Not Yet Diagnosed
Neurosis). Even the crack veteran divisions spearheading the assault on
the beaches suffered in the same way as other less-experienced ones.
They soon knew when a mate was getting 'bomb happy'.

They had all followed a bloody route indeed. D-Day casualties alone
totalled 10,000 dead and wounded. On Sword Beach, bodies formed a
khaki carpet from the water's edge to the cliffs. It was the same at
Omaha – 'Bloody Omaha', as veterans called it afterwards. And on
Gold Beach, men of the British Second Army took a terrible beating.

Nevertheless, those assault units pushed on, taking casualties all the
time but still moving, albeit well behind their scheduled progress
towards Caen. Losses were heartbreaking, as British soldiers battled to
take well-nigh impregnable defensive positions the Germans had been
preparing for four years. In some battalions, one man in three was
either killed or wounded. Nurses had been warned what to expect, but
the grim reality of it all was traumatic. Even battle-hardened war
correspondent Alan Moorehead, who had been with 50th Division in
Africa and Sicily, was sickened by the 'butcher's bill'. He noted: 'There
was a kind of anarchy in this waste, ... an unreasoning and futile
violence.... There seemed no point in going on.'[6]

Men could only take so much. The divisions with battle experience
fought in full knowledge of the inescapable fact that to continue fighting
against the enemy meant living with the continuous and immediate

prospect of violent death. Inexorably and inevitably many of them developed an anxiety neurosis – their stock of courage simply ran out.

In Maurice Pinkney's battalion, the 7th Green Howards, cases of 'exhaustion' increased, and morale dropped to such a low state during a 'minor' action at La Taille that the ADMS of Number 50 Division made a special visit to the battalion's regimental aid post on 8 July to see for himself what was happening. The regimental medical officer confirmed the situation. The ADMS went back to headquarters to note in his war diary his 'concern about the number of young men leaving the battle on the excuse that they are exhausted.'[7]

He was not to know then how widespread the problem of anxiety neurosis was. It affected all three fighting services alike – Navy, Army and Air Force. Indeed, one of the best-kept secrets of the Second World War was the establishment of twenty-two pyschiatric hospitals in remote parts of Britain specializing in cases of disturbed neurosis: five centres for mild neurosis, four psychiatric centres and thirteen NYDN centres.

Nurses dealing with badly shaken young men close to the front line often had to try and find their own solution. It was not easy and just as difficult in all hospitals on the evacuation route home to Britain.

Just eighteen hours after the landing in Normandy, casualties were arriving at the Midlands and North Staffordshire Royal Infirmary, where half the beds had been allocated especially for them. Sister Hilda Smith was there, ready and waiting.

> We had been warned and told to go to our rooms and if possible sleep, because we would get little once the casualties arrived. We lay on our beds but could not really rest. We were too worked up and wondering what was shortly going to confront us. It was more shocking than we ever imagined.
>
> They came by train to Trentham Gardens and from there in an army convoy to the Reception area. There we had four 'stations' each with a Consultant, Houseman, and Sister for each patient. Every soldier had a label attached to his uniform. Some would have a large 'T' on the forehead denoting tourniquet, others might have an 'H' indicating haemorrhaging, and quite a few would have the letter 'M' for morphine, all marked with indelible pencil.
>
> The Reception area had supports for stretchers so that Consultants could examine each casualty and make an appraisal of where he should be sent. Some were sent immediately for a blood transfusion, others to one of the three operating theatres in the basement; there was another on the first floor and they all worked non-stop for the next forty-eight hours. No wonder we were told to get some sleep before the convoys arrived.
>
> The kitchen was ready with meals for those who could

tolerate food. Everything was so efficiently organized but just
in case there was a problem, the hospital Matron was ready
to react to whatever situation arose. She was marvellous, a
perfect lady. From the moment the ambulances arrived until
all had been admitted she never stopped dashing from one
ward to the next, down to the kitchen or along to operating
theatres. She really was an inspiration to us all.

Some patients were in a terrible state. One sailor was the
sole survivor of a ship which had gone down in flames. There
was not a patch on his body, except for his face, which was
not severely burnt. Fortunately for such patients, and there
were many like him, we had a plastic surgery unit with a
superb surgeon, John Grocott, who had worked with
Archibald McIndoe, later knighted for his work, in the
Queen Victoria Hospital at East Grinstead. He worked
wonders. I was Theatre Sister.

Some cases are forever imprinted upon my memory. There
was a young woman brought in. An exploding bomb had
blown off both her hands, taken out her eyelids and eyes,
and seared her face. Added to this, she was pregnant. Such a
pretty girl, we saw later from her photograph which was
brought in to help the plastic surgeon rebuild her face.

We nursed her for months through her pregnancy, and
after the baby was born Mr Grocott built her a thumb and
two fingers for each hand and then taught her how to bath
her baby.

Our hospital helped to pioneer the treatment of using
saline baths for burns. Salt came by the train from
Merseyside. It was made absolutely sterile and then used in
arm baths for elbows and also for complete submersion of
the whole body. I can still smell the stench of those burns.
We had to go over the burnt area with tweezers picking off
the slough and dead tissue.

Another nursing sister, Margaret Jackson Browne, has never been able
to eat Camembert cheese since working with Sir Harold Gillespie's
plastic surgery at Park Prewett. 'The smell of it reminds me so much of
the stench of a septic burn.'

Sister Hilda Smith recalled what a slow and painstaking business
plastic surgery was.

One soldier who had his ear blown off, had a skin graft taken
from skin from his abdomen until a flap grew from there on
to the inner side of his forearm. When enough of this 'flap'
was ready the forearm was strapped up to where the man's
ear had been and in that position he was kept for weeks.

When the flap was attached to the ear position it was removed from the forearm and then sculpted to the shape of an ear. It just happened that Mr Grocott was a good engineer as well as a surgeon. He could make things with his hands – even a motor car!

The physical wounds were shocking enough but equally upsetting for the medical staff were those young men whose minds had gone completely with the trauma of what they had witnessed in battle; men who no longer knew what was happening to them, who cringed and shouted out, panic-stricken. When they had gone to sleep for the night they would wake with screams, tortured by nightmares we could do nothing about. And we knew that those nightmares would go on for years to come.

Whether the wounds were physical or psychological, nursing care, from casualty clearing stations back to base hospitals in Britain, was of the highest standard. Mary Webb (now Pinkney), then at the Royal Hampshire Hospital, recalled what it was like there:

With men suffering from gross wounds to the chest and abdomen we did our best, monitoring individuals closely; giving a little sedation, fluids, sometimes plasma, rest, warmth and the reassurance of a few encouraging words given whilst holding the patient's hand. Even when there was little hope of recovery we tried everything that could be done for the men. They deserved no less. Frighteningly wide gashes in the chest and abdomen were packed with vaseline, gauze, tulle and sulphanilamide, and we told patients the wound would gradually heal from the outside inwards.

Obviously, speed of evacuation was essential for those with penetrating head wounds and those needing eye and facio-maxillary care, and this is where a magnificent job was done by the 'Flying Nightingales' – the nurses of the Air Evacuation Service. The importance of speedy air evacuation of casualties was noted by war correspondent Alan Moorehead. He saw that it not only improved a wounded man's chances of survival but that it was important for the resolution of soldiers still fighting. He reported how demoralizing it was for infantrymen to see so many of their pals being killed and lying wounded on the battlefield waiting to be evacuated to casualty clearing stations where nurses and doctors barely had time to care for their injuries. He noted too how this very heavy casualty rate was affecting the self-assurance of young officers who often felt there was no point in going on. 'No future but a bloody end for themselves.'[8]

Field Marshal Montgomery came to the same conclusion and wrote to the Chief of the Imperial General Staff to say that casualties would have to be evacuated more quickly by air.[9]

Iris Ogilvie took one of the first convoys of wounded to the airstrip. 'As we approached I could see amongst clouds of white dust, the familiar shape of the RAF *Dakota*. I learnt there had been a counter-attack when the plane landed and a tank battle was going on in the wood at the end of the air strip.'

Waiting on board the *Dakota* were WAAF medical orderlies. They were the first to care for casualties on the flight. The wounded were quickly loaded, but the testing-time came when the aircraft took off in a cloud of dust, as Iris Bower recalled: 'The forward landing strip came under mortar and shell fire. We heard later that the *Dakota* was hit as it flew out and that seventy flak holes were found in the fuselage.'

That essential air evacuation operation was going to be a hazardous business.

10   The Flying Nightingales

It is a terrible, sad business to total up the
casualties each day and to realize how
many youngsters are gone for ever.[1]
Supreme Commander,
Dwight D. Eisenhower,
in a letter to his wife.

By the time she was seventeen, Myra Roberts was quite sure in her mind
that she wanted to join the Air Force and become a nurse. Nursing was
something for which she had a natural aptitude, and her love of Air
Force life came from hearing her two brothers talking enthusiastically
about flying whenever they came home on leave.

She wasted no time. In 1941 she volunteered to join the WAAF and
tackled her training in such a zealous manner that all her instructors
graded her in the rare terminology of 'exemplary'. It came from no
effort on her part. She just loved the life.

So it was that after completing her specialist medical training as a
nursing orderly and putting it into practice at RAF Sawbridgeworth,
Hertfordshire, the Station medical officer came up to her one day when
she was alone in sick quarters and hesitantly put forward a proposition.

He said, awkwardly at first, 'Corporal Roberts, I have been asked to
make recommendations for a nursing orderly with the essential skills for
a ...' He paused, as if seeking the right words – words that would bring
the response he wanted. 'You see, we need to find suitable personnel to
staff a new unit, an experimental unit, for the evacuation of wounded
soldiers by air. An Air Evacuation Ambulance Service. But ...' He
looked directly into Myra Roberts's twinkling blue eyes. 'But it could be
dangerous work. And it's not going to be an easy job. There'd be some
extra hard training for you to do as well. And so ...' He seemed to be
reluctant to put the question. 'Well, I can only recommend nurses who
volunteer.'

Myra did not wait to be asked. 'I'd like that a lot,' she said, beaming
from ear to ear. Here was an opportunity for her to fly and be like her

119

brothers. Within days, orders came for her to pack her kit and draw a travel warrant from the Orderly Room.

Like all RAF postings, it was an early-morning start. She looked at her posting order, a puzzled frown creasing her pert face.

> 'Blake Hill Farm, Cricklade. What on earth and where on earth is that?'
> No one in the Orderly Room had the faintest idea.
> 'Probably one of those hush-hush units,' suggested a bespectacled corporal who always liked to be the knowledgeable one who could quote RAF form numbers to suit every occasion.
> No one at the railway station could enlighten her either.

That was not surprising. A small Hillman pick-up was waiting for her at Cricklade and drove her through the wide main street, flanked by seventeenth-century houses, and out into the countryside. 'Better get ready for it,' said the driver in answer to her query, 'we're in a God-forsaken place midway betwene Cirencester and Swindon.'

He was not kidding. It was one of those so-called satellite airfields which were popping up like mushrooms all over the countryside at that time to cater for the increasing number of squadrons arriving from all over the world.

When Myra arrived, Blake Hill Farm was being built for utility rather than comfort. The essential features were being readied first – runways and dispersal areas for aircraft, administrative buildings, squadron offices and various messes. Last to be considered, it seemed, were comfortable sleeping-quarters.

> It was grim [Myra recalled]. We lived in a cold, damp Nissen hut which had rivers of condensation streaming down the walls. Around the buildings were water-logged tracks of churned up mud. It was everywhere. We floundered about in wellingtons. The training was tough but interesting.
> It really was hard. Anyone who was not fully committed soon dropped out. Perhaps that was the idea of the gruelling routine. A sorting out process. We realized why later.
> We learnt what to do if our aircraft came down in the sea by going to the swimming pool to practise how to inflate and get a huge rubber dinghy right-side up in the water, how to climb in it and how to pull wounded men into it also. We were taught how to put the stretcher in the opening made for it in the plane, how to give oxygen and how to recognize the effects of lack of oxygen and judge when to give it. Once in the aircraft, keeping the patients alive was our responsibility.
> Most of this specialist nursing training was given at RAF Wroughton hospital. All this was purposeful and enjoyable.

It was when we got airborne that my troubles began. I think I must have drawn the short straw when I was allocated to my Dakota for air experience training, because the pilot seemed definitely against the whole idea of having a woman aboard. I could understand that part of the air experience training was to sort us out into those who could cope with being airborne and those who would be more of a liability than an asset. But my pilot went much too far.

I had never been troubled with air sickness but whenever I went up with my allotted pilot, a Scottish Warrant Officer called Jock McCannell, he would fling the aircraft about the sky as if he were a circus stunt flyer at a pre-war Air Display. He did this every time we took to the air, whatever the weather. At first I thought this was something all the air-women on the course were having to face. It was not. The inhospitable Jock McCannell had a deeper motive for his awful tactics. I guessed he was just trying to get rid of me. Well, he had picked the wrong woman.

I waited until after one particularly gruelling flight which left beads of perspiration standing out on my forehead and my stomach feeling more queasy than it had ever been. I felt weak but so very angry. It gave me strength to vent to my feelings!

What did he think he was doing? Not one of the other pilots had been cutting such a caper. Was he trying to get rid of me?

His reply made me wish I had turned on him before. In his broad Scottish brogue he confessed he came from a small village in the north of Scotland where fishermen would never put out to sea with a woman in their boat because it brought bad luck. There was nothing personal about it.

Oddly enough, whether it would ever have happened again I shall never know. A few days later all women of the Air Evacuation Pool were grounded. It was 6th June, D-Day. Every available aircraft was committed to the airborne assault on Normandy.

Jock McCannell's Dakota was in the great armada taking 8,000 British and 16,000 American airborne troops to land by parachute and glider. His aircraft was one of the few that did not return that day.

'When I heard that news, a shiver went right through my body because I thought right away of his fisherman's superstition about a woman in the boat!' added Myra, still with that strange feeling pulsing through her.

Three days later all members of the Air Ambulance Unit were called to headquarters. The station commander introduced a senior RAF officer with gold braid on his cap and broad ribbons of rank on his arm. He was the Director-General of RAF Medical Services, Air Chief Marshal Sir Harold Whittingham. He looked around the men and women gathered before him and told us what a worthwhile job we had been training for and that very soon we should be putting all that good training into practice. It was a very short address as pep talks go, which we all appreciated. Then he surprised us all by almost using the apocryphal Service joke of 'I want three volunteers. You, you and you.'

Except this time he named the volunteers as Lydia Alford, Edna Birkbeck and me, Myra Roberts. He told us to stay behind and dismissed the rest of the gathering.

We had to send someone for our night clothes as we were told not to go out nor speak to anyone about our mission. A WAAF Sergeant came along and brought us soft hospital blankets to sleep on and a tray with hot sweet cocoa on it. It felt a bit like the prisoner eating a hearty breakfast before the execution.

No backing out now.

Dawn was breaking when they were called. This time they really were treated like other aircrew for a change and enjoyed a traditional aircrew breakfast, including the rare pleasure of one of those wartime scarcities, a real fried egg with the bacon.

Briefing afterwards was short [said Myra]. We were to land close to the front line in Normandy, unload vital stores of ammunition and then load as many casualties as we could fit within the narrow confines of the Dakota fuselage. Because they were transporting ammunition on the outward journey the aircraft carried no Red Cross markings. We were however to be given fighter cover.

We were all in our seats and about to close the side door of the Dakota when the Air Chief Marshal strode across the muddy field from his jeep and handed a folded newspaper to me. 'You can read this as you go over. Pass the time,' he said.

Myra and her friends have since giggled a lot about that. She had far more interesting things to be looking at on that short trip across the Channel and over the assault beaches. She gazed down in wonderment at the extraordinary shambles of wreckage piled on wreckage, tanks sunk up to their turrets in quicksand, a wasteland pitted with thousands of shell-holes and craters, of concrete pillboxes wrenched apart by the barrage of naval shells and bodies lying about their blackened entrances.

Then the Dakota swooped down low over a cornfield, bounced along a makeshift runway of honeycombed metal matting and came to a jolting stop. Men ran alongside, swung open the side door and began offloading as fast as they could. Then off they ran. A new gang of medical orderlies appeared, carrying bloody, bandaged soldiers on stretchers.

Myra's team excelled themselves. Within record time they had all the stretchers crammed inside. Myra has never forgotten the sight of those wounded men packed together in the fuselage.

They looked awful. Many of them lay twisted in odd attitudes, faces white and eyes shut. Others stared vacantly about them, cold fingers plucking at the rough blanket covering them. They were all dirty and unshaven, with battledress torn and soaked in blood, all of them tired beyond belief.

We were about to close the door prior to take-off when a jeep raced up alongside.

'Hold it. Hold it please!' shouted a medical officer. 'Sorry to do this to you but I've a badly wounded soldier here and no place for him here. His only chance is with you. He probably won't make it but for God's sake don't let him die on the plane. He's very brave and very young. Do your best.'

Gently they lifted the stretcher upwards. The young soldier's face was twisted in pain, his teeth clenched as if to keep back his screams. The left sleeve of his battledress blouse lay empty and soaked in blood. One of his trouser legs was nothing more than a tangled, flat-looking mess. His face was pale, his skin clammy and covered with sweat, his breathing deep and noisy. I took hold of his hand gripping the edge of the stretcher.

I could see by the colour of his face he needed oxygen. Quickly I coupled him up, gradually increasing the flow. As I was doing this he began to mutter a few words. Swear words in Welsh. I looked at the label tied to his jacket. I stared in disbelief. His home town was Tywyn. My own home town!

I could see he was in a very bad way. Not only had he lost an arm and a leg but he had terrible stomach wounds. I knew I'd have to do something. I had to get to the wireless operator. Gingerly I stepped over bodies on stretchers, at times toppling and grabbing stanchions for support. At last I was near enough.

'Radio ahead for a doctor to meet the aircraft when we land. Every minute counts now with that lad back there. We've got to do everything we can for him now.'

She went back to that soldier. His breathing was shallow. His face pale with the indelible blue pencilled 'M' for morphine on his forehead. And she did not give him much of a chance. Never would she have believed the sequence of events which would follow this one trip. Like so many wartime experiences, this first trip had an ending more coincidental than a fiction writer would dare to make up ...

The ending came six years later.

> I was living with my husband in Bryncrug. He came home one day and said that an ex-soldier riding round in an invalid carriage had stopped him and asked, 'Who was that lady with you last night?' My husband said it was his wife. The man told him that he remembered my face as he had seen my picture in the paper the day after I'd brought him home from Normandy in the Air Ambulance. I met him the next day and we celebrated with a drink. He was without one arm and a leg but lived for another twenty years afterwards.

On that memorable day when the Air Evacuation Service made its first experimental flight, Rosemary Gannon was on duty at Number 1 Casualty Clearing Station, RAF Hospital Wroughton, Wiltshire, waiting to receive the first of the D-Day's wounded.

> We had been sworn to secrecy about the work we should be doing and on arrival at the hospital we had been divided into two teams comprising surgeons, Sisters, Operations Room Assistants and Plaster Room Assistants.
>   We were confined to camp and told 'It's all about to happen,' and that a hooter would sound to tell us the invasion had begun and we should report to our respective operating theatres to receive the most severely wounded from the invasion beaches.

The casualty clearing station had theatres in which ten operations could be performed simultaneously by surgeons working in teams on a shift system covering twenty-four hours. The Movement Control Office kept in constant touch with airfields, with every ward in the casualty clearing station and also with RAF base hospitals throughout the country so that the surgical and medical staff were able to have up-to-the-minute information on the disposal of patients.

Ambulances, driven by WAAFS, could be called from their dispersal points by direct radio. These young women were seeing the grimmer side of war for the first time, but far more nursing orderlies turned up for duty when a convoy arrived than were actually detailed. They willingly worked on in their off-duty hours.

Rosemary Gannon recalled the first day that the air evacuation scheme got under way.

I had just returned to the barrack block, 'on my knees' as we used to say, after a hard day in the 'clean' theatre upstairs. I lay back on my bed with my feet raised on my kitbag relaxing with a cup of tea which my friend brought from the NAAFI, when it sounded. *The Hooter*!

Gone was the lethargy and tiredness as I rushed to the operating theatre. In no time we were all ready and waiting. For what? No one quite knew. We were being thrown in at the deep end. But no one could have prepared us for what we were about to see. We waited with apprehension. Would we be up to it?

We scanned the skies looking for the air ambulances bringing the wounded to nearby airfields. From there they'd come by road to Wroughton.

At last they arrived.

Convoys of them to be booked in, X-rayed, sorted into groups and sent on their way with the smoothness and efficiency of a huge assembly line all on ground level – no doors, just curtains to separate rooms.

It was horrendous. In the large Resuscitation Ward, we washed them and prepared them for surgery. I haven't words to describe just how awful it was. When we turned some of them over we could see daylight through them. A lot of them with deep gaping holes in their stomachs and chests died. We did all we could for them. We had some of the famous Harley Street surgeons there – Wing Commander Alec Badenoch and the Canadian Wing Commander Scott. And the Sisters too came from well-known London hospitals such as St Thomas's. Everything though went so smoothly. It had been so well planned down to the smallest detail for expediency.

There was no panic. We were all so absorbed in our jobs. The hours passed very quickly. I felt privileged and humble as I carried out my duties with those boys, for they were the 'Bravest of the Brave'. And we were a good team working together in harmony. As we went off duty the next morning it was with a very deep sense of satisfaction. More than a hundred seriously wounded soldiers had passed through our hands. We were a very big hospital and we kept them all until they were fit enough to be dispersed to other hospitals. But so many were beyond saving even with all our specialist care. So many died, so many. It was so sad.

This was only the beginning of many, many more nights of waiting, receiving and dealing with convoys which brought the wounded to No. 1 Casualty Clearing Station at RAF Wroughton.

A few days after that first 'experimental' air evacuation trip, Myra
Roberts had just landed in Normandy when the weather settled in and
low cloud prevented aircraft from taking off. Whilst she was waiting for
flying conditions to improve, she accepted an offer from a war
correspondent to visit the forward positions where the action was fierce.

> We could see the artillery shells landing and the aerial
> bombardment too. As we made our way back to the landing
> strip we too had to take cover from shells. When we got
> going again we passed an infantry battalion making its way to
> the front. Their khaki uniforms were covered in dried mud,
> their weary faces sunburnt red. They trudged along as if in a
> trance in which all their senses had been anaesthetized. Ten
> paces between files, four paces between the men in each file.
> Along the poppy-lined track on which they marched were
> graves, some marked simply with a stick with a British
> helmet above the mound of earth.
>   One of the soldiers looked at us in the jeep and yelled,
> 'Blimey! Women!' It was almost as though they all felt
> reassured. As if it could not be so bad further forward if
> women were actually there.

When Myra got back to the landing strip the aircraft was loaded with
casualties, and as the weather looked all right they set off. And only just
in time.

The next day, the weather deteriorated as one of the worst gales for
half a century hit the coast of Normandy. For three days and nights it
raged. It drove 800 vessels ashore, wrecked most of the 'Mulberry'
artificial harbour off the American beachhead and severely damaged the
'Mulberry' sections off Arromanches. No further air ambulance flights
were made until it died down.

For everyone in Number 50 Mobile Field Hospital then, life was not
easy, as Sister Iris Bower recalled:

> I think it was one of the most difficult times. The advance
> seemed to have come to a halt, the anti-aircraft gunners were
> firing most of the time and the air was full of falling shrapnel.
> It rained down on the canvas of our tents and clanged and
> banged upon the trucks and ambulances. At night time,
> when I did my rounds, one of the older medical orderlies
> insisted on coming with me from tent to tent. Many a time we
> had to make a dash for it from one tent to another. As if
> having a canvas overhead made us feel safe. Added to all this
> there was torrential rain and casualties began to pile up, for,
> due to the storm, air ambulances could not fly and the
> shallow draft hospital carriers could not leave the beaches.

There were some pitiful sights arriving from Army Casualty Clearing Stations. The same ones would reappear three or four days in succession. They lay on stretchers waiting and travelling backwards and forwards in ambulances over bumpy roads. Those who were in our tents waiting to be evacuated were in a poor state too. One night, which was particularly noisy due to gunfire and shelling, we were all busy dashing from one wounded man to another. I was stopped by one of the lads, who was very poorly, lapsing into periods of unconsciousness. He had the familiar intravenous infusion and, in addition, tubing being retained in his stomach. I noted that he was unconscious, made certain all was well with his tubing and then hurried off to do other things. After a little while I returned to look at him again. This time he had his eyes wide open and said in a perfectly clear voice, 'Where's your tin hat? Who do you think you are, a blinking fairy?' I had forgotten I was not wearing one. I went to find my helmet and put it on. I returned to reassure him. He had just died. I have never forgotten that young lad's concern for me.

When the air ambulance shuttle started again it was always a race against time – time so valuable for those lying on the stretchers. And as the front line moved painstakingly forward, so the landing-strips followed, always getting as close to the fighting as possible.

We went right into where the action was going on [Myra Roberts recalled]. At times it was unforgettably dreadful, especially when we knew some of those boys: and now we were seeing those same faces lying, bloody, dirty, upturned to flies and the sun in ditches and hanging from hedges.

One trip I'll never forget. I said many a prayer that day. The aircraft was being tossed about in bad weather, casualties were air-sick and vomiting over each other, missing the sick-bags I had tried to wedge between the stretchers. And amongst it all there was a soldier choking to death. He had a tracheotomy tube in and I had to clear it and fix it back into his throat so that he could breathe. Then I felt like spewing up myself. Please, please, God, I prayed, don't let me start vomiting now. I knew that once I started then I'd not be able to stop. That's the way it is with me.

When we got back that day we had a plate of fatty tinned bacon and beans put before us. I couldn't eat a thing.

As the battle progressed, airstrips were laid ever closer to the front line. The closer to the action, the better chance of survival the seriously wounded had. The area director of medical services for Number 50

Infantry Division was a firm advocate of this. Understandably, with the
front line never static – moving forward one day and sometimes
backwards the next – it became a risky business to put aircraft down on
improvised landing-strips close to the forward areas.[2]

Apart from such tactical problems, however, there was often a more
pressing and personal one for the nurses, as Myra Roberts recalled with
a grin on her face:

> Finding a suitable hedge to get behind to spend a penny,
> when the air ambulance was in the middle of a field, was
> often a problem. I remember one day when several planes
> were on the strip and two of us felt the need to relieve
> ourselves. We were doing a little reconnoitring to find
> somewhere suitable when a young pilot officer came by and
> said, 'Can I help you? Are you looking for something?'
>
> 'Yes,' said Rose, 'We're looking for a hedge we can get
> behind.' Poor chap, he blushed so red that he did not know
> what to say and walked away muttering apologetically. He
> must have said something to someone though, for soon we
> had a little canvas contraption rigged with a bucket and two
> RAF chaps on guard, bless him.
>
> With the air strips being so close to the front they were
> frequently shelled. One day we were walking round the
> aircraft to stretch our legs when an elderly Army officer with
> a lot of gold braid and a red-banded cap came up to us and
> said, 'This is a very historic moment, ladies. Here you are,
> British women on French soil risking your lives for your
> country.' The next moment there was a sound like ripping a
> sheet of calico and he was flat on his face on the ground. We
> thought he had fainted with the emotion, but not a bit of it!
> He'd recognized the sound of shells coming down and was
> yelling to us to get down too. They were giving the air strip a
> real stonking. Shells were bursting nearer and nearer. We
> made a very quick get-away from that place. And we never
> went back.

Other nursing orderlies were not so fortunate. They became
casualties themselves, not only from shelling but also from being shot
down by enemy aircraft. No fighter cover was provided for the
ambulances after the first few days.

Margaret Campbell, Myra's friend, took off one day from a
Normandy airstrip without any casualties aboard. Cheerfully she stood
in the doorway of the Dakota and shouted to Myra, 'I'll keep that date
with you and your friend. We'll be in touch.'

Her aircraft never got back to base.

Once more for Myra, the long arm of coincidence which stretched out
so frequently in wartime to touch everyone, came into action again.

It happened some years after the war when I was nursing in the Central Middlesex Hospital. A shiver ran down my spine as I got the message from a Catholic priest who was visiting patients on my ward. In those days of clothes rationing, he was dressed in an old RAF greatcoat but with civilian buttons. As an ex-WAAF, I recognised it and we got chatting. Then, when I told him what I had been doing, flying over the battle areas bringing out casualties, he surprised me by asking if I had ever known a girl called Margaret Campbell. The picture of her standing in the Dakota doorway all those years ago flashed back into my mind's eye. I told him that she had been lost and presumed killed. Then he told me a strange story about when he had been a prisoner of war and had been asked by the German commandant to carry out a burial service for the crew of a British aircraft that had been shot down near to the camp. He had agreed to officiate and as part of his duties made a record of those interred. Amongst all those names he had remembered was that of one woman: Margaret Campbell. Somehow, I felt that my friend had now kept that date with me. She had been in touch after all. From the dead.

But to those young nursing orderlies the thought of death never seemed to bother them unduly. Like many a soldier, they had the attitude that being killed in action was always something that happened to other people. Edna Birkbeck, who was on the first experimental flight with Myra Roberts and Lydia Alford, said, 'I never thought of anything happening to me. I suppose we all believed we were invincible. Until something did happen. And then it was different.'

We were flying over Germany when our plane caught fire. The pilot and crew tried everything they could but the flames would not die down.

Then it all happened too quickly for us to be frightened.

'Hold tight. We're going to crash land,' shouted the pilot. In seconds we were skimming over fields and on to an Allied airfield. The propellers of our aircraft were still spinning as we chewed up the turf with them. The undercarriage just collapsed under the impact.

Our cargo was a stack of jerry cans full of petrol. The shock of the landing tore them from their securing ropes and they fell all over the floor. I caught my foot in the tangle of ropes and cans and had to struggle to get out, expecting every second the aircraft to explode in flames.

But I made it in time. Curiously the engine fire was put out by the crash and the spilt petrol did not catch fire. Our day of reckoning had not yet come.

Nor was it to come for many of those stalwarts of the air evacuation pool. They led a charmed life, surviving countless near misses. Myra Roberts recalls a similar crash landing when her aircraft was in difficulties. The pilot was circling the airfield near Oxford to use up as much petrol as possible before attempting a crash landing with his damaged aircraft.

'Get your parachute on!' the pilot called to Myra. She didn't fancy that idea at all and decided to take her chance with the crash landing. 'I just curled myself up into a ball with my hands behind my head so that I could roll with the impact of hitting the ground. We skidded along and got out all right.'

> Somehow we survived one thing after another. We were on duty so much, over-worked really, sometimes doing two or three shuttles in a day and evening. It was dangeorus work, yet none of us showed signs of suffering from nerves. We were often carrying ammunition on the way out and were often sitting on bombs as we flew over. We didn't think about the risks. It was our duty and we just got on with it. I supposed we just got acclimatized to death and the handling of bloody bodies.

As the armies battled on through France and Belgium the Air Evacuation Service expanded, with many more WAAF medical orderlies and Sisters of the Princess Mary's Nursing Service working together to save so many more lives because of the speed with which wounded were taken back to hospitals in the UK. They all did a magnificent job, especially in the breakout from the Normandy bridgehead in the late summer of 1944.

11   Break-out from the Bridgehead

You're so intent on helping to relieve the
suffering of those young lads that you don't
think of the bombs exploding around you.
You don't think, let's get out of here.
You're too busy. It's a wonder how we did
it.

Sister Flora Whyte (later Urquhart)

For the survivors of those early battles from the beachhead, more chaos,
confusion and squalor lay ahead. It was especially terrifying for the
infantry; a hell where machine-guns burrrped and metal sliced into flesh
in a bloody struggle which seemed to have no end save death or
mutilation.

For Sister Marie Sedman, who had already seen her fair share of
terrible wounds, the sight of the infantry going forward into battle was
upsetting. 'I don't think I shall ever forget the sight of those young
infantry soldiers plodding steadily along French roads towards the front,
heads bent down against the sagging packs and kit piled on their backs.
Sweat streaming down their faces. They looked neither to the front nor
the side. I was reminded of cows being led to the abattoir slaughter
house.'

The end of July 1944 saw the beginning of a tremendous build-up of a
million American and British troops, packed into the bridgehead. More
hospitals and field dressing stations were arriving. More nurses were
there waiting for the flood of casualties the next phase of the campaign
was sure to bring.

Ironically, amongst all this, an echo of normal life went on. Iris Bower
recalled:

In the midst of all the hectic activity, I was astonished to see
the odd civilian walking about in a field beyond our hospital
and even more surprised to see an old woman leading a cow.
She seemed to appear from nowhere. She had a milk churn
on a little cart and was bringing it towards the field kitchen.

131

After a long time on nothing but powdered or sickly sticky condensed milk, some of us took our mugs in anticipation. I saw the catering sergeant pour out the milk from the churn into a container and hand her some pig swill. To our horror we saw the woman pour the swill back into the churn. I thought if that container ever saw a cold water rinse it would be lucky. We decided not to touch the milk.

The fighting throughout the front then had descended into the dirtiest kind of infantry slugging. Advances were slow and gains measured in terms of yards rather than miles. In these conditions, infantry losses were high, particularly in rifle platoons.

It was then that nurses and doctors began to be aware of a kind of wound that aroused suspicion that it could have been self-inflicted. Consequently, on 11 July, Number 3 Casualty Clearing Station received a signal saying that henceforth all patients who might be suffering from a self-inflicted wound should be sent to Number 84 British General Hospital.[1]

The twenty-one cases already admitted to Number 3 CCS received a visit from two sergeants from the Special Investigations branch of the Military Police. Inquiries were swiftly completed. On 13 July, twelve men were tried before a Field General court martial. Four days later four more men were tried and sentenced. Coincidentally (or was it?) on that day Prime Minister Winston Churchill visited the unit where soldiers were being tried. (Files on courts martial in the Public Record Office, London, are not available to give information on sentences imposed, but seven years' imprisonment appears to have been the usual one.)

Having all suspected cases sent to one hospital, Number 84, allowed medical personnel to learn more about the nature of such wounds. With one SIW patient came a short note from his commanding officer: 'Watch this soldier particularly carefully. He is credited with more escapes than Houdini himself.'[2]

At first, such casualties had been 'accidentally' shot through the foot 'whilst I was cleaning my rifle'. Sometimes it was the hand. Soldiers in desperation became more cunning. Two mates could shoot each other from a distance to avoid powder-marks. The problem affected both British and American infantry units. When Supreme Commander General Dwight D. Eisenhower visited a hospital at Verviers he found hundreds of men with wounds suspected of being self-inflicted. Later, casualties termed as 'self-inflicted' would be coming in as 'frostbite' or 'trench-foot'. Even VD became 'self-inflicted' unless the man could prove he had been to a prophylactic clinic after sexual intercourse.

The strangest of cases arose. The war diary of Number 3 CCS records a unique case of an officer casualty being brought in unable to speak, gasping for breath and panic-stricken. It took some minutes to diagnose his condition. He had swallowed his dentures. 'We had to evacuate him by air to the UK, as we had not got a bronchoscope,' wrote the unit commander.

Despite the stringency of battle conditions during the build-up for the break-out from the Normandy *bocage* (an area criss-crossed by dense and heavy hedges growing out of high banks), there were times when the nurses' workload eased enough for them to accept an occasional invitation to a social evening at neighbouring support units. 'We worked hard and we played hard,' laughed Hilary Lewis, then with Number 101 BGH.

Nurses were very much in demand for such occasions. Not surprisingly, it was a time for whirlwind courtships and engagements to be married. In those rare off-duty moments, romance burgeoned. Serious romantic relationships developed in an atmosphere of almost indescribable tension, as forces in the bridgehead built up. With many of those soldiers about to be sent into action there was a feeling that time was running out, and if they did not snap up their girl when they had the opportunity, then someone else would.

Even in the most difficult circumstances peoples' personal lives seemed to continue, and romantic love flourished almost as if Fate approved. Nurses could not help but be influenced by the drama of the whole situation. Pamela Thompson looked back somewhat nostalgically to those memorable days when they were doing a worthwhile job on the beachhead yet where occasionally there were rare opportunities for relaxation and romance.

> When we went to a party in a neighbouring officers' mess I sometimes felt it was like being in a film, unreal and yet real enough to be swept along by the general mood of eat, drink and be merry, for tomorrow ... Well, you don't think at times like that, do you? It was too thrilling. We danced to a scratchy wind up gramophone playing Victor Sylvester's ballroom dancing tunes, and smooched around the floor in semi-darkness to the soothingly reassuring voice of Vera Lynn telling us that we would all meet again some sunny day. And when you're in the embrace of a handsome and determined young man you could find yourself saying all kinds of romantic things you might never have said back home. So no wonder there were quite a few amorous adventures. Generally innocent enough, though. Looking back, I think most nurses were very 'good'. Sex didn't seem so important then. Love was.

War aphrodisia really was at work, possibly even more powerfully on the bridgehead than at home in London's Palais de Dance. Relationships begun at a social evening soon developed into more serious liaisons. These were brave decisions for those nurses who every day saw maimed and terribly disfigured men brought back for their care. Tragically, many of those romantic engagements ended with a brief note from a loved one's commanding officer or colleague breaking the news that he had been killed in action. Yet there are today many who are celebrating fifty years of happy marriage which began in those frightful days half a century ago. They can look back and wonder how it could possibly have happened when battles raged around them and fiercer ones were about to begin.

Such was the situation at the end of July 1944 when it was clear that a crisis-point in the campaign was approaching.

Field Marshal Montgomery was still commanding all Allied troops from his headquarters near Bayeux, but his erstwhile opponent Field Marshal Erwin Rommel was fighting for his life in a Luftwaffe hospital at Bernay. A Spitfire flying at treetop height along a Normandy road had seen a staff car raising a cloud of dust as a worthwhile target and had let loose a burst of cannon-fire. Rommel's war was over.

Along the makeshift roads in Normandy, traffic moved in slow-moving queues, as the Allies moved into position for the crucial battle of the break-out. Waiting to move close behind them were the smaller mobile field hospitals, newly stocked with essential medical stores, blood, plasma, the new wonder drug penicillin, and the sulphur drugs. Once again the doctors and nurses of the Allied armies, together with a most efficient evacuation system, were in a state of peak readiness. They had already proved their worth, as Supreme Commander Eisenhower was later to say in his book *Crusade in Europe*. He maintained that Allied doctors and nurses and evacuation teams were so efficient that the percentage of wounded dying was less than one-half of the ratio in the First World War.[3]

Now, though, that efficiency was to be tested even more severely. On 7 August 1944, he sent a personal message to all units. It urged them to go forward with the determination to force the enemy to surrender and to ensure that no foot of ground once gained should be relinquished.[4] Number 50 Mobile Field Hospital drove as far forward as possible, and ambulances were directed into a field. 'It's safe enough; the engineers have cleared all the mines,' they were told. Sister Iris Bower recalls being in the sixth ambulance in the convoy. 'We had only just got into the field when there was a loud explosion. Our leading vehicle was blown up and the sergeant in it very badly wounded. Yet we still continued to occupy the field and set up our tents with the large Red Cross sheet again prominently displayed in the centre.'

The great attack went in on 24 July 1944. It was a disaster on all fronts. Allied bombers dropped their load right on to the positions of Number 120 Infantry Regiment, killing 111 American soldiers outright and severely wounding more than 500. Whilst the Americans attempted to break through the *bocage* with such high cost in casualties, the British and Canadians suffered greatly on the front by Caen. They too were subjected to successive bombing raids by their own air force. These euphemistically termed 'shortfalls' alone brought 300 wounded into British casualty clearing stations. After the Canadians suffered a further 1,500 casualties attacking Caen – a third of them killed – the British divisions were thrown into the attack. Day after day the guns thundered. Day after day ambulance jeeps and boxcars brought their bloody load back to the field ambulance units.

In the casualty clearing stations and field hospitals the feverish work never stopped. Doctors often worked on a triage system. The wounded were divided into three categories: those whose lives could be saved by immediate attention, those whose lives could be prolonged, and those whose usefulness to the war was limited. Abdominal and head cases had to be evacuated as soon as possible, fractures and gunshot wounds were treated as soon as time permitted, but little time was spent on those brought in with little chance of survival – a tremendous responsibility for medical officers under pressure. Such was the situation in the last days of July: nurses and doctors stepping over stretchers feeling pulses, ripping off clotted dressings and sniffing at the gaping wounds for the cloying stench of gangrene. In wards for those too seriously wounded to be moved, men lay braced up in strange postures, swathed in dressings. At night, in their drugged sleep, they would sometimes scream out loud as they relived their battles.

'We couldn't do much for those men in the grip of horrific nightmares. Some would suddenly sit up in bed, shout out commands and give a piercing shriek before slumping back on their pillows, still muttering. Often it took a sharp command from a senior sergeant to shake them out of their dreams. They just responded to orders,' recalled Pamela Thompson.

Men whose minds were affected by their experiences were liable to act completely irrationally. Sister Iris Bower remembers how a walking casualty went suddenly berserk one day when there was a lot of loud gunfire coming from all directions. 'He took off from the tent and ran wildly across the fields. Medical orderlies brought him back still shaking and shouting.'

The next move for Number 50 Mobile Field Hospital was to a field close to the action around Caen, still intent on their main task of arranging the air evacuation of casualties. Many of the wounded suffered from severe burns which were treated in the operating theatre. After initial cleansing, the affected area was given a thick application of Tulle Gras impregnated with an antibiotic, and then the limbs, and body if necessary, were encased in loose plaster. This was found to be the most efficient way, in the prevailing field-dressing conditions, of treating casualties with gaping and raw wounds before their subsequent journey by air.

Unfortunately, however, there could be some unexpected side-effects
with this form of treatment.

Iris Bower recalled:

> I do remember our consternation once and it's not a very
> pleasant thing to talk about but it did actually happen. Due
> to the bad weather the burns cases were lying in the tent for
> several days encased in plaster. To our horror one day, a leg,
> on examination, had maggots creeping out from under the
> plaster. We removed all the plasters and reapplied all
> dressings. To our great surprise, the healing process was very
> evident. We sent a note with this soldier to the burns unit and
> received a reply saying the soldier's leg was recovering well.
> The message ended with: 'Congratulations! The maggots did
> a good job!'

Further back down the line at base hospitals, some relief from tension
came with a concert. Nurses realized it was not easy for either the
amateur or the professional artiste to perform in a ward full of
pain-racked men with shattered limbs, men with splintered jaws and
formless faces. Men with features newly moulded with fear, despair and
uncertainty. Such pitiful sights appalled even the most experienced of
professional entertainers, and often it was up to the ward sister to advise
them on what acts might be best for their patients.

Some entertainers just could not face the task. Even a hardened
trouper like Marlene Dietrich asked to be taken off hospital duties. She
confessed she was too tender-hearted. 'It's only with difficulty I can
keep back the tears, and the wounded notice that immediately. I can't
endure the pain in the eyes of the bedridden, the despair in their
voices ...'[5]

It took a special kind of performer to cope. Comedians went down
well, comics of the calibre of Bob Hope. He learnt that what wounded
soldiers appreciated most was not sympathy but jokes that made fun of
their plight. Elizabeth Patteson, a VAD nursing in Bayeux, was at a
concert one night when gale-force winds lashed torrential rain on to
their tents. 'The crack of the evening came when the comedian shouted:
"Hey! the VAD marquee has blown down." We all laughed heartily.
When we came out we found it was true!'[6]

As casualties were brought in, others were moved out. It was the only
way to deal with such a flow. But not all the casualties in that heavily
wooded countryside reached those forward hospitals or casualty
clearing centres. Some lay bleeding from multiple wounds, hidden by
the undergrowth in which they had taken cover as their unit fought its
way forward. There were never enough stretcher-bearers to go round.
Consequently, the wounded were often left longer than they should
have been, or were missed altogether. One of these was Sergeant

Maurice Pinkney of the 7th Green Howards, boyfriend of Nurse Mary Webb. He was lying just off the road on the edge of a wood with machine-gun wounds in his shoulder, elbow and knee. And the battle had moved on.

At last the Allies' infantry and tanks crashed through the smoking ruins of cottages and apple orchards and out of the *bocage* of high hedges. They passed abandoned enemy tanks, wrecked trucks, looted civilian cars out of petrol and twisted Tiger tanks, some with a body hanging half out of the turret. The door to the east – towards Berlin – was finally open.

The cost to the Allies was terribly high. Since D-Day the Americans had suffered 124,000 casualties and the British 64,000, which together with the Canadian losses brought the total Allied casualties to 206,000 men.

It is hard for anyone to imagine then just how nurses coped with the horrifying and harrowingly awful carnage of the battles of Falaise. Eisenhower found it traumatic when he saw what had been happening on that front line. Of the battlefield at Falaise he wrote: 'It was literally possible to walk for hundreds of yards at a time, stepping on nothing but dead and decaying flesh.'[7]

Every day, nurses faced survivors. Despite all their training they could not see their patients merely as surgical cases needing dressings changed and pulses monitored. It was not easy to distance themselves. They still saw their patients as young men in pain, with sweat glistening on their white faces.

They were soon faced with another problem. In the height of that hot summer the fat bluebottle flies fed on putrefying flesh and laid their piles of white eggs on the orifices of eyes and nose which turned into writhing white 'carnations'. Swarms of flies were an ever-present menace, settling on food wherever it was being eaten. Soldiers and nurses came down with painful stomach cramps. On 19 August, Number 75 BGH received an urgent message from the Area Director of Medical Services: ALL HOSPITALS PREPARE TO ADMIT CASES OF DYSENTERY AND ENTERITIS.

'I don't know how I escaped that,' said Marie Sedman. 'As we left the mess tent after every meal we dipped our mess tins first into one large vat of boiling water, then into a second which was cleaner, and finally into a third which supposedly was absolutely clean. In fact by the time a few less scrupulous ones had passed through they were all greasy with scum floating on top.'

Another problem for the nurses came with the German wounded. Sometimes there would be an interpreter to help, but more often than not communication was a mixture of charade, sign language, and the traditional English habit of mouthing English words more distinctly and loudly. Fortunately, most of the young Germans were co-operative, only too pleased to be in a hospital and out of the fighting forever.

Occasionally there was the arrogant one from an SS battalion who was difficult, deliberately refusing medication and even spitting in the face of a nurse wanting to help.

Hilary Lewis tells an amusing story of some Germans she was looking after. 'We had a batch who complained they could not sleep at night and pestered me for a sleeping pill. At last I agreed. In fact I gave them a vitamin C tablet. The next morning they all said they had slept well and wanted a pill every night. The placebo treatment. But effective.'

Systematically, nurses dealt with thousands of badly wounded soldiers almost every day. Number 75's war diary of 31 July, for example, records 3,000 admissions in three weeks. As soon as they were fit enough to travel, they were sent back to Britain by air or sea. All this was part of a very efficient evacuation chain of hospitals.

Nurse Mary Webb in the Royal Hants County Hospital in Winchester saw thousands of them brought up the hill from Southampton docks in red buses. Each day she scanned the admissions book, apprehensively reading the familiar regimental names in Maurice Pinkney's Northumbrian division, East Yorks, Green Howards, three battalions of the Durham Light Infantry, and for reasons she could never understand, those of the Devons, Dorsets and Hampshires in the south country. When the list ended with no mention of her loved one, she would breathe a sigh of relief.

It was on 3 September, 1944, exactly five years since the war had begun, that the shock came. But not from perusing the list. A nursing colleague brought a copy of the *Northern Echo* newspaper to her. Tentatively she asked her if she had seen the paper. It was folded at a page of photographs of servicemen. Amongst the names of other local men was that of 'Sergeant Maurice William Pinkney, missing, believed killed in action'. Stunned, Mary sat down, unable to believe it had really happened. Her Maurice! The only mail she had received from him since he had gone across to Normandy was one of those printed cards, which for security reasons all soldiers had been given just prior to embarkation, where he had ticked a box against a sentence which read: 'I am in good health and will write soon.' Then nothing more. But people said the mail was not getting through, and she would probably get a batch all at once. And so she had continued to write to him every few days.

All through the next week she worked in a daze. His parents too were overwhelmed by this 'bolt from the blue'. Eight days later, on 11 September 1944, they received a short official form on which was a typed message.

From Infantry Record Office, York.
Regret to inform you that
4391686 Sergeant William Maurice Pinkney
has been posted as missing whilst serving in North West

Europe. This does not necessarily mean killed. He may be a prisoner of war or missing.

Now came the waiting. A terrible time for families and sweethearts.

> What had happened to me [recalled Maurice Pinkney fifty years later over a cup of tea in York's Theatre Royal Café], was that I caught a burst of machine-gun fire in my shoulder, elbow and knee which laid me low in the long grass at the side of a wood. We were attacking a copse and were being stonked too with those moaning minnies, the six-barrelled Nebelwerfer mortar. There was all hell around and I got left behind. Our own medics somehow missed me and I was picked up by Americans who took me through their own medical evacuation chain to a US hospital in Cherbourg. It was only when I got a bed there that I could write home and to Mary.

He looked across the table, reached out and laid his hand on hers. She smiled, but there was a hint of mistiness in her eyes and she gave a wry smile when she spoke. 'By the time I'd got the letter he was back in the thick of it again with the Green Howards. He came through all right though and we got married as soon as we could after he was demobbed. We've just celebrated our golden wedding.'

Back in Bayeux at that time, in the midst of all that awe-inspiring slaughter, romance flourished too. Patients fell in love with their nurses, and medical technicians and doctors were also captured by the charm of these young women in battledress and berets worn jauntily at an eye-catching angle.

No finer example could be found of true love flourishing from D-Day to that bloody August of 1944 than in the remarkable love story of Sister Marie Sedman and Sergeant Geoffrey Norris. (His real name was Floyd-Norris but he modestly thought it was too much of a mouthful for the army to swallow.) Marie had met Sergeant Norris very briefly at Angmering when Number 75 BGH personnel were being kitted out for the Normandy landings. She recalled:

> My room mate asked if I would go to 'The Lamb' pub with her. She was meeting a sergeant she had just got to know. 'I don't drink,' I told her. But she was insistent, so, to please her, I agreed to go. There were two soldiers sitting on a settle when we arrived and we all sat down in a line against the wall. The sergeant leant forward and asked if he could get me something to drink. 'No thank you,' I said, 'I don't drink'. But he said I could have an orange juice. So I accepted. A

little later he leant forward towards me and asked if I would like a cigarette. 'No thank you. I don't smoke.' He leant forward again and took a long look at me, smiled, and then said slowly: 'You're just the girl I'm looking for.' It was love at first sight.

Fate brought them together on HMS *Invicta* when it was rolling up and down the south coast of Britain, marking time until it could cross to Normandy. It happened that Marie Sedman was a good sailor and was not at all seasick. Neither was Geoffrey.

Our hammocks were down on the mess-deck and the air was stifling. So bad in fact that when I stood up from my hammock on the first morning I fainted and fell flat on my face. That fall changed my life for ever. When I recovered I made my way up on to the deck for fresh air.

It was very cold for June. This Sergeant I had met briefly before, came and stood by me. We leant against the rail under a very grey sky as the ship sailed slowly between wrecks, their masts sticking out, short and tall at varying angles. At that time of year you'd have expected us to be looking away at a coastline of green fields and chalk cliffs but the grey sea merged with the grey sky blotting out everything else.

We talked about our lives before the war. I had been a Girl Guide, Geoffrey had been a Boy Scout. We had so much in common. Liked the same things and disliked the same. It really must have been love at first sight for both of us. On that very first morning we had only been standing together for ten minutes when he turned to me and said, 'I want to marry you. And I'm going to.'

Once ashore with the 75th BGH, working all hours God sent, we still saw a lot of each other. Sometimes, when I was on night duty he would help me in the ward with the drip feeds. He was a skilled medical technician and with a full ward it was difficult to get through all we had to do in the time available. Patients were given three hourly injections of penicillin, then in an orange powder form mixed with distilled water, and there were also the anti-gas gangrene injections. So Geoffrey was a great help and the more we saw of each other the more our relationship flourished.

It was not easy for them though. The Army frowned upon liaisons between officers and other ranks. Such was the class structure of Britain that there could not possibly be in the British Army the cameraderie between officers and other ranks which was such a feature of the

American or 'colonial' armies. King's Regulations – the Army's Bible – forbade officers from 'consorting with other ranks on the unit or in public places, such as parks or cinemas'. It was considered 'prejudicial to good order and military discipline'. Commanding officers had junior officers on the carpet in their office to reprimand them and award extra duties as a punishment if they were seen walking out with an 'other rank'. Hospital Matrons could be just as severe and were often more so. But neither Sister Marie Sedman nor Sergeant Geoffrey Norris were going to be put off by ridiculous red tape and petty regulations.

Fortunately those very regulations were already in question in the summer of 1944, thanks to a hitherto unknown public health committee chairman for Westmorland, Eric Crewsdon. He wrote a letter to the Air Ministry asking whether the rule that an officer could not walk in a park with an airwoman was an Air Ministry order or was one depending upon the whim of the station commander. He refused to be brushed off with a vaguely worded official reply and reinforced his enquiry as the Chairman of the County's Public Health Committee, saying he was worried about the rise in figures recording veneral disease. 'One of the ways in which it is best combatted' he said, 'is by allowing young officers to make friends of decent Service girls. By forbidding such friendships, these officers are driven into the arms of diseased harlots.'[8]

A flurry of letters and memoranda passing between the Air Ministry and the War Office ultimately brought a decision from the Under-Secretary of State, who said: 'The Inspector General points out that it is desirable that we should, as far as practicable, march with the Army and Navy in matters of this kind. The War Office attitude is apparently to let sleeping dogs lie. The Admiralty apparently do not keep a dog at all. My own feeling is that we should be well advised to follow the War Office example.'[9]

Discreetly, Marie and Geoffrey met as often as possible. On 5 August – two months after their first meeting – they announced their engagement. No date was set for the wedding. Then, a rumour which spread round the hospital forced them to make a decision. Geoffrey heard that drafts of nurses were being prepared for postings to the Far East. He immediately went to the office for the 'Application to Get Married' army form. Straight away he took the form to Marie's ward, slapped it on the table and said, 'Here, sign this before anyone has time to put your name on one of those drafts. It'll be too late then.' It was not a very romantic proposal, but Marie gladly signed without worrying about what her commanding officer might say.

When, however, she asked her hospital matron for time off to get married, the immediate response was not encouraging. 'You, Sister! You, of all people!' And she marched off to see the commanding officer. His reply settled the matter once and for all: 'Well, if they want to get married, let them.'

On 7 December 1944 they had an unusual and memorable wedding in

Bayeux. It was the third on record as being held under special wartime regulations for weddings 'conducted by an appointed officer whilst on active service overseas'. They made their vows in the Matron's office.

The hospital colonel stood in for her father to give her away. Marie recalled:

> Nobody had a camera so one of the technicians made one from cardboard and used X-ray film. Someone placed a plank on trolley wheels and we sat on it for the photograph. It came out very well considering the makeshift cardboard camera. Two sappers from the Royal Engineers made a wedding ring from perspex and welded a gold band on to the outside.
>
> We had a party afterwards in the Sergeant's Mess and then slipped quietly away. We spent our honeymoon in the Laboratory that night. There was nowhere else to go.

That sleeping dog of the Army, however, would not remain lying down. It would not do for a married couple to work in the same hospital when they were of commissioned and non-commissioned ranks. Shortly after their wedding the unit moved to Brussels, and Marie was posted to the other side of the city to join Number 8 BGH. That did not cause any heartache because they were only a tram ride away from each other. Whenever they had a spare half day they would take a tram, passing through streets that had a surprising number of florists' shops ablaze with roses and forced flowers of all varieties, which were grown to cater for German occupation troops who, apparently, loved expensive flowers so much that the shops did a tremendous business. The tram took them out to Waterloo, the battlefield where so many soldiers had died in the past, and there they would walk through the countryside. It was all too wonderful a love story to be true, it seemed. In fact, it was the beginning of fifty gloriously happy years of married life together.

12   Finale in Italy

> It will not be a walk-over; a mortally
> wounded beast can still be very dangerous.
> You must be prepared for a hard and bitter
> fight.
>> Special Order of the Day,
>> General Alexander, April 1945[1]

Almost forgotten now – during the months following October 1944 –
were the men and women on the Italian front line. There, as winter
fastened its iron grip on the high peaks of the Gothic Line, Eighth and
Fifth Army soldiers were suffering the rigours of the worst winter of the
war. In slit trenches, seven thousand feet up, gales of snow and sleet
made life almost unbearable. It was so cold that even the fast-flowing
mountain streams froze over. Men shivered in their shallow foxholes
with only a wet blanket for cover. Small wonder so many came down
with pneumonia and filled the beds of hospitals, along with the
thousands of American and British casualties incurred in the desperate,
never-ending battles of attrition for that Gothic Line.

To look after such casualties, Number 66 General Hospital had
moved up to Ancona. 'We learnt later that we should have been going
to Bologna,' said Margaret Jennings, then in Number 66 GH, 'but that
city had yet to be taken, so we sailed up from Bari to Ancona on the
hospital ship *Leinster* and then moved up to Rimini to be as close to the
front line as possible.'

> Towards the end of March 1945, there came the disquieting
> order, to clear the wards. We were left with rows and rows of
> empty beds ominously waiting to be filled with the mangled
> remains of yet another battle. The soldiers must have
> wondered if it was to be their last battle and for many of
> them it was. I shuddered for them.

But was there a glimmer of hope for them all? On 30 March,
appropriately on Good Friday, when nurses were attending mass in the
grandiose Byzantine churches of Rimini and Florence, a rumour went
round that the war in Italy would be ending quickly and postings were
coming through for the Far East.

Indeed, the rumours were well founded. Lady Louis Mountbatten (later Countess Mountbatten of Burma), who had visited over 170 hospitals in the Far East, was pressing for more nurses to be sent to the 'forgotten army' there.[2] And news of that possibility for nurses was automatically linked to other rumours about the Italian campaign ending very soon.

Indeed, months before, in December 1944, Germany had taken steps towards a negotiated peace. Baron Konstantin von Neurath, German consul in Lugano, had made contact with Allen Dulles of the US Office of Strategic Services. General Albrecht Kesselring, commanding all German troops on the southern front, had been brought into the negotiations in January 1945. Then too SS General Karl Wolff, who commanded the SS and the police in Mussolini's Salo Republic, had come to the conclusion – as had his superior Heinrich Himmler – that for Germany the war was lost. And so secret approaches were made.[3]

Towards the end of March 1945, German proposals for peace in Italy, backed by Supreme German Commander General Kesselring and his successor in Italy, General Heinrich Vietinghoff, were indeed presented to Allied Force Headquarters in Caserta, and for those who were privy to information it looked as if the surrender of all German troops in Italy would be secured in no time.[4]

But time, unfortunately for the troops and nurses, was running out. Some inexorable force was driving generals to commit their troops to battles in Italy, which could have been won more easily by simply staying where they were. For the war then was virtually over. On 8 March the Russians had stormed into Vienna, General George Patton's Seventh Army had breached the Rhine and were racing southwards to the Austrian Alps, British troops in the north of Germany were heading towards a meeting with the Russians who were near Berlin. German divisions were crumbling daily.

Arguably, there was no need for those weary troops in Italy to be thrown into assaults against the almost impregnable German defensive positions of the Gothic Line stretching for 200 miles across the peninsula from La Spezia on the Ligurian Sea to Pesaro on the Adriatic Sea. Along this line the Germans had dynamited every village into shapeless brick rubble and felled all the trees to give the infantry and gunners a clear field of fire. In front of the flattened villages they dug deep tank-trap canals. In front of these they laid down their barbed wire and never-ending fields of mines – the simplest and deadliest weapons in Italy. In the range of mountains were 500 pieces of artillery built into bunkers of concrete and steel, and from dominating positions on mountain crests were over 2,500 interlocking machine-gun emplacements.

On the eastern flank, the Eighth Army, astride the via Emilia, was faced by Germans dug in behind a maze of fortified river and canal lines stretching right up to the River Po itself. Manning these positions were Germans of the elite parachute divisions.

In the autumn attempts to break through the Gothic Line, the Fifth Army had lost over 17,000 men and the Eighth Army 14,000.

In view of the peace negotiations and the strength of the German defences nurses might then have wondered if it was really necessary to empty their wards in March 1945 to take yet another load of casualties. Was it really necessary for thousands of young men who already expended most of their stock of courage to have to make the supreme sacrifice at that stage of the war? Today, many of them speculate upon what it was that drove commanders to commit their troops to such costly battles.

What did the commanders say?

Alexander, Clark, Truscott and McCreery were determined to finish their own campaigns on a completely victorious note. General Mark Clark, commanding the 15th Army Group, was perhaps the most adamant about launching a final offensive to destroy the German army in Italy. Otherwise, he argued, the whole campaign made little sense. In any case, a decisive victory in Italy would add so much to his laurels. He wanted the final glory of delivering the mortal blow to a tottering enemy. He feared, as he wrote to his wife, 'that the war might fold up with me sitting on my royal behind.' It still irked him that the glory of being the first general to capture Rome from the south had been eclipsed within twenty-four hours by the D-Day landings in Normandy.

As for 'Roaring Dick', as General Sir Richard McCreery was known to Eighth Army soldiers, he was determined that his magnificent army should end its long march from the dusty railway station at El Alamein on an equally glorious note.

And so the Allied commanders who, despite the German proposals for peace, had already made their plans for the final offensive against the impregnable defences of the Gothic Line, went ahead. They were not going to be deprived of their glory or their bloodbath. Clark himself described how bad that final offensive was in a letter to his mother: 'It is just as bloody, as desperate as any in Europe.'[5]

The nurses in those Italian hospitals and casualty clearing stations would vouch for that.

Sister Diana Sugden (now O'Brien), then at Number 66 BGH, has never forgotten the day the offensive was launched. 'Suddenly it all started. A dreadful noise began just after mid-day when hundreds of heavy Allied bombers came over, dropping bombs on German positions. Then we could hear the roar of the guns firing. I'd never heard such a barrage. A patient told me later there were a thousand guns – far more than at El Alamein.'

There were in fact 1,500 guns of all types used in support of the attack. Infantry waiting to go into the attack said the air seemed solid with the roar and bangs of battle. As soon as that kind of noise stopped there came another even more frightening one for the nurses and patients of Number 66 BGH – low-flying fighter-bombers skimming over the roof-tops. Then the programme seemed to start all over again with the same variety of noises well into the evening.

Ambulances started rolling into Number 66 BGH surprisingly early, one after the other. The first of the casualties were from the unlucky Polish corps. They had been forming up for the attack when Allied bombers missed their target and dropped their load right in the midst of the Polish ranks.

'Stretchers were lined up in rows on the floor of the reception hall – Poles, British, Sikhs, Italians, Germans, Canadians, Australians, South Africans,' recalled Sister Margaret Jenkins. 'It was grim. Bedlam reigned as voices in all tongues called out as best they could in spite of their injuries.' In the casualty clearing stations doctors and nurses worked amidst the unearthly cries of the wounded and dying too, going through the mechanical motions of uncovering wounds, applying dressings and re-bandaging. Hundreds passed through their hands. Most came on stretchers; others were slung like sacks on the backs of friends. Some, who started as 'walking wounded', crawled the last few yards before collapsing. There seemed to be no end to all the pain and suffering.

There was to be an end to it all, though, for thirteen days from the start of that last offensive German soldiers fought with fanaticism to observe Hitler's decree that every soldier should hold his ground and fight to the last man.

In the first five days of that last offensive, the Eighth Army broke through all the river defences that stood between them and the River Po, but at a heavy cost in casualties and with the prevalence of one particular type of wound. Diana Sugden O'Brien said:

> I don't know if it was because of the marshland and water in which wounded soldiers lay that caused it, but we had such a lot of cases of gas gangrene wounds in the hospital then. So many limbs had to be amputated that patients feared being taken into the operating theatre.
>
> The hospital, which was housed in a big school, was filled beyond capacity. Not a bed free. Casualties lay on their stretchers wherever they could be placed – in corridors and hallways. We had to go round them on our hands and knees. Poor men.

During the last few days of April 1945 and for the first time in the whole Italian campaign, every unit of every nationality – and there were twenty-three of them on the Allied side – raced forward to a fantastic finale. But even in this desperate retreat the German Army was still to prove a formidable opponent, inflicting heavy casualties so that medical services had to keep up with the troops. Sister Flora Whyte Urquhart remembers how their Number 59 General Hospital had to move rapidly northwards in the wake of the forward units. 'We had often been called the Fighting Fifty-Ninth because we were so often near or in the front line but we fairly flew across that Italian plain beyond Ravenna during that final battle. And very soon we had three operating theatres going all the time. Troops were amazed to see women so close to the front line.'

Night duty for some Sisters was a veritable nightmare – and Diana Sugden O'Brien still wakes up with those nightmares.

I remember I had two wards to look after with 84 patients and only two orderlies. We had to give the penicillin injections every three hours. Mainly it was through a tube in the plaster of Paris cast. There were also the plasma drips to look after. We gave them plasma then and not blood. No sooner had I finished one round than it would be time to start the next. As morning drew near I began to try and write the reports for the night superintendent and matron. Sometimes it just wasn't possible to get the report done for looking after the patients. But the night superintendent was very understanding. My recurring nightmare even now is not so much of the wounded but of trying to get that Night Sister's report finished!

The faces of men I tended at night, dying men, still come into my mind though. And I cry. As I cried then. One young lad had been caught in the abdomen by a burst of Spandau machine-gun fire. We had packed all the many holes with gauze. On my rounds I would always take a close look at him. Towards dawn as I came to him I saw that he was pulling out yards of bloody gauze from his wounds. He was half conscious and in a delirious mental state. I took his hands and tied them down to the bed. Then I repacked the gauze and stood watching him for a few minutes before I had to get back to the penicillin round. When I came back to him later, I found him lying with his eyes wide open. He was dead. And I cried because he had died alone. And I wished I could have been with him.

On 22 April the Allies reached and crossed the River Po. Six days later, Mussolini was captured and shot with his mistress Clara Petacci by Partisans or British or American Secret Service agents, depending upon whichever of the many stories surrounding their mysterious deaths one wishes to believe.[6]

The following day, the German army in Italy capitulated completely. Nearly a million men surrendered, unconditionally. Churchill announced the triumphant conclusion of the Italian campaign to a packed House of Commons in London on 2 May 1945 and praised all those divisions in Italy as 'gallant an army as ever marched' and the surrender as 'one of the most famous episodes of the Second World War'.

But that final assault on the Gothic Line and the advance northwards to the river Po was one of the most costly battles, in terms of casualties, of the whole bloody campaign in Italy. In fourteen days, between 9 April and 2 May, the Allies lost 16,747 men.

The news of the German surrender reached the hospitals and fighting formations in Italy on the wireless. Nurses in Number 66 General Hospital in Rimini gathered round and listened to the cheers coming from jubilant crowds in Piccadilly and outside Buckingham Palace.

Those cheers seemed to come from a different world.

In the real world of war of that General Hospital, Sister Margaret Jennings remembered how nurses there received the news of victory.

> Nobody felt like dancing in the streets. Grim reality was all about us. I could have cried at being surrounded by so much agony and loneliness. I was on the maxillo-facial ward where young men lay with their jaws wired together, to immobilise the bones and allow them to heal. Mealtimes involved giving patients liquidised food they could suck through straws. I remember one boy calling me back. I turned, wondering what was the matter. He looked at me and with a stifled chuckle he forced out a line from one of Bing Crosby's songs through his clenched teeth: 'Or would you rather be a fish?' I was amazed that he could still see humour in the situation. It was just the sort of thing that helped us to press on through that recurring nightmare of work. To see the bravery of those boys carried in with smashed-up, bleeding faces, to see them calling out in their nightmares, reliving their battles and struggling out of bed dragging their blood transfusions with them, brought tears to my eyes. No, we did not feel like celebrating.

Today there is little in Italy for the tourist to see of the efforts made by those young men of the Fifth and Eighth armies. The beaches they stormed are covered with promenades and multi-storey hotels. There are no real monuments to mark the blood shed by battle-weary young men of both sides who still refused to give in. Except for the cemeteries which stretch right across the length and breadth of Italy. Cemeteries where often the young men of Allied and German armies lie side by side, and the casual visitor is left wondering why so many had to die.

It was no wonder that when that grim campaign, in which each river line and mountain ridge had to be captured at appalling cost, ended, no one felt like celebrating victory.

They did not feel like celebrating in Germany either. It had been a long and painful haul from the time the armies broke out of the Normandy bridgehead to the bitter end at Belsen.

13 To the Bitter End in Europe

> And it is awful to die ... when you are
> young and have fought a long time and
> when you remember with all your heart
> your home and whom you love, and when
> you know the war is won anyhow.
> Martha Gellhorn, war correspondent[1]

September was a happier time for nurses and for the weary Allied soldiers in their drive from France into Belgium, Luxembourg and finally into southern Holland. Those battles in Normandy had ended in a crushing and decisive Allied victory, and it seemed as if the German power of offering effective resistance had gone.

It was for the Allies a time of hope, as they moved forward towards the German frontier, a time when citizens and villagers rushed into streets to cheer and shower them with flowers, food and wine. Nurses, however, were still in the midst of dealing with the legacy of the horrific battles of July and August.

'You never knew what to expect when you were removing wound dressings. I remember a nineteen-year-old soldier who was sitting upright on the bed. When I took off his dressing he had no flesh at all covering his posterior rib cage – his lungs were exposed. He never murmured as I re-covered his chest with sterile padding,' said Monica Dixon (now Carhart-Harris).

Despite all the horrors of war, it was generally, for the Allies, a time of euphoria. In Britain, the lights were going on again. Black-out restrictions were relaxed and modified street-lighting reintroduced. On the continent, American troops of Number 28 Infantry Division liberated Paris, and on that day nurse Myra Roberts, of the RAF's air evacuation service, flew into Le Bourget with part of General de Gaulle's entourage as passengers. She recalled: 'We had to circle round for ages whilst the engineers on the airfield repaired holes in the runway so that we could land. But we had to leave the celebrating to the Top Brass whilst we flew back for more essential work. We still had hundreds of casualties to evacuate to the UK.'

There was time too for nurses to relax. Monica Carhart-Harris recalls 'Early in September, when 121st General Hospital moved forward to Arques-la-Bataille, the villagers were delighted to see us. We had umpteen invitations to dinner on meagre rations, and dances were arranged for us. A French girl would bring along her whole family to act as chaperone. One evening, an interesting matriarch of the village pinned a tricouleur on to my tunic. I was dancing with a British Army captain carrying on a normal conversation when he stupidly asked, "Are you French?" and I stupidly answered "Oui". He immediately broke into pidgin English, then was as mad as a hatter at my ruse and I saw him no more.'

Meanwhile, British divisions, anxious for the kudos of capturing a capital city after the American troops had entered Paris, fought their way into Brussels, five years to the day after Britain declared war on Germany. Amidst the excitement and celebrations at being liberated, the Brussels radio stations announced that Germany had surrendered. The news immediately spread throughout Europe, and in Britain the *Daily Herald* reported how 'men and women left their homes and came into town to join the celebrations. There were taxis full of singing soldiers.'2

It was not surrender at all but the beginning of yet another phase of horror, as the first of 1,200 flying bombs was launched upon London, the southern counties of Britain and later upon Antwerp. Nurses, once more, were in the thick of it all.

In one church in southern England the morning service had just begun, attended by nurses from the nearby hospitals at Carshalton. At the lectern a member of the congregation was about to read the first Lesson. Suddenly, with a shattering roar, a robot flying-bomb plane hurtled through the roof, and in a flash the building crumpled into a mass of rubble. Only one wall remained, that where the altar stood undamaged, with the words of the text 'Glory be to God' gleaming through the rising dust upon a scene of death and destruction. Many of the 150 worshippers in the church lay dead, while others lay crushed and bleeding, pinned to the ground beneath piles of masonry. Shocked and bespattered with debris and blood, nurses in the congregation helped the rescue services to recover the injured.

Those 'flying bombs' or 'doodle-bugs', as the public came to call them, were nothing compared with the V2 rocket bomb. With a warhead of 2,000 pounds of high explosives, it travelled at 3,000 miles per hour, and had a range of 200 miles. The V2s hurtled down upon London and the southern counties day after day. Hospitals were often hit, St Hellier's twice in one week.

Hitler hoped that the V2 would demoralize the civil population enough to make them call for peace and so stave off the defeat which faced him in the field. A vain hope.

*   *   *

Meanwhile, racing on beyond Brussels, British armoured units smashed across the Dutch frontier and reached the town of Breda, 12 miles inside the border north-east of Antwerp. Now it was time for the Number 75 British General Hospital and others to move from their muddy tents of Normandy to more civilized quarters in Brussels. There they looked after the wounded from the Grenadiers and Welsh Guards who had stormed down different routes in a neck-and-neck race into the city. Nurses revelled in the luxury of their new living-quarters. They went on shopping sprees, had their hair cut, shampooed and permed in the fashionable salons of Brussels, and sent their smart scarlet-and-grey uniforms to be cleaned and pressed.

It was both a hopeful and yet daunting time for other hospital units driving forward through those summer battlefields still reeking of death. 'You couldn't get away from it. The dead still lay in the fields, faces blue-black, bodies swollen and the sickly sweet smell that reminded me of my mother's kitchen when she was pickling green tomatoes with lots of vinegar, sugar and herbs. Cows lay on their backs in grotesque positions with four legs pointing to the sky, their eyes wide, with flies feasting on every hole of the head and body. German horses, still in harness, lay swollen to an incredible size. The air all around stank to high heaven and the smell clung to our clothes like the smell of stale tobacco does after a night in a crowded pub,' recalled Pamela Thompson.

The local farmers suffered terribly and to a degree that made many of them completely apathetic. Sister Iris Ogilvie was astonished to find three old ladies at Camilly who had stayed in their little stone house all the time the shells dropped around them and infantry fought in their fields. 'I shall always remember them. We never saw them dressed in anything other than black from head to toe which seemed to accentuate their very white faces. Mollie, Mary, Robbie and I visited them whenever we could. Fortunately Robbie had a very good command of French and we heard grim tales of atrocities before the arrival of our troops in the area. They kept repeating tales of how French collaborators, whom they hated, had betrayed resistance fighters to the Gestapo. These three dear old ladies showered us with kindness and showed their gratitude for being liberated.'

It was whilst the Number 50 Mobile Field Hospital was at Camilly that an amazing and frightening incident occurred. A doctor in his blood-spotted white coat ran out of his tent and pointed upwards, shouting instructions which sounded like, 'Get them down! On the floor!' Roaring overhead and obviously out of control was a pilotless Liberator bomber. The crew had baled out, and the aircraft now circled crazily above the tents of the hospital. Iris Ogilvie rushed out from her tent to see a cook, still with a pan in his hand, running across the field.

I knew something terrible was about to happen and rushed back into the ward to find that some of the more mobile

patients had already put one who was seriously ill on the
floor, drips and all. I stayed with him and he was very much
alert, listening to the roaring of the bomber's engines. It
circled, flopping and sliding sideways, above the camp,
slowly losing height for about fifteen minutes which seemed
an eternity. Suddenly it dipped its nose and hurtled
earthwards and burst into an inferno of flames as it hit the
ground just four hundred yards from our tents.

Shortly after this incident, towards the end of August the
Field Hospital moved forward from Camilly passing batches
of German prisoners under guard, young lads, trudging in a
slovenly fashion. It was difficult to reconcile these men with
those once proud faces of the German army seen in news reel
films. It was the face of an army in defeat.

However, by the time the American and British troops reached the
River Scheldt, the steam was going out of their great drive to the
German frontier. Slowly but surely the Allied advance ground to a halt
with the capture of Antwerp.

Now, as the Allied armies stood on the threshold of Germany,
Churchill warned that the war was not yet won and that 'supreme
efforts' still had to be made. 'This is no moment to slacken,' he said. It
was indeed a time for the overstretched Allied armies and the hospitals
to consolidate their positions and prepare for the next phase – the
assault on the Rhine.

As part of this preparation, the RAF's Air Evacuation Service set up
their landing-strip in a field on the outskirts of Antwerp. All too soon,
whilst other troops were busy 'getting their feet under the tables' of
hospitable Dutch families, the air ambulances were in action. And some
of their first casualties came from their own unit. Myra Roberts recalled
what happened:

Our landing strip was in a quiet piece of land with grass short
enough for the lads to use part of it as a football pitch. They
used to go out there with a football for a kick at about
lunchtime, and in the evenings have a scratch game with
Dutch lads who lived nearby. We never gave a thought to
impending danger. But suddenly we were right in the midst
of it all. Hitler had launched his secret weapon upon the
citizens of Antwerp determined to make the port unusable for
the support of Allied troops.

I'll never forget the scene that sunny September dinner
time. There was a happy sound of a ball being booted about
and everyone was having a good time, calling for a pass,
cheering the scorer of a goal as if it were the FA Cup Final
and then there was a terrifically loud bang and there was

nothing there, just a big crater and what might have been bits of bodies or bundles of old rags lying about. On the fringes of the field, men were lying bleeding. A V2 bomb had landed right in the middle of the pitch. We soon realized those V2s came in faster than sound so you could not hear them coming and there was no time to take cover.

It was the beginning of a crippling attack by V1 and V2 rocket bombs launched by the Germans in the autumn of 1944. The great port of Antwerp was obviously going to be valuable to the Allies – being so far forward – and would make supply lines so much shorter. Naturally the Germans were keen to obliterate the whole port area and prevent its use. Rocket bombs showered down, day after day. Compared with the rocket-bomb attacks on London, those on Antwerp were much more horrific because of their concentration. A total of 5,960 bombs out of the 8,696 launched against the city fell within eight miles of the city centre; more than 4,000 people were killed, 3,470 civilian and 682 of the Forces. Nurses worked round the clock, snatching catnaps whenever they could.

The Air Evacuation Service flew out casualties in a regular shuttle. 'We tried to get in and out as fast as we could in between raids. The trouble was there was no warning of when the bombs would be falling. It was a great strain on everybody's nerves. Now when I look back upon those days I just say to myself "How on earth did we manage?" I still can hardly believe we did keep going,' recalled Myra.

Then, in the midst of all the V2 casualties, came those from another operation. On the momentous Sunday morning of 17 September, the newly promoted Field Marshal Bernard Law Montgomery launched the ill-fated 'Operation Market Garden', planned to be a 'lightning stroke' which would finish off the Germans completely.

From airfields all over Britain's eastern counties the most formidable airborne force of parachutists and glider troops since D-Day took off. The British First Airborne Division and the US 82nd Airborne were flying south to link up with their comrades of US 101st Airborne. From then on they flew in three awesome columns, ten miles broad at times and at least a hundred miles long, towards Arnhem. They were to land behind the German lines and capture key bridges across the rivers Waal, Maas and Rhine to allow the advancing Allied armies to break through the right flank of Germany's whole defence of the west. To cope with the heavy casualties expected, Army casualty clearing stations were moved as far forward as possible. So too was Number 50 RAF Mobile Field Hospital. Hurriedly, air landing-strips were laid ready for Dakotas of the Air Evacuation Service to use.

As soon as those aircraft crossed the orange smoke flares of the Allied front line, intense anti-aircraft fire battered the tight formation. Planes streamed to the ground in flames, scattering white, blossoming parachutes. It was the beginning of a nine-day battle that cost the Allies nearly twice as many casualties as D-Day.

Casualty clearing stations and mobile field hospitals were overwhelmed and sometimes, in the resulting chaos, found themselves right in the front line itself. Iris Ogilvie Bower remembers how she went forward by jeep with one of her medical officers to reconnoitre a new location; they noticed on the way back a strange lack of Allied soldiers and vehicles on the road. She recalled: 'Suddenly the driver saw something and put his foot hard down on the accelerator. He drove at a terrific speed for miles until we reached our unit and got an incredible welcome. For a few moments we could not understand why everyone was so demonstrative. They told us the Germans had retaken that area and cut the road along which we had driven. We'd had a very lucky escape.'

Things went wrong with 'Operation Market Garden' right from the beginning. The narrow road leading towards the bridges was clogged with traffic moving at a British Bank Holiday pace. When traffic thinned out somewhat, Number 3 CCS found themselves travelling down a road alongside which infantrymen lay in ditches, their rifles aimed towards the fields on either side.

No sooner had the nurses set up their casualty reception area, housed in a small school, than shells landed in their midst and convoys of wounded came in.

Whilst casualty clearing stations waited to advance along the narrow forty yard corridor, the infantry fought to get through to Arnhem where the beleaguered parachutists were now in a desperate situation. The bombardment was so intense and unremitting that many men broke down altogether. By the time they reached medical care, nurses passed them quickly down the line to base hospitals in Belgium. Little could be done for their mental condition as long as they were in range of the guns.

After nine days of the most bitter fighting, it was clear that the Arnhem adventure was over. There was little to do but to pull back as many men as possible and consolidate. In Arnhem itself, now securely in German hands, physician Major Guy Rigby-Jones and a handful of medical orderlies scoured the houses in the area of the Hotel Tafelberg, serving as a makeshift hospital, to bring in wounded men, swathed in bloody, dirty bandages. Often they had to carry them by hand before loading them into German trucks, ambulances and jeeps. At last, as many accounted for as possible, they drove away eastwards into captivity.

All the while the fighting was going on, and despite all the shelling of their area, nurses in the casualty clearing stations worked on without having any idea of how the battle was going. In number 50 Mobile Field Hospital, the four nursing sisters received the flood of wounded and passed them on to the air evacuation teams at the landing-strip. 'For us,' recalled Myra Roberts, 'it was particularly moving, for we had trained with those young lads of the Airborne Division, we had danced with them, joked with them and knew so many of them and their badges. Now they were pathetic blood-stained bundles on stretchers packed closely together in the fuselage of our Dakota.'

Statistics told a more complete story of 'Operation Market Garden'. The First Airborne Division had been sacrificed and slaughtered. Of the original 10,000-man force, a little more than 2,000 of them came back from across the Rhine, exhausted, hungry and bearded, beaten in body but not in spirit, though many were in a state of shell-shock. After nine days the division had 1,200 dead and counted 6,642 missing. The combined losses of the nine days' operation in killed, wounded and missing amounted to 17,000 men.

Summing up that heavy cost, Dr John C. Warren (author of *Airborne Operations in World War Two*) was to write: 'In return for so much courage and sacrifice, the Allies had won a 50-mile salient – leading nowhere. The verdict of history seems to be that it was a defeat that prolonged the war.'[3]

Many a nurse who tended to the wounded in those fateful days so long ago must no doubt have shaken her head in dismay when reading what Montgomery wrote in his memoirs about that disastrous operation: 'I remain an unrepentant advocate of Market Garden.'

The autumn of 1944 became increasingly dreary. Hospitals were filled with casualties from attacks made by Number 21 Army Group from the Nijmegen bridgehead, whilst further south, infantry battalions were slugging it out, making gains measured in terms of yards rather than miles.

The nurses of Number 3 Mobile Casualty Clearing Station commanded by Lieutenant-Colonel J.J. Myles were so close to the front line they often had to take cover from mortar attacks as well as from long periods of shelling. Often the unit war diary was brief. The entry for 10 October simply read: 'Heavy shelling all day. Very uncomfortable'. A case of familiarity breeding contempt! On another day Lieutenant-Colonel Myles wrote: 'All the windows of the acute surgical ward were blown out by a salvo from our own guns.'[4]

Infantry losses were high. And, as nurses were soon to discover, many of the casualties were not due to enemy action alone.

Hospital beds were being filled by infantrymen who had been exposed to the terrible weather for too long; cases of frostbite, trench foot, and respiratory diseases were so numerous that hospitals were urged to get men back to their depleted units as soon as possible. Returning these men to the front after only a short spell in hospital created another problem – that of morale. Once again, nurses were having to build up patients mentally as well as physically.

As the coldest winter for thirty years wore on, it was clear to everyone that there would be no short cut to victory. With their backs to their own frontier, the reinforced and re-equipped German armies were resisting stubbornly.

Meanwhile, in hospitals all over north-west Europe, nurses – true to tradition – were planning to bring a little joy to the faces of children in their area. Christmas was coming. Iris Bower recalled:

> On December 6th, St Nicholas's Day, we gave a wonderful party for Dutch children. Planning and preparation had taken weeks. Airmen in the hospital had saved up all their chocolate ration for the children who had never tasted it. We made up a small sack of presents for each of the two hundred children invited from around the hospital at Eindhoven. They filed forward, a row at a time, to receive them from a fatherly figure who shook each little hand. When all of them had received their gifts, the lights were switched off and a huge Mickey Mouse was flashed on to the screen. The children shrieked with joy throughout the film. And when it came to an end they all went into the dining room for a feast. Those little ones left the building with such happiness on their faces and left us with even more happiness in our hearts.

Ten days later it was a very different story. At dawn on 16 December, Hitler unexpectedly launched two giant Panzer armies, comprising over half a million men, at the weakest point of the Allied line in the Ardennes, now thick with winter snow. Catching the Allied High Command completely by surprise, they very quickly drove deep into Allied lines, creating havoc. For days the crucial battle raged back and forth in blinding, blanketing snow. Casualties were brought into hospitals in ambulances driven by men wearing no gloves to get a better grip on the steering-wheels which slipped this way and that as vehicles skidded over frozen roads. Windscreens became solid sheets of ice. In the end, the army had to go back to using horses and mules to bring the wounded from the battlefield.

Ironically, the most popular song in the hospitals that year was Bing Crosby's 'White Christmas', but for most men in those wards it was in fact the blackest. Thousands of them were flooding into overcrowded wards, wounded and exhausted, suffering from swollen, gangrenous feet, frostbite, pneumonia and combat fatigue.

To the north, New Year's Day brought the bombardment to the Number 50 Mobile Field Hospital at Eindhoven, as Iris Bower well remembers:

> Without warning the deafening noise of bombs exploding reached us. I was in the middle of attending to a patient and I think he instinctively knew, like I did, how close to us the bombs were falling. The main target was the nearby airfield

used by the Dakotas of the Air Evacuation Service. Quickly the casualties arrived; eighty-two within an hour, all in a serious and dangerous state. Everyone gave a hand.

Nurses, physicians and surgeons hurried from stretcher to stretcher, taking some for immediate surgery, giving blood transfusions, intravenous infusions and morphia. One of my vivid memories is of seeing aircraftsmen continuously mopping up blood from the floor. It was a gruesome task and a gruelling New Year's Day for us all.

The unexpected happened the next morning. Mollie and I were told that our names were in the New Year's Honours List. We had been nominated members of the British Empire, Military Division. We both appreciated the honour but felt we had been privileged to have served with the 50th MFH.

By the time the Battle of Ardennes finished, the hospital beds were fully occupied again. Altogether the Allies lost 77,000 men, of whom 8,000 were killed, 48,000 wounded and 21,000 captured or missing.

It was a very sad time for us to be watching those young men coming in so badly injured when we had thought the war was coming to an end [recalled Monica Carhart-Harris, then with Number 121 British General Hospital]. The less severely injured soldiers were laid on a bed to have their dressings checked before quick evacuation to England. Sadly we learnt of more than one hospital ship being sunk on the way home with all lost.

While we were at Arques-la-Bataille, we had a convoy of German prisoner of war patients brought from a hospital where medical supplies were exhausted. Men had been held down for amputations – a quicker way employed by that hospital for men to recover from horrendously mangled limbs. Many had plaster of Paris casts which reeked like manure heaps.

Night duty for me was harrowing. Caring for terribly wounded soldiers in their last hours was awful. We could only give comfort to a man black as charcoal with no skin left when extricated from his blazing tank.

The leading divisions were now pushing hard eastwards against a German army that was now conscripting all boys of sixteen years and over. On the morning of 7 March, American troops reached the Rhine at Remagen and, to their utter amazement, found the railway bridge spanning the river intact! The leading platoon raced across the bridge and disconnected the demolition charges. Just over a fortnight later British and Canadian forces crossed the Rhine at Rees and Wesel.

Now, British general hospitals, mobile field hospitals and casualty clearing stations went forward rapidly, as more and more Rhine crossings were made – but at a cost of 35% casualties. There was still a tremendous job for the medical teams. And here one must give high praise to all the RAMC and regimental medical orderlies too. Men like Corporal F.G. Topham, for example, who saw two of his fellow medics killed during the battle for Wesel whilst trying to get to a wounded man lying in open ground. Topham ran forward crouching and a bullet smashed into his jaw, but he kept going and carried his badly wounded comrade back to safety through heavy fire. His own wound was treated, and then he begged to go back to the front, where he once more went forward over open ground under fire, to help three men who had been badly wounded in a carrier. For his gallantry 'of the highest order' Corporal Topham was awarded the Victoria Cross. And there were many more like Topham; many who did not survive to receive an award.

One battle followed another. It was almost as if those in command could not face calling it a day. Germany's position was hopeless, and surrender to the Allies could have prevented the loss of thousands on the field of battle and avoided further destruction of German cities and industries. On 31 March 1945, Supreme Commander Eisenhower issued a proclamation to the German troops and people, urging them to surrender and for the people to begin planting crops. His purpose, he said, 'was to bring the whole bloody business to an end.'[5]

But Hitler and his sycophantic generals, with nothing to lose personally, fought on, possibly in the desperate hope that the Allies would fall out amongst themselves and consequently fail to complete the conquest of Germany. Whatever the reason, the fighting went on, and the casualties flowed into the wards.

The resilience of the human spirit showed itself, however, in the most trying of times. Monica Carhart-Harris was intensely aware of the stark contrasts of her experience:

> When I look back now I find it incongruous that though we were so busy, often within the sound of gunfire, we could still accept invitations to dances at neighbouring officers' messes. In fact it was whilst I was at the Life Guards mess in Brunswick that I heard that one of their members was in our hospital. When I made enquiries the following day I found he was actually in one of my wards. I went to talk to him, we immediately liked each other, and very soon we were married.

The next big move for Number 121 BGH was a two-day journey up to Celle. 'It took us two days to cover 150 miles through devastated countryside but when we reached Celle itself we were surprised to find it had not been bombed as heavily as other towns. We took over a commodious college-type building with large classrooms which lent themselves to conversion into wards with 600 beds in all.'

There, local German women worked in the hospital, and one day Sister Michelle Carey was attending a patient close to where these women cleaners were talking. Michelle, whose home was in Guernsey, spoke German fluently. She heard the arrogant German women talking very disparagingly about the 'English pigs' who told them what to do. Michelle rounded upon them and in their own vernacular told them that henceforth they would not be working for 'English pigs' but would be sent to a camp for transfer, eventually for work with the Russians. That quickly deflated their arrogance. They cringed and pleaded, but they were sent packing.

With Number 121 BGH then was Number 5 Maxillo-Facial Unit. It was small, mobile, and specially staffed and equipped to deal with men who had terrible injuries to the face. Some had lost the whole of their lower jaw, while others had gaping holes in the side of their mouth; many could only breathe through a tracheotomy tube in the throat, and many were blinded too. The task for nurses was a painstaking and harrowing one. The priority for them was to ensure the wound was cleaned up and made as healthy as possible so that reconstructive surgery could be carried out in base hospitals back in Britain.

It was not easy for nurses not to show horror on their own faces as dressings were removed from casualties whose faces were mutilated beyond belief. Many a tremor of apprehension shot through them as they bent to look under a dressing. But, as Sister Brenda McBryde wrote in her authoritative book *A Nurse's War*: 'They were such brave men. Uncomplaining beyond belief.' Nurses fed them on fluids through tubes, and they displayed incredible courage, such as the 'Guardsman who was being kept alive on eggnogs poured down his nasal tube'. 'He would hand me little notes: "Steak and chips tonight, Sis? Or shall we try the Duck a l'Orange?" '6

Sister Monica Dixon (now Carhart-Harris) found that nurses dealing with these horrendously disfigured men day after day had to have a special kind of courage.

The war's end was so near, and yet the casualties kept coming in. One of these was perhaps the most memorable of all for the nurses of Number 74 BGH. Pat Bradley (now Stephens) was on duty when they brought in a little man with a crooked nose and a deep scar which ran from his right ear to his mouth. As soon as he spoke there was no mistaking his identity, for his voice on the wireless was, after Churchill's, the best known to the British wireless listening public. And best hated by them. He was William Joyce, the ex-British Fascist known to millions of listeners as Lord Haw Haw, who began his nightly broadcasts with a snarled nasal introduction of 'Jairmany calling. Jairmany calling'. He had made his last broadcast, from Radio

Hamburg, drunk, and been shot in the buttock resisting arrest. After his wound was dressed in Number 74 BGH, he was dispatched to the UK to stand trial as a traitor (though he was born an American citizen of Irish descent and had become a German citizen before America entered the war) and was hanged in London on 3 January 1946.

That was not the only memorable sight for Pat Stephens in those days of May 1945.

> We had been invited to a neighbouring officers' mess and I was dancing with an army captain who suddenly turned to me and said: 'Would you like to see Heinrich Himmler, the Head of the SS?' I said I would and he led me off the dance floor to a small room at the back of the Medical Room. He opened the door, switched on the light and there, lying on a stretcher beneath a red blanket, was the body of the evil man himself. I shuddered and we went back to the officers' mess.

Pat Stephens, who would soon be seeing very much more of that corpse, was not told then how it came to be lying in that back room. Military historian Charles Whiting, then serving with the Reconnaissance Corps in Flensburg, described what happened to Himmler after he had been arrested and brought before the local camp commandant, Captain Selvester:[7]

> Things started to move fast. Selvester ordered Himmler to be searched for the same kind of poison phial with which von Friedeburg had killed himself that very day in Flensburg; no poison was found. Colonel Murphy, General Dempsey's Chief of Intelligence then, rushed in to take charge of the prisoner. Again Himmler was searched. Again no poison was found on him. But Murphy was not taking any chances. He ordered his doctor to stand by at HQ. Then, Himmler, clad only in his underpants and shirt, but wrapped in a grey army blanket [he had refused the offer of a British Army uniform] was whisked away to Lüneburg.
>
> The MO there, Captain C. Wells, started immediately to examine Himmler, while Major Whittaker watched and noted afterwards: 'I was not at all impressed by the man who had terrorized Europe with his SS, Gestapo, concentration camps and "final solution" for the extermination of the Jews. There was no arrogance about him. He was a cringing figure who knew the game was up.' Captain Wells examined Himmler's finger nails, chest and buttocks, his feet and toes, looking for signs of concealed poison. Finally, he came to Himmler's mouth. Inside he saw a small blue tit-like object sticking out of the lower sulcus of his left cheek. He knew

what it was. A cyanide capsule. He put his finger into Himmler's mouth. Himmler bit it hard and wrenched the doctor's finger out. He swung his head away and then with a disdainful look crushed the capsule of cyanide between his teeth and took a deep breath.

Whittaker then acted swiftly, upended Himmler and got his mouth into a bowl of water, trying to wash the cyanide out whilst Himmler groaned and spluttered. His face turned purple, contorted with pain. Wells tried artificial respiration. Whittaker shouted for cardiac stimulants. An officer ran to the nearest MI room. There he found a doctor's farewell party taking place. 'Must have a cardiac stimulant!' shouted the officer. Everyone thought it was a huge joke. Someone pushed a whisky at him. Thus Himmler's life ended in a kind of tragicomedy at twenty to twelve that night. The dentist wanted to pull a couple of his teeth as a souvenir but Major Whittaker said 'No!'[8]

Pat Stephens next saw Himmler's body on the post-mortem slab. 'It was horrible, yet funny in a way.' At that time a lot of people were thinking about souvenirs. Someone had already taken Himmler's pince-nez. The pathologist, Dr John Glyn, cut a lock of hair from Himmler's head and gave it to Pat Stephens and gave another to a nursing pal of Pat's. She sent it home for safe custody, but her mother misread the letter and thought it was just a piece of pony's hair and threw it in the fire. Unknown to the pathologists, one or two medical orderlies sneaked into the room and also cut off locks of Himmler's hair. 'He must have been nearly bald by the time they carted him off,' laughed Pat. 'But at the time these things happened, during the war, you took them all in your stride without thinking much about them. But now I do think. I wonder what happened to his body?'

Charles Whiting's account continues: 'It was wrapped in camouflage nets, tied up with telephone wires, thrown into the back of a truck and driven to a lonely spot and buried by Major Whittaker, Sergeant Major Austen and Sergeants Reg Weston and Bill Ottery. No one has ever discovered the grave. Major Whittaker has taken that secret with him to his own grave.'

No one cared much anyway during those memorable weeks of May 1945. Too much was going on. Nurses still had plenty to keep them busy with the unlucky soldiers who had been wounded so near the war's end.

But there were bright spots to lighten the days, as Pat Stephens recalled:

I was on duty in the operating theatre one day and for some reason we had a few men from the Pioneer Corps working with us in place of the usual RAMC orderlies. These

Pioneers were willing but not always very bright. We were all masked up and the surgeon was grunting away in the midst of an operation, having trouble with gas coming from the patient's stomach. He called to me, 'Get me a Flatus tube, quick.' [pronounced as 'Flaytus'] I leaned across the table and said to the man opposite me, 'Quick, bring a Flatus tube!' He walked off and was away ages. The surgeon worked on, wondering where the man had gone. Then he reappeared, walking carefully. Balanced precariously in his hand was a plate of soup!

In Number 74 BGH then, everyone was beginning to enjoy life.

Molly Wiskins, a VAD, recalls one of the much-appreciated luxuries of life then – hot baths. 'We were living in ex army barracks. Here the baths were six in a row, and we could emulate the Romans and hold a public debate while bathing or carry on private conversations if one wished.'9 Hospital orderlies were driving about in abandoned German cars, and nearly all the nurses had a pony from the local stables, to ride over the Lüneburg heath.

Then came the horrific time they were ordered across the heath for a job which filled them all with such horror that they can hardly speak about it to this day. They had to help in sorting out the ghastly looking inmates of Belsen.

It was a camp of sheer murder, one of many throughout Germany like those at Dachau, Buchenwald and Auschwitz where millions of men, women and children were killed in circumstances of particular horror. Camps where butchers' hooks, ovens, gas chambers, torture cells, whipping-posts, multiple gallows and pits of lime were used to perpetrate some of the blackest deeds ever committed by one human being against another. They were camps where the physical cruelty suffered by prisoners at the hands of Nazi gaolers was not the worst thing that happened. By mental torture they reduced them to subhuman level where pity and mercy for one another were abandoned. As the senior medical officer of the British Second Army said after his own visit: 'Prison doctors told me there had been cannibalism. Prisoners were so far gone that they took out the heart and kidneys of people who had died.'10

It was into this place of absolute degradation that medical officers and nurses went to help survivors. 'We had to go round the starving victims of the Nazis and tag those who would live to separate them from those who could not be saved. There were hundreds of people who could not even speak because they had been locked up for so long. One nurse caught typhus and died,' recalled Pat Stephens. It was a risky business for everyone going into that camp. Monica Carhart-Harris also remembered the experience. 'Two of our doctors contracted typhus,' she said.

Edwin Tetlow, war correspondent of the *Daily Mail* who went into the camp during a temporary truce before the war ended, recorded his experience of that horrific day. 'The Germans set it off to a bad start by sending, in a mood of horrible savagery, four fighter bombers to bomb and machine gun our ambulances, water supply points and electricity system in the camp.'[11]

Sisters of Number 32 and later Number 35 CCS were faced with terrible problems on their wards in requisitioned buildings away from the camp itself. Their patients were suffering from all kinds of sickness and disease as well as from starvation. Mollie Budge Jennings, who had served in the Western Desert and Italy, as well as in Germany, saw the horror in Belsen from a different perspective. 'I was posted to Denmark to look after children who had been evacuated from Belsen concentration camp. They were in a terrible state. We had to give them a little to eat and often. I remember watching one child to whom I'd given a slice of bread. When she thought I was not looking, she hid the crust under her pillow. That was the way they had been living, never knowing when the next crust would be coming.'

Sister Iris Bower remembers how doctors of the RAF 50th Mobile Field Hospital came back from duty in the camp.

> They had found 40,000 half dead prisoners, corpses in great heaps and thousands of cases of typhus, typhoid, and tuberculosis. There was a pile of naked bodies of women which stretched eighty yards long and thirty yards wide and four feet high.
>
> Those doctors came back shocked and stunned as never before. They admitted being physically sick. Then it was our turn. We had the job of flying out a few of the victims who would benefit straight away. They arrived on stretchers and we loaded them on to the Dakota with the help of the WAAF of the Air Evacuation Service. The stench was awful. The pilot told us that when they flew over the camp, the smell would penetrate right into the plane. All those former inmates had the same look in their eyes, haunting, staring and lifeless. It was as if they did not know what was happening to them. Most of them seemed to be old people but when I looked at the medical cards pinned to their clothing, they were mostly young.
>
> In looking back now, the extraordinary thing was that I don't think I smiled at any one of them. I find that unbelievable now that I could not bring myself to smile and yet in the past I had smiled a good deal to reassure badly wounded soldiers.
>
> When the last stretcher was loaded, the plane took off leaving us standing there gazing into the sky and thinking. It

was against this sort of bestiality we had been fighting these last six years. Fighting to get rid of everything that Belsen and all the other camps like Belsen stood for, and to get rid of it forever.

At 2.30 p.m. on 29 April 1945, Adolf Hitler went through a bizarre form of marriage ceremony with his mistress, Eva Braun, and then, after she had taken poison, he put a pistol in his mouth and shot himself. Eight days later the so-called 'Thousand Year Reich' came to an ignominious end, a mere twelve years since it had been launched with triumphant fanfare. Twelve years of bloodshed and evil were finished.

But, at the other side of the world, there was still an equally repugnant story of atrocities, bloodshed and evil to be terminated. And nurses were already being posted for duty in that Far Eastern theatre of operations where their sisters in the profession had already endured so much.

14 Horror in the Far East

On horror's head horrors accumulate
William Shakespeare
Othello, Act III, scene iii, line 371

Tuesday, 10 March 1942. In Britain the relatives of nurses stationed in Hong Kong read their morning newspapers with hands shaking with shock and anguish. What had happened to their loved ones?

They read how the House of Commons had sat in horrified silence as Mr Anthony Eden, Foreign Secretary, rehearsed the catalogue of atrocities committed by the Japanese army in Hong Kong against the garrison and civilian population after the capitulation. Reading steadily through his prepared script, the Foreign Secretary had paused to look round the House and, choosing his words carefully, went on to say:

> Out of regard for the feelings of the many relatives of the victims, the Government have been unwilling to publish any accounts of Japanese atrocities in Hong Kong until these had been confirmed, beyond any possibility of doubt.
>
> Unfortunately there is no longer room for doubt. The Government are now in possession of statements of reliable eye witnesses who succeeded in escaping from Hong Kong.
>
> Their testimony established the fact that the Japanese army in Hong Kong perpetrated against the helpless military prisoners and the civil population, without distinction of race or colour, the same kind of barbarities which aroused the horror of the civilized world at the time of the Nanking massacre of 1937.
>
> It is known fifty officers and men of the British Army were bound hand and foot and then bayonetted to death.
>
> It is known that ten days after the capitulation, wounded were still being collected from the hills and the Japanese were refusing permission to bury the dead.
>
> It is known that women, both Asiatic and European, were raped and murdered ...

One horror after another. How had it all come to pass?

In the first week of December 1941, a sense of impending danger was beginning to pervade the military and naval bases in Hong Kong, though the nurses there were going about their tasks in a pleasant, peacetime way in their lightweight summer uniforms. It was, after all, more than 70°F in the shade. In the harbour below, the sun tinted the sails of the Chinese junks as they drifted along with the strong tide. The clear blue sky was streaked with long, rich brown streamers of smoke from the ferries and passing launches. A truly peaceful scene. The last for the next four violent years of hatred and passion.

Earlier that week, the only problem facing the nurses on the wards was that of how to organize the forthcoming Christmas parties. A pleasurable, traditional task.

For the 2,000 British infantrymen stationed on the island, life had rarely been better. Each pay-day they drew more than enough to keep them well-supplied with cigarettes, beer and, for some of them, a Chinese woman who would look after their laundry, pressing their uniform and occasionally satisfying other more personal needs.

In many ways it was a token force. Even though in October 1941 it had been reinforced by two battalions of Canadian infantry, it was still too small to provide any real defence for the prized British possession of Hong Kong. Indeed, when the Far East Commander-in-Chief, General Ismay, had urged Churchill to reinforce Hong Kong, the blunt reply he received was that, 'If Japan goes to war with us there is not the slightest chance of holding Hong Kong or relieving it. It is most unwise to increase the loss we shall suffer there.'[1]

And so the garrison soldiered on 'regardless', making the most of their cushy situation. No one was giving any thought to the possibility of actually having to fight one day.

But on that black Sunday of 7 December 1941, everything changed. At 7.55 a.m., over 300 Japanese bombers and fighters struck in ruthless succession, and without any declaration of war, at the American warships lying at their moorings in Pearl Harbor, Hawaii. The proud American fleet was all but eliminated.

That same evening, bombs crashed into the central district of Hong Kong and also around the Royal Naval Hospital. By that time, though, Superintending Sister Miss Olga Franklin, who one day would be Matron-in-Chief, had been very busy preparing for such an eventuality. Patient numbers had been reduced to a bare minimum, and the whole of the hospital cleared except for the ground floor where the remaining seriously ill patients were placed in the charge of Sister Rollin. The acute surgical ward and casualty department were also moved to the safer area of the ground floor, with Sister Griffith in charge. This arrangement left Miss Olga Franklin free for administration and relief night sister duties. Typically, she kept notes of the momentous events of the next few days which later formed the basis of a detailed report to the Matron-in-Chief. And there was much to note!

On the morning of 8 December, nurses were awakened by the deafening slap and crash of exploding shells. The impersonal whine and crash of the howling missiles left patients trembling in their beds. Now there was an air of urgency in the wards as nurses moved rapidly from bed to bed ministering to those seriously ill.

Further down the road, Major George Gray of the 2/14th Punjabis waited for the first sight of invading Japanese troops. Suddenly, he could not believe his eyes. Marching towards his men, as if on a routine training exercise, was a tightly formed column of Japanese infantrymen. An ideal target. The Punjabi riflemen and machine-gunners held their fire until the little men marched cockily to within 300 yards. Then, on Major Gray's command, 'Fire!', they let loose a deadly hail of bullets, hosing the Japanese column from front to rear. The road was strewn with bodies, bleeding men who were sliding, crawling and screaming. Hundreds of them were lying in grotesque postures, cut to pieces by the murderous fire from close range. They were blood-sodden bundles in khaki rags. The Hong Kong garrison had won its first victory. And its last.

Then, one after another, Japanese planes thundered down, machine-guns rattling in awful metallic fury. Bombs fell from them, wrecking the empty upper wards of the naval hospital.

The next day, shells whistled with a sudden rising shriek, bursting on and around the hospital buildings. The Chinese staff took flight, looting as much of the hospital gear as they could on the way. More shells hit the hospital, shattering windows and doors, as staff took refuge in the strongest part of the building, the pharmacists' store. Gas, electricity and water supplies failed, and there was no means of heating and no means of using sterilizers, kettles or X-ray equipment. Emergency water-tanks were holed by shrapnel, and water was so scarce that one bowl of water in the morning had to be used by many of the staff for scrubbing up and for washing up to a dozen patients.

During the continuous bombardment only one member of the sick berth staff could be used for each ward, whilst all the rest, including the two nursing sisters, 'were required for fire parties, demolition squads and so forth', wrote Superintending Sister Olga Franklin in the calm, objective style she used in her report.

When one bomb fell right outside Ward Five, shattered window-glazing flew in all directions; plaster, bits of masonry and parts of wooden shutters clattered on to patients' beds. In the dark corridor leading from the operating theatre to the ward the Surgeon Commander was in the midst of amputating a man's arm by candle-light, but the operations went on. Soon the whole hospital was a wreck, as a hundred shells fell on the building itself. Somehow, with its small, dedicated staff, the hospital continued to function as casualties – European, Chinese and Indian – were brought in.[2]

On 11 December, the Japanese launched a ferocious attack against a Royal Scots battalion, forcing the British army to fall back from the outer defences to the so-called 'Gin-drinkers' Line, but this did not hold, forcing a withdrawal to the island itself.

Whilst these battles were being fought, Japanese 105 mm gun shells tore through the air into the naval hospital buildings. One afternoon, when the Commodore visited the hospital, his car was wrecked in the hospital grounds. Nurses even got used to the various sounds of the shells. Those passing overhead roared like an express train and burst beyond the grounds with a rumble, like rocks tumbling down a gulley. Others bursting in the garden area filled the air with red-hot swishing metal. The noise was deafening, but there was little to be done except 'getting on with the job' of tending to the patients.

On 18 December, Japanese infantry battered their way through the British defences. Twenty-five anti-aircraft gunners began to walk from their weapon pits with hands raised. A Japanese soldier charged the first man with his bayonet. As he fell, writhing and screaming with hands clasped over his stomach, the next Japanese charged. Twenty-five times, blood-crazed Japanese ripped into the gunners with their bayonets. That done, they ran into the nearby Regimental Aid Post, indiscriminately bayoneting stretcher-bearers and wounded soldiers.

Pockets of British troops fought on spiritedly. Sergeant-Major John Osborne, with a small group of Winnipeg Grenadiers, drove the Japanese from a hilltop position and held out against everything the Japanese could throw against them until only eight Grenadiers remained. Then a grenade landed in their midst. Osborne shouted 'Get down!' and then dropped his own body on top of the grenade. Osborne had saved the mens' lives, by sacrificing his own. Canada had acquired its first Victoria Cross of the war.

And so the ordeal went on until Christmas Eve. True to tradition in the naval hospital, the nurses and staff made a special effort for their patients in those broken-down wards. Charles Strong, the chaplain, managed to obtain chocolate and cigarettes to distribute round the two wards at lunch-time, and in the afternoon he organized a carol service. During the whole service the shells were dropping on and around the hospital, but it did not deter LSBA Baggs who played the harmonium without faltering.

By Christmas Day the RN Hospital was virtually untenable. On that day, though, the rich prize of Hong Kong surrendered to the Japanese Army. The flag of the Rising Sun flew over the government buildings. It was then that in the neighbouring hospital of St Stephen's a time of unimaginable horror began, as Japanese atrocities mounted to a final cataclysmic crescendo.

Not only were many of the Japanese assault troops now out of control, lusting for blood and sex, but they were also drunk. A group of them pushed their way into the St Stephen's school buildings, then serving as a hospital. Two medical officers, Colonel Black and Captain Whitney, who saw the rowdy mob approaching ran to the front door to bar their way. They were shot dead, their bodies flung to one side. Horror-struck nurses then watched almost in disbelief as sadistic Japanese soldiers ripped bandages and dressings from wounded men before plunging their bayonets into their bodies. It was all too much for one nurse, who ran screaming to the bed of a patient about to be given the same treatment and flung her own body protectively across his. The Japanese soldier thrust his bayonet through both of them at the same time. Fifty-six wounded men were slaughtered within minutes. Then came the terrible ordeal for the nurses. In their blood-spattered white uniforms they were herded into one room and then brought out, one by one, to be raped. Repeatedly they were taken and sent back throughout that Christmas night and the following day.

Five days later, on the night of 30 December, Japanese soldiers came to the Royal Naval Hospital and demanded to be taken to the women there. It was a time for quick thinking. Surgeon Commander Cleave, at the point of a revolver, led them away from the women and instead took them to the sick berth staff mess. There the soldiers were diverted from their sexual gratification to that of greed and occupied themselves with removing watches and rings from the staff. The nurses were spared.

The official surrender had already taken place. Hong Kong had held out for barely eighteen days. Just ninety-nine years from its formal cession by China to Britain, it had fallen to the Japanese. Now those Japanese soldiers, previously despised as a fighting force, were seemingly successful everywhere.

Within weeks they were threatening Singapore, the symbol of Western power in the Far East. During the weekend of 14–15 February it was clear the city would soon fall. In view of the news from Hong Kong, hospitals were cleared. Nurses were bussed to the quayside, where a launch waited to take them to the *Kuala*, a small ship already packed beyond safety capacity with 400 women and children and 300 servicemen and nurses from several hospitals with four of their matrons.

Immediately, another ordeal for nurses began. 'There was an air raid whilst we were trying to get on board,' recalled one of them. 'Jap planes dived low and after dropping their bombs, machine-gunned the crowded decks. Sisters were killed from this and from bomb splinters on the boat itself.'[3] Desperately the captain of the *Kuala* tried to manoeuvre his ship away from the blazing buildings on the waterfront and out of Singapore's doomed harbour. The captain steamed a course through the night among the many small islands in the seas around Singapore with the intention of keeping away from the major shipping lanes. When dawn broke he anchored in a shallow bay close to one of those tropical islands, hoping he could lie there unseen by patrolling Japanese aircraft. But luck was not with those nurses or passengers aboard the *Kuala*.

At seven o'clock the next morning a Japanese reconnaissance plane flew over the silvery calm waters of the bay, circled and then headed off north. *Kuala*'s captain feared the worst. He issued a strange order to all nursing sisters: 'Get out of your white uniforms and into something less conspicuous, dull, grey colours.' Hurriedly and by dint of borrowing and with even a bit of nervous giggling they threw off their whites and donned sombre clothing. Meanwhile the four matrons aboard met to confer on contingency plans for the possibility that the ship might be bombed and sunk. They did not reach any conclusion. The first bomb from six attacking aircraft pierced the ship's bridge and exploded in the engine-room, killing all four matrons.

'Those bombers came over four times,' wrote one survivor. 'The ship sank quickly and when we were swimming towards bits of floating debris, the aircraft machine gun bullets whipped the water around us.' Hundreds drowned. There were insufficient lifeboats and lifebelts on that overcrowded ship.[4]

Similar fates awaited other nurses evacuated from Singapore that day on the cargo ship *Empire Star*. Again, seriously overloaded with a total of 2,154 passengers, it sailed from Singapore on 12 February. Australian nurses sat with others packed into the ships' meat-hold. Hardly had the ship cleared the harbour than it was repeatedly dive-bombed. Three bombs landed directly on the ship. During one of those raids, staff nurses Margaret Anderson and Veronica Torney were caught on deck while tending to the wounded. They continued to nurse and at times lay across their patients protectively as the bullets hammered into the deck. Later, for their conspicuous bravery, Anderson received the George Medal and Torney the MBE.[5]

But the worst fate befell the sixty-five Australian nurses who sailed on the *Vyner Brooke* on that fateful 12 February, hoping to reach the safety of Java. Two days later it was attacked, set on fire and sank swiftly. Nurses, well trained in boat-drill, got everyone off the ship before attempting to get off themselves. Only thirty-two managed to do so. By that time though, less than thirty minutes from the beginning of the bombing, all lifeboats were full and drifting rapidly away in a strong current. Miraculously, nurses swam to floating spars, pulled each other into groups and survived the night to find themselves at daybreak drifting towards the shore of a small island, Banka.

Their relief was brief. Twenty-three of them were lined up by the Japanese at the water's edge. 'They all knew what was going to happen to them, but no one panicked,' recalled the sole survivor of the atrocity, Sister V. Bullwinkel. As commanded they waded forward into the sea, which had just reached waist-height when Japanese machine-guns fired at point-blank range. 'I don't think anybody screamed ... We just accepted it as our lot,' said Sister Bullwinkel in a statement to the Australian War Crimes Board in October 1945.[6] Bullwinkel was hit in the thigh, fell forward and feigned death. She drifted in to the shore and later crawled into the jungle. Of the twenty-two other nurses, not one survived the massacre.

Not far away, just off the small island of Pompong, the captain of the *Tanjong Penang* went ashore to ask for nurses who would go aboard his ship to nurse the wounded he carried. Sister Margot Turner and several other sisters volunteered, knowing full well they would have been personally much safer staying on the island even as prisoners than being at sea running the risk of Japanese dive-bombing attacks. As soon as they were on deck their work started. Dressings had to be applied and others to be put on, and by sunset they were so exhausted they collapsed on to the bare deck and slept. Suddenly they were awakened by the bright beam of a searchlight. A Japanese warship had them fixed in their sights. Guns fired at point-blank range. Their murderous fire sank the ship and left its passengers struggling for survival in the shark-ridden Java Sea.

Few of those who could swim survived the next few days of exposure without food and water under the blazing tropical sun. One of those tough enough to withstand the ordeal was Sister Margot Turner, a tall, athletic young woman who excelled in all sports, but especially swimming, hockey and tennis. For four days she drifted on a raft, keeping herself alive by eating bits of seaweed and drinking drops of rain-water that she caught in her powder-compact. Ironically it was a Japanese ship which rescued her. Its medical officer treated her with remarkable concern and eventually carried her ashore on a stretcher where she was taken to a prisoner-of-war camp. There she would endure three and a half terrible years of captivity.[7]

For the record, nurses with Sister Margot Turner in that prison camp were released in August 1945 and flown to Singapore for medical treatment at the Alexandra Hospital staffed by British doctors and nurses. The matron who had trained with Sister Turner at St Bartholomew's Hospital in London could not believe that this thin gaunt woman with two missing front teeth and hobbling on an injured foot was the strong, healthy woman she had remembered.

However, Margot Turner made a good recovery, and she lived to achieve the highest rank in the Queen Alexandra's Royal Army Nursing Corps – that of Brigadier, Matron-in-Chief and Director of the Army Nursing Services. In 1965 she was made Dame of the British Empire and on retirement became Colonel Commandant of the Corps and a legend in her own lifetime. She died in December 1993.

The end came for Singapore on Sunday, 15 February 1942. That evening General Arthur Ernest Percival went out under a white flag to capitulate to the Japanese commander. In doing so he surrendered 32,000 Indian, 16,000 British and 14,000 Australian soldiers. More than half of them were to die whilst prisoners of war in Japanese hands.

In Singapore itself the Japanese rounded up 5,000 Chinese civilians. They were all killed within the next two weeks. Many of them, with their hands tied behind their backs, were beheaded. It was to help in the fight against such barbaric men that nurses were now being recruited.

Winifred Beaumont smiled ruefully as she remembered how she came to be wearing a sweat-stained and dusty QA army uniform in the heat of besieged Imphal, India.

I had a very cushy job in wartime London as Sister in Charge of what was little more than a Casualty centre and First Aid Post in Whitehall. They called it a small hospital and I had my own living quarters there. To this day I can't explain how it all happened but I was sitting alone, toasting my knees in front of a nice red fire I'd built up for the Sunday night session of knitting and listening to the wireless. The nine o'clock news had just finished and then I heard the Principal Matron of Queen Alexandra's Imperial Military Nursing Service calling for experienced nurses to volunteer for service with many new hospitals which were being set up. Goodness knows what got into me – I often wondered later – but I dashed off a letter offering my services. I never thought then I should be sent to the Far East. And so quickly too. I told them at the War Office I only wanted duties in Britain and a Senior Matron in the War Office actually wrote on my forms 'For Home Service only'. But, as I found out later, nobody ever read army forms. Whenever I arrived at a new unit nobody expected me. Few people knew what was happening until it had happened.[8]

What had happened was that with the loss of Singapore the Japanese quickly made further conquests in Burma, which took them within a hundred miles of the border with India, and menacingly close to Australia. A new South-East Asia Command was formed under Lord Louis Mountbatten, with the main part of its strength based on the newly formed 14th Army commanded by General William Slim. Now an offensive against the Japanese was possible.

It was for this 14th Army that Winifred Beaumont was destined when she eventually arrived, dusty, dishevelled and without luggage at Number 92 Indian General Hospital at Comilla, to be met by the querulous, bad-tempered principal matron of the district, who embodied all the traits of a matron caricatured in the theatre. Winifred was in no mood for her outburst.

She dressed us down like schoolgirls just because the Rail Transport Officer had lost our luggage. She snorted and shouted with flecks of spittle spurting from her lips. 'Lost your luggage! How do you think you'll run a ward if you can't take care of your own bits of luggage? Did you lose it on purpose to dodge going into a battle area? Did you?'

No doubt my lip curled and eyes gave away my thoughts at such a stupid outburst but neither I nor my companions, Mac, Jill and Taffy, deigned to reply. One wasn't expected anyway.

'If that was your game then you've made a great mistake. You'll go up the line whether you have your kit or not. You'll go if you haven't a tooth brush between you.'

By that time we would have gone anywhere rather than stay within miles of that harridan. She whisked us straight off to the airfield to put us on a flight to the front. She got a flea in her ear, as my mother would say. The Wing Commander must have met her many times before and was not in a sociable mood.

'Can't do it! Not a space to be spared. My God, Matron, you don't know what you're asking. We lost three Daks yesterday, flying to Imphal.'

That Principal Matron had not reached her lofty rank without a strong streak of determination in her make-up. She would not be deterred. The Wing Commander could no longer withstand the continuous barrage of words. He gave in. He'd fly us in, somehow. But it was just that word 'somehow' that made us wonder what was in store.

Things then began to look better for us. The RTO telephoned to say he'd located our luggage. A truck went to pick it up from a rail junction twenty miles away and we were told to be ready to board the next morning's flight to join the 41st and 88th Indian General Hospitals.

We were pleased to be going by air and not in a bumpy dusty truck but we didn't think it would be such a hair-raising journey. First of all the aircraft was a very old Dakota which had a 'dodgy' undercarriage. When we got on board we had to squeeze ourselves alongside piles of equipment and our own baggage. It was far from reassuring when the loading sergeant said: 'For goodness' sake keep away from the tail. This old crate won't carry any more weight at all down there.' Then he took a bundle of old newspapers from under his arm, and gave half to me and half to another nurse, Jill. You'll probably need these,' he said.

Wedged also in that packed fuselage were two airmen. They were spotters. Just before we set off the Sergeant said to them: 'You'll be all right today, I think. You've got cover from Spitfires.'

I'll never forget the way that over-loaded Dakota took off. It bumped and rattled along the runway as if it would never get airborne. The pilot seemed to be wrestling with the plane as it half flew and half ran from one side of the air strip to the other. One wing rushed perilously close to the blurred muddy ground. Suddenly the bumping stopped. We were airborne and into a stunningly blue sky. It was like a tonic to us after all the dust and dirt of travel by rail and truck.

Then air pockets began to toss the aircraft up and down. We began to feel hot, and the air was thick with all kinds of smells. We all felt sick. We all vomited. The smell got worse. We needed all those newspapers. We lay there dozing and longing for death.

The old Dakota suddenly lurched and then fell rapidly to land in a shallow depression surrounded by hills sloping gradually upwards like a soup dish with curved edges. The engines cut and the fuselage door banged open to let in the glare of the midday sun as a harsh voice shouted, 'Wakey, Wakey!'

We stumbled out squinting around the rough air strip where piles of mangled metal lay heaped. There were burnt out skeletons of aircraft that had landed once too often, and all the detritus of war, Bren carriers pitted with jagged holes, a Humber staff car tilted on its side and five gallon petrol cans.

We might have expected those first welcoming words: 'Women! By God! No one told us you were coming.' And our first words were, 'Where are we? What's the name of this place?'. The officer hesitated and then said, 'Imphal'. We'd heard of Imphal when we were in Ceylon. It was in the newspapers and on everybody's lips. You know, headlines such as IMPHAL BESIEGED and ROAD TO IMPHAL CUT.

Across the front now in Burma, nurses were arriving in response to appeals made by Lady Louis Mountbatten for doctors, nurses and auxiliaries to volunteer for service in the Far East. They were joining hospitals where conditions were often primitive beyond belief. Edwina Mountbatten, in her capacities as wife of the Supreme Commander South-East Asia Command and also as Superintendent-in-Chief of the St John Ambulance Brigade, had repeatedly said so in her reports after visiting 172 hospitals in the Far East. Those reports pointed out that most hospitals were understaffed and many of them lacking in equipment. 'Commanding Officers and Matrons', she wrote, 'had to use ingenuity and near genius to improvise even for operating theatres. In one hospital, operating theatre lights and reflectors had been improvised out of petrol tins.'[9]

These were not inspections made by a distant figurehead travelling in cosseted luxury. She poked her nose into every nook and cranny, amazing senior officers who went around with her. She travelled light and lived rough, with seeming enjoyment. Once, when her route lay across a swiftly rushing river, she strode into the dark waters and swam to the opposite bank. Visiting advance dressing stations in Burma, she went by amphibious DKW down the Irrawaddy River to meet stretcher cases brought from the front line.

Her appeals certainly produced results. Nurses responded to her call for them to serve with the 'Forgotten Fourteenth Army', and their experiences formed a bond which still pulls them together for reunions with the Burma Star Association and as guests of the 'Not Forgotten Association'.

Answering Edwina Mountbatten's call was VAD nurse Joy Wilson (now Hobley) – another public-spirited young lady who decided to swap the comfort of Shottesbrooke Park Hospital to travel half-way round the world to nurse in a bamboo hut.

At first Joy Wilson found the hospital at Comilla a real culture shock, with its canvas beds and basins.

> The hospital, 74th Indian General, was a real Clapham Junction for casualties coming from the jungle fighting. There was a small airstrip nearby from which the wounded were flown in Dakotas to Dum Dum or Alipore airfields near Calcutta. Seriously wounded casualties had to be accompanied by a nurse and it was a great treat for one of us to go with them for it gave us a free day in Calcutta afterwards. One of those Dakotas was full of terribly wounded Gurkhas who had been in hand-to-hand fighting.
>
> Conditions in that bamboo-built hospital were in many ways primitive but the dedication of those doctors and nurses was as good as anywhere in the world, of that I'm sure.
>
> Inside it was unbearably hot and at night, lit only by hurricane lanterns, the air was even hotter. As we went from bed to bed giving injections, huge flying beetles flew straight into the glass of the hurricane lantern, others missed their mark and got entangled in any loose hair protruding from our caps.
>
> But there were compensations. Sometimes we could get to the local officers' club and dance to records of Glenn Miller. It was there one night that a handsome young Gurkha officer asked me to dance. He was wearing a very smart pair of brown leather boots which he said he had taken from a dead Japanese officer. We started to meet as often as our off duty hours allowed. He asked me to marry him and I then asked Matron if I could have two days' leave to go to Calcutta to buy a ring. He bought me a beautiful blue Zircon ring and I bought him a gold signet ring. When we got back to Comilla

he was posted to Simla for a course in Japanese. He could already speak Chinese. We were so happy together and so much in love. Later, though, he told me how well off we'd be when we were married. He said he had a nice flat and a car back home. I then said, 'By the way, where is your home?' His reply brought me down to earth. 'Why, in Shanghai of course.' What a shock. Much as I loved him I had no wish to live anywhere but England. And that was the end of that love affair.

As events turned out, however, I met another very handsome officer who also wanted to marry me. I agreed and then things happened very quickly. He said he did not want anybody else to snap me up. That same day he asked permission from his Colonel, came with me to see my Matron, and within a very short time we flew to Calcutta and had a lovely wedding in a church there.

So much for responding to Edwina Mountbatten's appeal for volunteers for Far East nursing service.

Joan Morgan, who joined the QAs at that time, thought she was going to be nursing in Mombasa and Nairobi, but hardly had she arrived than she got four hours' notice to be ready to embark for the Far East and was soon advancing with the 14th Army in 'Operation Cannibal' in its drive for the reconquest of Burma. 'Our hospital was under canvas and soon after I got there we were machine-gunned,' she recalled.

For Joan Morgan, too, there were compensations. She was later posted to Akyab where the British offensive of 'Operation Cannibal' came to an unsuccessful end when the Japanese forces defending that important Burmese port went over to the offensive. It was there however that she was invited to a neighbouring officers' mess and met a personable young officer who quickly found her to be the type of woman he had always wanted to marry. And in fairy-tale fashion they were quickly married in Chittagong.

Meanwhile, the brutal fighting in Burma went on.

'Casualties came to our 41st Indian General hospital in rushes. It was a thousand bed hospital and convoys of wounded men would come in filling all our wards and any space we could put stretchers. We had to treat more than their wounds, for every patient had a skin infection and most had jungle sores and a touch of dysentery as well. Moreover, they nearly all suffered from bouts of malaria.' It was this pressure of work which gave rise to a situation which Winifred Beaumont regrets to this day. It was one which other nurses may have experienced as was the case with Marjorie Bennett in the North African desert.

It happened like this [said Winifred to the writer]. The mail had come in and as usual some of the letters were tied together after they'd been sorted and some patients might get a batch of three or four. It was getting on towards evening, I remember, because the mosquito nets were all down and tucked under the patients' bedding and the lights were lit. They gave out a feeble light and I was dispensing medicine from a horrible tin medicine measure by the flickering light of a hurricane lamp. I was just approaching one bed when I heard a noise that I recognized at once. I ran to the bed, flung back the mosquito net and saw the ghastly mess on the bedding. The man had cut his throat with a razor blade right across the jugular vein.

The news spread round the ward. It upset everybody more than you'd expect in a ward of soldiers who had seen so much death and mutilation. But this.... Well, it was so sad because most of those men knew they were never going back into action again and as soon as they were fit to travel they would be on their way home.

This man though, I found out later, had news in a letter which told him he had no home to go back to. His wife had gone off with somebody else. A neighbour 'thought he ought to know'. Why did those self-righteous busybodies have to be so meddlesomely stupid? The news could have waited till he was home and well. I felt so sorry and wondered if I should have noticed something before.... But we were so busy.

A patient got out of bed and politely asked Winifred Beaumont if she thought it would be a good idea if he went round the ward and gave everyone a tot of rum. She agreed. Half way round the ward the soldier approached her with the communal measuring-tot.

There was a touch of mockery in his manner and, acutely aware of the listening silence, I knew this was a kind of test. Would I accept the drink from the communal measure as if I was one of them. Or, in refusing, show I thought myself superior? 'Please,' I said. He filled the measure to the brim with rum and I tossed it back in two large gulps. A great sigh of satisfaction ran round the ward. I was one of them.

One never knew what stomach-turning surprise would be encountered on those wards where African, Indians and Ghurkas were being nursed. Before Winifred's arrival, the fighting to keep the key features of Imphal and Kohima from the Japanese had cost the 14th Army dearly. British, Indian and Nepalese forces lost 14,700 men.[10]

The Gurkhas, who for 150 years had been leaving their mountain home in Nepal to join the British Army (and still continue to do so), suffered heavy losses and came into hospital with wounds the like of which Winifred Beaumont had never seen before – horrible ones from hand-to-hand fighting in which their curved, broad-bladed Kukri was often used with deadly effect.

She nursed some of the wounded from the most tragic of their battles, known as the 'episode of Scrub Ridge'. The 4th Gurkha battalion had been been ordered to retake the ridge, 'regardless of cost'. Very quickly three Gurkha officers were wounded. The battalion was pinned down just below the enemy on the crest. A young Lieutenant MacLeod, who had only joined the battalion two days before, took charge and rallied the men for another attempt, but before it could be launched he was killed. From a nearby picket, Captain Frankenberg dashed across and led the men as far as the wire, before he too was killed. One after another, officers rushed from flanks to push forward the attack. Altogether, ten officers, including the battalion's commanding officer, were killed and eight other officers badly wounded. The gallant mountain warriors fell by the score with each successive attack. Winifred Beaumont remembers those wards full of those wonderful young men.

> A Gurkha corporal came up to me in his pyjamas one night calling out, 'Mem-sahib! Mem-sahib! Come quickly.' He led me to the ward where my dying patients were gathered round little fires in groups. I was about to pause and look around when the corporal led me to a bed in the far corner of the tent where a young Gurkha soldier was throwing his arms about and writhing in the high delirium of cerebral malaria. He looked to me no more than a twelve-year-old boy. He was calling out in a voice that was just like a child's too. I could see he was seriously ill and sent immediately for the Indian Medical Officer. He knew right away what to do and put him on an intravenous quinine drip. I kept my eye on him all night, occasionally sponging him to bring down the temperature and trying to make him lie in a more comfortable position. Once, whilst I was moving him with the doctor by my side I saw a small smelly bundle tied to the young lad's waist and I was about to touch it when the doctor laid a hand on my wrist. 'Don't touch it!' he said. 'They are the ears of his enemies. He is a brave warrior.'

There were a lot of brave warriors in that 14th Army, fighting an enemy whose bestiality knew no bounds. Nurses needed no lectures on that score. They had heard enough as soon as they joined their units. Before leaving the embarkation camp in Britain they had all been issued with a Red Cross armband to wear over their khaki drill battledress, but that notion was soon knocked out of their heads when security officers told them that Japanese infantrymen made a special target of those wearing the Red Cross emblem. 'Our security officer thought that all nurses in forward areas should carry a loaded revolver so they could shoot themselves if they fell into Japanese hands,' recalled Winifred Beaumont.

As the British, Indian and Gurkha troops advanced towards the Irrawaddy River, the demarcation lines of the front became more confused. At night small Japanese patrols would creep silently forward, feeling their way through the undergrowth. One of them would call out to defenders, 'Hey Johnnie, let me through. The Japs are just behind me. They're going to get me.' No one ever fell for that old trick. They held their fire. Then, as soon as the defenders thought the enemy was close enough, mortars opened up and machine-guns fired on fixed lines. The night was hideous with screams and yells.

Time and time again the Japanese attacked and were beaten back and the 14th Army forced a bridgehead across the Irrawaddy, but at the cost of so many casualties that an appeal was made for nurses to go forward to help in the overworked field ambulances of Number 20 Division. Sister Barbara Carol Maunsell, QAIMNS, was one of many who volunteered. She worked under shell-fire and with the possibility of her position being overrun by Japanese at any moment. And the nurses knew what that would mean. They had come across some awfully mutilated women and children left in the wake of the retreating Japanese troops.

Barbara Maunsell tackled her work calmly and at times cheerfully as she began to improve the terrible conditions in which the wounded lay waiting for treatment. In that festering jungle, with its torrential rain, the temperature would drop and everyone shivered in their thin cotton uniforms. Tracks around the tents were little more than ribbons of red mud. Then, when the downpour stopped and the sun came out again, it sucked up steam from the sodden earth which mingled with the awful stench of dead bodies and gangrenous wounds.

On top of all this, cholera broke out. This did not deter Barbara Maunsell. The citation for the award of the Royal Red Cross stated that 'for long hours she gave of her best. Her devotion and nursing saved many lives.'

Mandalay fell. Rangoon followed. The Japanese were now virtually broken, many were starving, their pride was humbled and they were beginning to surrender.

At daybreak on 6 August 1945 the B-29 bomber *Enola Gay* dropped an atomic bomb on the Japanese city of Hiroshima. There was a massive blinding flash. In that moment 80,000 men, women and children died, and more than 35,000 were maimed for life.

The war was virtually over. Japanese guards, who had been marching Allied prisoners of war hundreds of miles away from the areas on which they thought the Allies might land, stopped their guilt-ridden activities. Some had stopped already, for of the 2,000 Australians taken out of their camp at Sandakan, North Borneo, only six were still alive when they reached Ranau.[11]

Nurses who had survived the brutality of their internment camps were about to be freed. Soon they would all be sailing home with the warriors of that 'Forgotten Army'. All of them, nurses and soldiers alike, had served to the best of their ability for the benefit of their comrades. And in so doing, they had learnt something of their true selves. And that, perhaps is the most important thought that remains with them all today.

Who else remembers those men and women of that 'Forgotten Army'?

Can those who were there ever forget what it was like? They cannot. Some nurses still have nightmares in which they see weary columns of men plodding forward to their inevitable fate. They see so many of them brought back, slung over jeep stretchers with ugly yellow shell-dressings already turning scarlet clapped over their wounds.

Sister Winifred Beaumont has but one souvenir of those days in Burma. 'It is a piece of tin bearing the words "Lest we forget", pricked out in holes by a nail and the heel of a boot. A soldier's tribute to a dead comrade. Like a bad conscience it lies at the bottom of my trunk, reminding me of a promise made and never kept.'

There is little in Burma today to show for all the effort and blood shed by those young men half a century ago. Occasionally groups of veterans – nurses, soldiers and their wives and widows – make the pilgrimage back to where their comrades fell, and they stand respectfully with eyes brimming as they gaze upon that lonely memorial on a lonely hill bearing the poignant message:

> For your tomorrow
> They gave their today

Epilogue

Oh, talk not to me of a name great in story;
The days of our youth are the days of our glory;
And the myrtle and ivy of sweet two and twenty,
Are worth all your laurels, though ever so plenty
Lord Byron
Stanzas written on the road
between Florence and Pisa

Suddenly it was all over. The most monstrous war mankind had ever known had ended. No one has ever been able to calculate, even within millions, the number of dead or those who were wounded, blinded and maimed for life. Furthermore, no one person could ever know the horror of it all. It was far too widespread.

Even in their own theatre of operations, fighting troops knew only what went on before their very eyes. It must be remembered also that only ten or fifteen of every hundred in the forces ever got near enough to the front line to witness the reality of all that bloodshed in six years of bitter fighting.

Nurses, more than most, saw the mass cruelty that mankind inflicted upon itself. They had to care for those young men and women whose final awareness of life was a bedlam of fire, and noise and pain. Understandably, few of those nurses have ever been the same again. It made them loathe war.

Yet many have said how their wartime roles could be vastly exhilarating, providing opportunities for self-fulfilment. Times when they discovered a greatness in themselves they had never before experienced; moments when they knew for sure what they were doing was the most satisfying and right thing for them. They were giving their best, nursing so close to the front line that a wounded man's chance of survival was far greater than it ever was during the First World War.

Those were the days of their youth when they were supremely professional, taking pride in providing medical care that no other soldier in history had received. In spite of the hardship, the tiredness, and the fear, they experienced also a wonderful feeling of comradeship – a comradeship that has stayed with them. Not all the cynicism in the world can ever deprive them of that.

Those nurses, however, are the first to recognize how much they were inspired by the courage, pain-bearing stoicism and cheerfulness of the young men in their care.

Many nurses also remember how those wartime days were not all an interminable nightmare. There was, even in the midst of frightening battle conditions, a good deal of gaiety when enduring friendships and romantic relationships were forged.

It is not surprising then that, today, they can look back with pleasure and pride, and perhaps even a little nostalgia, and say they were the best years of their lives.

References

1. Into France and Norway
The following have contributed to this chapter in letters, long accounts and/or
interviews:
Eileen Hawkin Haynes, Marjorie Doyle Bennett, Teresa Gladwin, Beatrice
Hownam, Helen Clark, Winifred Barnfather Reid.

1. *The Memoirs of Field Marshal The Viscount Montgomery of Alamein*, KG
   (Collins, 1958)
2. Public Record Office, File WO 177/14
3. PRO, File WO 177/14
4. *The Memoirs of Field Marshal The Viscount Montgomery of Alamein*, KG
   (Collins, 1958)
5. The term Fifth Columnist had originated in the Spanish Civil War, when
   General Mola, advancing on Madrid in 1937 with four columns of rebel
   troops, claimed that the Francoist supporters within the city were his Fifth
   Column, ready to undermine the defence from the rear
6. PRO, File WO 177/14
7. Ibid.
8. Norman Woodhouse in conversation with the writer
9. D. Flowers and J. Reeves, *The Taste of Courage* (Harper, New York,
   1968)
10. Ibid.
11. Ada Harrison, ed., *Grey and Scarlet, Letters from War Areas by Army
    Sisters on Active Service* (Hodder & Stoughton, 1944)
12. Cajus Bekker, *The Luftwaffe War Diaries* (Macdonald & Co Ltd, 1966)
13. A. Harrison, ed., op.cit.
14. Ibid.
15. PRO, File WO 177/1420

2. Front-line Britain
The following have helped with this chapter: Alexandra Croll; Iris Bower; Joy
Hobley; Dorothy Blackburn; Margaret Browne; Margaret Pritchett; G. Platts
Mungall; Beryl Allinson; Sylvia Suthren; S. Simonites; Betty Wragg.

1. Hugh Trevor-Roper, *Hitler's War Directives* (Sidgwick and Jackson, 1964)
2. Edward Bishop, *The Guinea Pig Club* (Macmillan, 1963)
3. Kathleen Harland, Journal of the Royal Navy Medical Service, *A History of
   the Queen Alexandra's Royal Naval Nursing Service*
4. Ibid.
5. *Daily Telegraph*, 14 November 1940
6. Ministry of Home Security publication, issued by the Ministry of
   Information: *Front Line 1940–41*
7. *Daily Telegraph*, 8 March 1941

3. The Middle East

The following have contributed to this chapter: Marjorie Doyle Bennett; Valarie Barron; Margaret Jennings (Boyce); Violet Bath (Leather); Norma Whitehead; Henrietta Hallows (Lee); Louise Robinson.

1. Fred Majdalany in *The Battle of El Alamein* (Weidenfeld & Nicolson, 1965)
2. Ernie Pyle, *Here is your War* (World Publishing Co., 1945)
3. Susan Travers and Bir Hacheim – from information from correspondence between the writer and Robert Barr Smith, Professor of Law, University of Oklahoma (Colonel retired), Timberdell Road, Norman, Oklahoma. *See also* Douglas Porch MA, PhD, *The French Foreign Legion* (Macmillan, 1991)

4. Greece, Crete and Malta

Interviews and letters from the following have helped with this chapter: Valieri Stavridi; Mrs Margaret Stavridi; Mrs Hadjilazaro; Colonel Neil Hamilton-Fairley; Marjorie Bennett; Violet Leather; Roger Keys.

1. PRO, File WO 177/1245, War Diary 26 BGH
2. Betty Wason, *Miracle in Hellas* (Museum Press, 1943)
3. *See also* Eric Taylor, *Heroines of World War Two* (Robert Hale, 1991)
4. Brenda McBryde, *Quiet Heroines* (Chatto and Windus, 1985)
5. PRO, File WO 177/1136
6. Letter from Colonel Neil Hamilton-Fairley to Valieri Stavridi, passed on to the writer
7. PRO, File WO 177/1136
8. Roy Farran, *Winged Dagger* (Collins, 1948)
9. PRO, File WO 177/1136
10. PRO, File WO 177/1287
11. Cajus Bekker, *Luftwaffe War Diaries* (Macdonald, 1966)
12. Hugh Trevor-Roper, *Hitler's War Directives* (Sidgwick and Jackson, 1964)

5. Tunisia – Springboard to Europe

The following have contributed to this chapter: Yvonne Hunter Lander; Beatrice Hownam; John Cooper; Marjorie Bennett.

1. Sir Harry Secombe, *Arias and Raspberries* (Robson Books, 1989)
2. Kay Summersby, *Past Forgetting* (Collins)
3. Ibid.
4. Ibid.
5. David Irving, *The War Between the Generals* (Allen Lane, 1981)
6. Ernie Pyle, *Here is your War* (World Publishing Co., 1945)

6. Sicily and Salerno

The following have contributed to this chapter: Marjorie Bennett; Pauline Greenway; Maurice Pinkney; Mary Webb Pinkney; Flora Whyte Urquhart; Iris Ogilvie Bower; Margaret Browne; Margaret Jennings (Boyce); Diana Sugden O'Brien; Noelle Starr; Stella Spence.

1. *The Memoirs of Field Marshal The Viscount Montgomery of Alamein*, KG (Collins, 1958)
2. *Daily Telegraph*, 10 July 1943
3. Farley Mowat, *And No Birds Sang* (McClelland and Stewart, 1979)

4. Christopher Buckley, *Road to Rome* (Hodder & Stoughton, 1945)
5. PRO, File WO 177/1431
6. Hugh Pond, *Salerno* (William Kimber, 1961)
7. Ibid.
8. PRO, File WO 177/1431
9. Ibid.
10. General Mark Clark, *Calculated Risk* (Harrap, 1951)

7. Naples and Bari
The following have contributed to this chapter: Pauline Greenway; Margaret Jennings (Boyce); Diana Sugden O'Brien: George Pfister (husband of the late Anne Watt Pfister).

1. Norman Lewis, *Naples 44* (William Collins, 1978)
2. Ibid.
3. Obituary, *Daily Telegraph*, 11 September 1995
4. The writer is indebted to former Nursing Sister Marie Sedman Floyd-Norris for this article from the *Washington Star*
5. PRO, File WO 177/1431
6. PRO, File WO 177/1374
7. Ibid.
8. Information generously supplied to the writer by the Ministry of Defence (Naval Policy and Finance 26 and the Department of Health and Social Security)
9. Ibid.
10. See also Hansard, written answers to questions dated 4 February and 14 February 1991

8. The Bloody Road to Rome
In addition to those in references below, accounts came from the following nurses and soldiers: Margaret Jennings Boyce; Mollie Budge Jennings; Kitty Jones Hutchinson; Bill Dilworth; George Pfister; Derek Ball.

1. C. N. Barclay, *History of the Duke of Wellington's Regiment* (Heinemann)
2. PRO, File WO 177/1431
3. Ibid.
4. 'With a Casualty Clearing Station at Anzio' in KSLI and *Herefordshire Light Infantry Chronicle* no. 92, January 1948
5. Ibid.
6. Bradley, *Beachhead Bailout at Anzio, The Retired Officer Magazine*

9. Into the Normandy Bridgehead
The following nurses have helped with this chapter: Iris Ogilvie Bower; Mary Webb Pinkney; Margaret Jackson Browne; Hilary Lewis; Monica Dixon Carhart-Harris; Hilda Smith; Marie Sedman Floyd-Norris.

1. Sister Mary Mulrey QAIMNS in *Unsung Heroines* by Vera Lynn, with Robin Cross and Jenny de Gex, (Sidgwick and Jackson, 1991)
2. PRO, File WO 177/1340
3. Ibid.
4. Ibid.

5. Ibid.
6. Alan Moorehead, *Eclipse* (Hamish Hamilton)
7. PRO, File WO 177/402 (ADMS Number 50 Division war diary)
8. A. Moorehead, op.cit.
9. *The Memoirs of Field Marshal The Viscount Montgomery of Alamein KG* (Collins, 1958)

10. The Flying Nightingales
The following have contributed to this chapter: Iris Ogilvie Bower; Myra Roberts Jones; Rosemary Gannon; Edna Birkbeck Morris.

1. Eisenhower, Dwight D., *Crusade in Europe* (Heinemann, 1948)
2. PRO, File WO 177/402

11. Break-out from the Bridgehead
The following have contributed to this chapter: Flora Whyte Urquhart; Marie Sedman Floyd-Norris; Iris Ogilvie Bower; Pamela Thompson.

1. PRO, File WO 177/628
2. Ibid.
3. Dwight D. Eisenhower, *Crusade in Europe* (Heinemann, 1948)
4. Ibid.
5. Marlene Dietrich, *My Life* (Weidenfeld and Nicolson, 1990); *See also* Eric Taylor, *Showbiz Goes to War* (Robert Hale, 1992)
6. Doreen Boys, *Once upon a Ward* (Photobooks, 1950)
7. D. D. Eisenhower, op.cit.
8. PRO, File Air 2/1019
9. Ibid.

12. Finale in Italy
The following have contributed to this chapter: Diana Sugden O'Brien; Flora Whyte Urquhart; Margaret Jennings Boyce.

1. John North, ed., *The Memoirs of Field Marshal Earl Alexander of Tunis* (Cassell, 1962)
2. Madeleine Masson, *Edwina – The Biography of the Countess Mountbatten of Burma* (Robert Hale, 1958)
3. Allen Dulles, *The Secret Surrender* (Harper & Row, 1967)
4. Ibid.
5. General Mark Clark, *Calculated Risk* (Harrap, 1951)
6. See PRO, File CAB 101/144 165363 for Churchill's views on the fate of Mussolini: 'Some may prefer prompt execution without trial.... personally I am fairly indifferent on this matter....' To have Mussolini tried as a war criminal could have proved embarrassing for Roosevelt bearing in mind the large number of Italian votes at stake in a forthcoming presidential election. It could conceivably have been convenient for Mussolini to have been shot by Italian Partisans, as some Italian historians have argued. See also article by Alberto Santoni in *Storia Illustrata* (June 1985) and *Rosso and Nero* (1995)

13. To the Bitter End in Europe
The following have helped the writer with this chapter through interviews, letters and their own accounts: Monica Carhart-Harris; Myra Roberts Jones;

Pamela Thompson; Iris Ogilvie Bower; Pat Stephens; Mollie Budge Jennings.

1. Martha Gellhorn, *The Face of War* (Rupert Hart-Davis, 1959)
2. *Daily Herald*, 3 September 1944
3. Dr John C. Warren in *Airborne Operations in World War Two, European Theatre* (USAF Historical Division, Washington, DC, 1956)
4. PRO, File WO 177/628
5. Dwight D. Eisenhower, *Crusade in Europe* (Heinemann, 1948)
6. Brenda McBryde, *A Nurse's War* (Chatto and Windus, 1979)
7. Charles Whiting's conversations with the writer. See also Charles Whiting, *The Last Battle* (Crowood, 1989)
8. Ibid.
9. Doreen Boys, *Once upon a Ward* (Photobooks, 1950)
10. *Lest We Forget* (Daily Mail publication, 1945)
11. *Daily Mail* 19 April 1945

14. Horror in the Far East
The following have helped with this chapter through conversations, letters and accounts: Pat Gould CBE, RRC; Winifred Beaumont; Joy Hobley; Joan Morgan.

1. Winston Churchill, *The Second World War*, Volume III (Cassell, 1948)
2. I am indebted to Pat Gould CBE, RRC for access to the Report from the Superintending Sister, Royal Naval Hospital, Hong Kong, presented on 30 October 1945 to the Matron-in-Chief of Queen Alexandra's Royal Naval Nursing Service, Admiralty, London
3. Ada Harrison, ed., *Grey and Scarlet, Letters from War Areas by Army Sisters on Active Service* (Hodder & Stoughton, 1944)
4. See Catherine Kenny, *Captives* (University of Queensland Press, 1986)
5. Ibid.
6. Statement by Sister V. Bullwinkel, AGH War Diary, part 2, Written Records 1939–45 1010/4178, Australian War Memorial, Canberra
7. For more complete details of Dame Margot Turner's life and career see Brigadier Sir John Smythe, *The Will to Live* (Cassell, 1970); Eric Taylor, *Heroines of World War Two* (Robert Hale, 1991); and *The Gazette*, Vol. 10, No. 10 (QARANC Association 1994–1)
8. This kindly lady, Winifred Beaumont, was well into her nineties and living alone in the village of Wormingford, Colchester, when the writer enjoyed many conversations with her. She was remarkably articulate, even at that age writing short stories and transcribing Chaucer's *Canterbury Tales* into modern English. She had a good recollection of her days in Imphal.
9. Madeleine Masson, *Edwina – The Biography of the Countess Mountbatten of Burma* (Robert Hale, 1958)
10. Field Marshal Sir William Slim, *Defeat into Victory* (Cassell, 1956)
11. Martin Gilbert, *Second World War* (Weidenfeld & Nicolson, 1989)

Bibliography

Alexander, Harold, *The Memoirs of Field Marshal Earl Alexander of Tunis* (ed. John North, Cassell, 1962)

Anderson, Bette, *We Just Got On With It* (Picton, Chippenham)

Barclay, Brigadier C. N., *History of the Duke of Wellington's Regiment* (Heinemann)

Bekker, Cajus, *The Luftwaffe War Diaries* (Macdonald, 1966)

Bishop, Edward, *The Guinea Pig Club* (Macmillan, 1963)

Boys, Doreen, *Once upon a Ward* (Photobooks, 1950)

Buckley, Christopher, *Road to Rome* (Hodder & Stoughton, 1945)

Burns, John Horne, *The Gallery* (Secker & Warburg, 1948)

Churchill, Winston, *The Second World War*, Vols I-VI (Cassell, 1949)

Clark, General Mark, *Calculated Risk* (Harrap, 1951)

Collier, Basil, *The Battle of Britain* (Collins)

Cotterell, Anthony, *R.A.M.C.* (Hutchinson, 1945)

Derry, T. K., *Campaign in Norway* (HMSO)

D'Este, Carlo, *Bitter Victory: The Battle for Sicily* (Collins)

—— *Fatal Decision – Anzio* (Collins)

Dulles, Allen, *The Secret Surrender* (Harper & Row, 1967)

Eisenhower, Dwight D., *Crusade in Europe* (Heinemann, 1948)

Farran, Roy, *Winged Dagger* (Collins, 1948)

Flowers, D. *Taste of Courage* (Harper)

Gelb, Norman, *Dunkirk* (William Morrow & Co.)

Gellhorn, Martha, *The Face of War* (Rupert Hart-Davis, 1959)

Harland, Kathleen, MA, *Queen Alexandra's Royal Naval Nursing Service* (Journal of Royal Naval Medical Service)

Harrison, Ada, *Grey and Scarlet: Letters from War Areas by Army Sisters on Active Service* (Hodder & Stoughton, 1944)

Hastings, Max, *Overlord* (Simon & Schuster)

Hinsley, F. H., *Hitler's Strategy* (Cambridge)

Iriving, David, *The War between the Generals* (Allen Lane, 1981)

Jackson, General Sir William, *The Mediterranean and Middle East* vol. VI, part III (HMSO)

Kenny, Catherine, *Captives* (University of Queensland Press, 1986)

Lewis, Norman, *Naples '44* (William Collins, 1978)

Majdalany, Fred, *Cassino* (Longman)

Masson, Madeleine, *Edwina – The Biography of the Countess Mountbatten of Burma* (Robert Hale, 1958)

McBryde, Brenda, *A Nurse's War* (Chatto & Windus, 1979)

—— *Quiet Heroines* (Chatto & Windus, 1985)

Miller, Russell, *Nothing Less than Victory* (Michael Joseph)

Montgomery, Field Marshal Viscount, *Memoirs* (Collins, 1958)

Moorehead, Alan, *Eclipse* (Hamish Hamilton)

—— *The End in Africa* (Hamish Hamilton)

Morris, Eric, *Circles of Hell – The War in Italy, 1943–45* (Hutchinson)

Mowat, Farley, *And No Birds Sang* (McClelland & Stewart, 1979)

Pyle, Ernie, *Here Is Your War* (World Publishing Company, 1945)

Ray, Cyril, *Algiers to Austria – History of 78 Division* (Eyre and Spottiswoode)

Secombe, Sir Harry, *Arias and Raspberries* (Robson Books, 1989)

Spaight, J. M., *The Battle of Britain* (HMSO)

Strawson, John, *The Italian Campaign* (Secker & Warburg)

Summersby, Kay, *Past Forgetting* (Collins)

Taylor, Eric, *Heroines of World War Two* (Robert Hale, 1991)

Toland, John, *The Last Hundred Days* (Random House)

Trevor-Roper, H. R., *Hitler's War Directives* (Sidgwick & Jackson, 1964)

Wason, Betty, *Miracle in Hellas* (Museum Press, 1943)

Watts, J., *Surgeon at War* (Allen & Unwin)

Whiting, Charles, *The Last Battle* (Crowood, 1989)

—— *The Long March on Rome* (Century)

—— *'44 – In Combat on the Western Front from Normandy to the Ardennes* (Century)

Index